Reporting in the MENA Region

Reporting in the MENA Region

Cyber Engagement and Pan-Arab Social Media

Mohammad Ayish and Noha Mellor

ROWMAN & LITTLEFIELD
Lanham • Boulder • New York • London

Published by Rowman & Littlefield
A wholly owned subsidiary of The Rowman & Littlefield Publishing Group, Inc.
4501 Forbes Boulevard, Suite 200, Lanham, Maryland 20706
www.rowman.com

Unit A, Whitacre Mews, 26-34 Stannary Street, London SE11 4AB,
United Kingdom

British Library Cataloguing in Publication Information Available

Library of Congress Cataloging-in-Publication Data

'Ayish, Muhammad Ibrahim.
Reporting in the MENA region : cyber engagement and pan-Arab social media / Mohammad Ayish and Noha Mellor.
pages cm
Includes bibliographical references and index.
ISBN 978-1-4422-3762-9 (cloth : alk. paper) — ISBN 978-1-4422-3763-6 (electronic)
1. Journalism—Arab countries—History—21st century. 2. Online journalism—Arab countries—History—21st century. 3. Social media—Arab countries. 4. Citizen journalism—Arab countries. 5. Digital media—Arab countries. I. Mellor, Noha, 1969– II. Title.
PN5359.A96 2015
079.174927'0905—dc23

2015024842

∞™ The paper used in this publication meets the minimum requirements of American National Standard for Information Sciences—Permanence of Paper for Printed Library Materials, ANSI/NISO Z39.48-1992.

Printed in the United States of America

Contents

Introduction

Several recent publications have addressed the role of social media in mobilizing collective action among young Arab generations; however, to our knowledge, there are only a few contributions regarding the role of social media in pan-Arab newsrooms. We hope this book fills this gap. The book investigates one significant feature of pan-Arab journalism in the second decade of the twenty-first century—namely, institutional and professional journalists' engagement with the emerging social media revolution. The authors draw on multiple data-gathering methods, including social media analytics and interviews, to describe and analyze how pan-Arab media journalists and institutions harness social space in their professional work. The aim of this book is to show how social media platforms, widely perceived as drivers of both public opinion and social empowerment, present Arab journalists with both opportunities and challenges in their professional careers. The book specifically looks at how pan-Arab journalists identify and apply social media tools in their communication strategies with the region's audiences. The turmoil sweeping the region has been partly attributed to new media, but the assumption that the power of digital communication can bring about political changes remains very tenuous, especially as the state remains the dominant player in the region's public sphere. This fact is highly significant in any analysis of new media regulations in the region; for example, in many Arab countries, new communication methods are regulated by traditional legal and ethical frameworks that, in many cases, would seem irrelevant in their application to the emerging media environment. New regulations have been introduced in some Arab countries to cope with online media activities, but most of them continue to be inspired by profound state visions about society and the public sphere. One of the critical questions we address in this book is how empowering social media has been for Arab journalists operating in severe state-controlled communication environments, on the one hand, and for audiences with substantial access to myriad online sources, on the other. Here, it is important to explore the traditional role of Arab journalists as gatekeepers and how social media have challenged that role by providing audiences with unprecedented opportunities to fill the function of journalists. This challenge has been brought to the fore, once again, by the wave of uprisings that have hit the region since December 2010.

JOURNALISM—POST-ARAB SPRING

The so-called Arab Spring, as it was reported from the Middle East and North Africa (MENA) region, suggests a central role for social media in order to disseminate information about the uprisings to the whole world. Social media have clearly provided new avenues for expressing significant political and social disenchantment across the region, but they did not cause the uprisings, which were the culmination of many years of social and political discontent. These media have been seen as a new platform for voicing citizens' concerns about critical political and economic issues in the region. Their significance, however, should not be measured by disparate statistics of the number of users but, rather, by how users engage with social media content compared with the centrally controlled legacy media.

The uprisings have brought about new forms of citizen journalism, argues Yomna Elsayed (2013), in order to meet the new demand for instantaneous updates on protests across the region. Mainstream news agencies faced pressure from authoritarian regimes to fulfill this need, which gave rise to new, albeit amateur, forms of journalism, driven by ordinary citizens who saw in it an alternative platform to circulate their version of the truth (Elsayed 2013). The YouTube video of the "blue bra girl," for instance, posted in December 2011 during the Egyptian protests, documented the violence of police forces against a female protester, prompting many international media to rebroadcast the video and the then US secretary of state, Hillary Clinton, to refer to it in her speech (Bebawi 2013). Social media have been used to challenge the traditional role of journalists as gatekeepers by offering raw YouTube footage from the Arab streets in order to seize the attention of audiences worldwide and present another perspective of the events on the ground; this footage is not always as clear cut as it seems, however, as activists also have their own agenda (Bebawi 2013). Several social media users took advantage of this in Syria—for instance, as a platform for presenting their version of the conflict at grassroots level by showing numerous sections of footage, stamped with the date and time, similar to what professional journalists and photographers would do (Bebawi 2013).

Social media in the MENA region, as elsewhere, have come to serve as new platforms for substantive virtual conversations, which tend to become quite heated during crisis situations, such as the Gaza conflict in July–August 2014. Both Israel and Hamas were highly active on social media sites in an attempt to rally support for their causes: Israel enlisted hundreds of students to take part in its campaign on social media, which, as one student explains, is "another place where the war goes on. This is another way to tell our story" (*Week* 2014). Hamas's Twitter account, on the other hand, witnessed a traffic surge during that conflict, with tweets in English, Arabic, and Hebrew showing distressing images of dead and injured children in the Gaza Strip. Numerous hashtags appeared on Twitter as part of Hamas's crusades such as #GazaUnderAttack, #StopIsrael, and #PrayforGaza (*Week* 2014). Gazan teenager Farah Baker was one of the Palestinians who rose to fame following her daily tweets about life in Gaza under fire, seeing the number of her Twitter followers surge from 800 to over 167,000 in a matter of days (Bora 2014). Supporters of either party had access to social media campaigns tailored to their preferences, with pro-Palestinians uploading videos of Israeli snipers and pro-Israel supporters uploading videos of Hamas's rockets fired from sites adjacent to hospitals. Those targeted campaigns, warns Gilad Lotan (2014), may end up building "personalized propaganda engines that feed users content, which makes them feel good and throws away the uncomfortable bits."

The use of social media by terrorist groups to propagate hatred and coordinate acts of violence has attracted much attention in scholarly and policy-making circles. Lebanese journalist Ali Hashem (2014a) is one of those who followed the so-called Islamic State's (IS or ISIS) social media propaganda, confirming that the group's strategy of warfare in Syria and Iraq drew much support by using new and social media to disseminate their ideas. This was evident, shows Hashem, in the way Abu Bakr Al-Baghdadi, the IS leader, appeared on July 4 in Mosul during the Friday sermon, with high-definition cameras placed inside and outside the mosque where he was praying. ISIS uses "cutting-edge tools and professional operators," according to Marwan Shehade, a Jordanian expert on Islamic movements: "I have to say that they are generous when it comes to their media machine, and they pay good money to professionals" (quoted in Hashem 2014a). ISIS depended on its own media divisions to create and disseminate online material by producing videos glorifying the group and its mission. Some of the stories circulated by Arab websites were (and are) simply based on rumors and fabrications, argues Ali Hashem (2014b). He gives the example of the Clinton-IS story disseminated by many Arabic websites, claiming that Hillary Clinton's memoirs, *Hard Choices,* include confirmation of past US support for ISIS in order to instigate divisions in the Arab world—a story clearly refuted by the fact that Clinton's memoirs include no mention of ISIS. The story seemed to have aimed at exaggerating the movement's threat to the region and was merely one of several baseless stories circulating at the time about the terrorist group's warnings, one that it would destroy Mecca, another that it would force female circumcision in Iraq. ISIS, argues Hashem (2014b), has dedicated moderators on each social media site such as Twitter and Facebook, posting news from their respective areas in order to spread the group's propaganda. It is against this emerging social media landscape that this book seeks to analyze pan-Arab media employment of social space to engage with their far-flung audiences.

NEW MEDIA, NEW RULES

The information and communication revolution of the late twentieth century has indeed been viewed as the most defining development in modern human history. Transitions from traditional analog to new digital media production and distribution modes and the advent of the World Wide Web have all revolutionized not only the way we communicate at interpersonal and mass levels but also how we conduct business and carry out a wide range of professional assignments in different fields, including journalism. Media convergence at corporate and technological levels around the world has been instrumental in changing not only the face of communication practices but the very business model on which conventional media have thrived. The rise of multimedia-based and interactive communication with a global reach has rendered the traditional one-way flow, sender-receiver communication model practically redundant. The steady transformation of the Internet into an ever-expanding communication platform has only accelerated shifts in how we perceive and practice our media work. A major implication of those transitions has been a decline of conventional journalism, as more legacy media outlets, brutalized by the financial crisis and an empowered public, struggle for safe cover in cyberspace. Newman (2009, 19) describes user-generated content (UGC) and social media initiatives in global newsrooms such as the BBC, the *Guardian*, the *Telegraph*, the *New York Times*, and CNN as including users' comments on published stories, users' videos and images, self-standing message boards with or without threads, blogs, rating polls, crowdsourced surveys published by newsrooms, and off-site engagements such as on Facebook and Twitter. Newman (2009) explores the issues raised by audience engagement in his study of participatory journalism in the UK and United States and how breaking news has been covered differently thanks to social networking and UGC, which compresses the news cycle and forces editors to find new ways of verifying and curating content created by users.

Social media also describes the use of web technology to launch different forms of interactive communication. The Internet provides an array of information sources such as *Wikipedia*, and journalists can consult such social media sites to stay tuned to online trends and be better empowered to cater to their audience's interests. Picard (2009) argues that journalists, who usually complain about being low paid, do not deserve higher pay because they no longer create much original value in their journalistic work. The exchange value of journalism is rooted in its functional benefits in providing information and ideas, emotional benefits, including enforcing a sense of community belonging, and self-expressive benefits in attracting users who can identify with the journalists' views or opinions (Picard 2009). Journalists and media professionals no longer monopolize the communication space, considering the abundance of information and news online. Once constrained by costly distribution, news suppliers were rather limited in number, leading to the enhancement of the economic value of their content, argues Picard. There is an array of sources of news and information now, however, which compete with newsrooms in providing immediate access to readers. The rise of citizen journalists who can report news and upload audiovisual material online means that professional journalists and editors no longer have exclusive access to information.

Arab journalism, in many ways, has not been detached from these global communication transitions. More Arab media organizations are embracing digital technology as developments in telecommunication infrastructures continue to be informed by global standards, especially in the oil-rich Gulf region. The Arab region is experiencing steady growth in a wide range of communication sectors such as the web, mobile telephony, and e-services, according to national and international reports. Over 150 million Arabs had access to the web in late 2013, while mobile telephony remains one of the most vibrant markets in the region. Electronic services in government and private sectors have made impressive headway in countries such as the UAE, Kuwait, Jordan, and Egypt; likewise, the telecommunications sector has demonstrated profound interest in catching up with global technological and business trends as national telecom providers work to diversify their services in order to embrace television and multimedia products. This dynamic communication environment has witnessed the notion of audiences gradually giving way to that of users, who are able not only to access limitless sources of information but to transmit that information to global audiences at the press of a button. Studies show more and more Arabs are turning to cyberspace to fulfill their need for news, entertainment, and information.

Pan-Arab newsrooms provide illuminating examples of the impact of this new technology on Arab journalistic practices. This book focuses on such pan-Arab media outlets because they have regional and global news agendas, they have built up large audience bases, and they have made significant progress in the emerging new media spheres. These outlets may be regarded as trendsetters by other national and local media institutions, as they employ a young, technology-savvy generation of media practitioners with global professional standards. The past two decades have shown that Arab investors tend to favor regional rather than national media operations, thereby targeting as wide an audience as possible, not only in the Middle East but also Europe, Africa, and Western Asia. These pan-Arab outlets, above all, operate high-tech newsrooms marked by significant national representations of their journalistic staff.

Pan-Arab media outlets covered by this study vary not only in their geographical, institutional, and political affiliations but also in their technological sophistication. BBC Arabic, France 24, Deutsche Welle, and Alhurra as well as Al-Jazeera, Al-Arabiya, Sky News Arabia, and Al-Mayadeen have made inroads into the cyber social media world. The first four outlets are based in different European and American cities and have largely integrated unique norms and practices into their newsroom operations in order to reflect the cultural diversities of their mother countries. BBC Arabic, for one, regards itself as an Arabic-speaking channel that provides public broadcasting services, critical for fostering a healthy debate culture across the region.

One unique feature of the BBC in general relates to its commitment to offer a tri-media platform through integrating radio, TV, and web content. This is also reflected in the role of journalists and producers in the BBC Arabic service, where there is a proactive integrative policy that encourages journalists to move among radio, online, and TV platforms.

OUTLINE OF THE BOOK

The aim of this book is multifaceted: (1) to describe ongoing digital media trends in the Arab world; (2) to analyze pan-Arab journalists' qualitative perceptions of social media, not only as empowering tools for their social and professional development but also as potential threats to their professional and social advancement; and (3) to analyze social metrics as an indicator of Arab journalists' patterns of social media usage, shedding new light on the future implications of the ongoing digital media trends for Arab journalism. A central theme emphasized in this book is the value of social media, not much seen in their reach or user numbers but more in the levels of engagement they are able to create in cyberspace. Some social media analytical firms have come up with several indices for engagement (based on Facebook "hits," "likes," "shares," and "comments"), but the development of operational definitions of this social media impact seems to be subject to ongoing experimentation.

Chapter 1 begins with an overview that places Arab journalism in a contemporary context, illustrating changes in journalistic practices in light of the recent technological developments, not only across the Arab region but also globally. Chapter 2 presents a discussion on the particular communication trends and their implications in the Arab world, drawing on data extracted from organizations such as the International Telecommunications Union, the Dubai School of Government, and the Arab Advisors Group. Chapter 3 focuses on the pan-Arab journalism sector, describing new developments in applying digital technologies in pan-Arab newsrooms and discussing the rising phenomenon of citizen journalism. Another emerging theme in this discussion is the impact of social media on changing traditional news values in pan-Arab outlets and on the preference of daily vernaculars as the most favored linguistic code, especially among young Arab audiences. Chapter 4 uses social media analytics to describe the use of social media in ten pan-Arab outlets, focusing on their Facebook and Twitter content in terms of topic, format, objective, and geographical reach. Chapter 5 shifts the focus to twenty-six individual journalists in ten different pan-Arab newsrooms who have won extensive followings on social media platforms as they seek to promote their shows or to disseminate their ideas in virtual space. Chapter 6 provides an analysis of journalists' engagement with their audiences on social media sites, demonstrating the audience's ability to influence content on social media and drawing on observations of social media traffic generated by the ten pan-Arab media outlets and the twenty-six journalists covered by the study. Chapters 7 and 8 draw on interviews with selected journalists in those newsrooms to describe their perceptions of social media use in branding their outlets, discussing further ways to improve social media services, and developing long-term strategies for audience engagement. Chapter 8 carries on the discussion by addressing the notion of citizen journalism as an emerging feature of pan-Arab media engagements in social space.

1

Arab Journalism

Values, Practices, and Regulations

This chapter places Arab journalism in a contemporary context, discussing transitions in journalistic practices as by-products of the recent changes in regulations and technology, particularly the proliferation of transitional pan-Arab news media targeting audiences not only in the Arab region but also globally. There are usually three levels of analysis of the practice of journalism: the society, the news organization, and the individual journalist (McQuail 2013, 5–7). The first level, in the context of Arab journalism, analyzes it in terms of the ideas circulated in the media, taking into consideration the way journalists interact with political and cultural elites. Some factors need to be included in the analysis of Arab journalism at the news organization level, such as the legal and regulatory system as well as models of ownership and control (McQuail 2013). Finally, at the level of individual journalists, it is important to look into Arab journalists' relationship both with their audiences and with other professionals. The objective of this chapter is to describe the political, legal, and professional journalistic milieu in which pan-Arab media operate.

The following sections provide an overview of these factors, focusing particularly on relations between journalism and politics, in light of the recent changes to the regulatory framework and press laws in the region. The media sector, as discussed below, has been subjected to increasing waves of market liberalization, paradoxically coupled with rigid media laws. Several media outlets have expanded their digital offerings in the meantime, in tandem with the rise of a new generation of online journalists who demand recognition as culture custodians. The chapter argues that Arab journalism in the twenty-first century continues to embrace much of the traditional values of nationalism and mobilization, despite recent upheavals and liberal market developments. The recent uprisings have, in fact, accentuated the political role of journalists as "mouthpieces" for the state or as voices of the opposition. Professional codes of objectivity and impartiality, therefore, shall be analyzed within the local and regional political context in the Arab world, where state control as well as self-censorship define newsroom practices. A brief discussion of journalism as a political and ideological tool follows, in view of the unique relations Arab journalists have had with political and business elites. These enduring journalistic traditions are believed to have a bearing on how Arab journalists and audiences deal with pan-Arab communications.

JOURNALISM AS A POLITICAL TOOL

The birth of the Arab press in the nineteenth century followed the introduction of printing by mostly Christian missionaries and colonial powers. The spread of literacy helped create a new generation of journalists, particularly literary journalists, in both Egypt and Lebanon, where Egypt had some of the first newspapers in the region and Lebanon hosted the largest per capita number of newspapers (McFadden 1953, 2). The emergence of the printing culture correlated with the emergence of a bourgeoisie class in the Arab region during that period, especially in Egypt, Lebanon, and Syria (Khodour 1997, 5; Kendall 1997, 216). Scholars such as Khodour and Kendall argue that Arab literary journalism was important for the development of modern literature and that "journalism was itself an actual part of Arabic narrative discourse." Journalism was regarded as a literary product, which explains why veteran journalists such as the Lebanese Ghassan Tueni of *Al-Nahar* newspaper (1926–2005) and the Egyptian Fathy Ghanem believed poets and novelists were "a kind of journalist" (Mellor 2011, 31).

Journalism in the Arab World was not a source of profit (Abu Zeid 1993, 17) in its formative phases, with many of the pioneering journalists considered to be part of the intellectual elites who saw the press as a new vehicle in the struggle against the Ottoman Empire and, later, against European colonialism. Arab intellectuals soon realized the power of the press: as a political mobilization instrument and a means of disseminating their political and ideological beliefs. Muslims in the Maghreb countries paid considerable attention to the role of the press for enhancing Islamic identity, or *shakhsia islamiyya* (Abderrahmane 1998). News in the Arab world, from a historical perspective, was not mass produced; its main aim was to provide instruction to officials and governors on how to improve their performance (Ayalon 1995, 15); by the middle of the nineteenth century, however, rulers seemed to recognize the influential role the media had. Isma'il (1863–1879), the grandson of Khedive Muhammad 'Ali, the powerful nineteenth-century Egyptian ruler, bought shares in the French paper *Le Temps* to publicize his policies and offered generous subsidies to *Al-Waqa'i' Al-Misriya* (*Egyptian Affairs*), the local newspaper (Ayalon 1995, 19).

The early newspapers in the region not only served as a platform to communicate official messages by political establishments, they were also tools for voicing the concerns and ambitions of Arab intellectuals by contributing to the national struggle against colonialism. The delivery of the intellectuals' views and opinions on questions of national identity and cultural roots was far more important than communicating the news—probably one reason why the press prospered as a forum of political debate at the time in countries such as Egypt, Lebanon, Syria, and Algeria, in which European colonialism was seen as the most serious threat to national identity. Saudi Arabia and Jordan, which enjoyed political stability and independence, did not develop the same press tradition (Ayalon 1995, 74). It is also clear that the Arab press had (and has) always been linked to politics since its inception (McFadden 1953, 1). High illiteracy rates in the region in the early twentieth century, combined with meager advertising revenues, also forced newspapers to depend on subsidies from various political factions for their survival, which, in turn, saw in the press an opportunity to promote their ideologies (McFadden 1953, 7–8); several Arab governments, such as Nasser's Free Officers–led one in Egypt, often saw the press and journalists as their most important allies, even after independence, and sometimes even as spokespersons for the new regimes. The press had then become a communication platform for the new governments' development policies, goals, and views about regional and foreign affairs. This has been the role of Arab journalism for so many decades, interrupted only, albeit briefly, by the War of 1967, when journalists voiced their harsh critiques and disappointment in the failing Arab policies.

The press in the Arab world has been used as an indispensable tool of political publicity and diplomacy; historically, Western governments have supported Arabic-speaking media ventures since the nineteenth century, when some diaspora initiatives were backed by former colonial powers (see Abu Zeid 1993). London and Paris, in particular, were used as "publication centers and listening posts for Arab politicians and journalists" (Tunstall 2007). Arab press undertakings were not confined to the Arab region but overflowed to European cities such as London and Paris, where it was possible to freely express political views. *Kashf al-Niqab*, for example, published by Amin Arsalan in 1894 in Paris, was established in order to defend the Ottoman authorities, and *23 July* magazine was set up in London by the Egyptian Mahmoud Al-Saadani after fleeing the Sadat regime (1970–1981). Al-Saadani's aim was to fight Sadat through overseas media, which allowed him free expression—he returned to Egypt following Sadat's assassination in 1981 (Mellor 2011). Those ventures usually addressed Arabs inside the region rather than those in the diaspora, thereby creating a shared pan-Arab identity and solidarity against other nations (Rinnawi 2006). The media did not necessarily contribute to a "multiethnic public sphere" but rather to the public debates within. They were viewed as examples of press contributions to shifting political debates across frontiers, from the Arab region into a more global arena; consequently, they were transcending traditional territorial boundaries, supported by historical ties to the former colonial powers like Britain or France. Saudi businessmen became the main funders of these ventures between the 1980s and 1990s by setting up several channels such as the ART bouquet, the MBC Group, and so on. Several pan-Arab newspapers were also launched, such as *Al-Hayat* and *Asharq Al-Awsat* in London. The main concern for such dailies was not necessarily to create controversy in the region, as they could not afford "to lose millions of dollars in advertising revenue" (Khazen 1999). Lebanese veteran journalist Hazim Saghiya from *Al-Hayat* once warned that the "media investment is a field that is left to the regimes and those close to them who believe that preserving the status quo is a prerequisite for the continuity of their concessions and interests" (Saghiya 2006, 565). National news media outlets are therefore centralized in terms of geographical locations (usually the capital and large cities) and ownership, while several pan-Arab media outlets are dispersed across the region and Europe, particularly London. It is important to include both the role of the state as well as private businesses, driven by commercial interests as well as by close links to ruling elites, in the analysis of pan-Arab satellite channels. Some scholars (El-Sherif 1980, 8) argue that journalism and entertainment have served as signs of modernization in the Gulf states, and others, such as Qatar, "would rather live without an army as long as they have their television channels and newspapers." Qatar's most impressive diplomatic achievement so far was the establishment of the Al-Jazeera (Arabic) channel in 1996, followed by an English-language channel in 2006, with financial support from the royal family. The channel was said to reflect Qatar's ambition to take an important place on the world political map and to improve some Qatari initiatives as part of that nation's international branding endeavors (Cooper and Momani 2011). Al-Jazeera is believed to have lost much of its glamour since 2010 in view of what has been perceived as its biased reporting of Arab upheavals in the Middle East and North Africa.

Arab journalism has moved through several phases of development, starting from the independence of Arab states in the 1950s to the uprisings taking place during the so-called Arab Spring. The 1950s saw that journalism was very much influenced by the nationalist discourse prevailing in the region, as journalists regarded their role as mobilizers and supporters of the postindependent Arab states. Journalists subsequently clashed with the newly appointed governments, which applied harsh censorship rules in the name of preserving national unity and sought to control rather than give free rein to the media. The proliferation of nationalist discourse in Arab newsrooms does not undermine or contradict other discourses such as Islamism (see Pintak 2011); it would be difficult, however, to define and trace attributes of religiosity in pan-Arab journalistic practices or to conveniently divide Arab journalism cultures into the binary of Islamism versus nationalism; attributes of religiosity, on the other hand, are clearly emphasized in dedicated religious channels such as Almajd or in channels supported by Islamic movements, such as Al-Manar (funded by Hezbollah) or the Muslim Brotherhood's Misr 25 channel (which ceased to broadcast in the wake of Morsi's government being phased out in July 2013).

Increased commercialization and regionalization of the Arab TV market caused several Arab journalists to attempt to take up a new role as social reformers in order to shed light on critical deficiencies in their societies. One of Al-Jazeera's star presenters, Faisal Al-Kasim, host of the controversial program *The Opposite Direction*, replied to his critics who saw it as a show based on sensationalism: "I am an academic [referring to his doctoral degree from a British university] and I could have produced an academic program . . . but unfortunately, it would only be watched by the elites. I do think, however, that only this mix in the program made teenagers, youngsters and housewives, an unpoliticized audience . . . , watch this kind of program" (Mellor 2011, 43). Another example is Egyptian Hala Sarhan, one of the popular TV stars in the Middle East, who said what distinguished her programs were the topics and personalities invited to her talk show. She notes, "We would bring normal people to discuss social problems, politics, and religion—everything they don't discuss on government TV. That idea came from my 'American heritage,' from the years that I lived and studied in America" (Schudder 2007).

Arab journalists have recently become the focus of several studies (Zayani and Sahraoui 2007; Ramaprasad and Hamdy 2006; Pintak and Ginges 2008) that tend to favor a "gatekeeper" approach, presuming "that cultural items simply appear at the 'gates' of the media—or culture-producing corporation where they are either admitted or excluded" (Negus 2002, 510). This discounts the role of journalists as cultural intermediaries, however: in their engagement in sifting out certain types of information and their endeavors to legitimize their own products and expertise as cultural intermediaries, journalists help produce and maintain cultural forms that signify some cultural authority in the public sphere (Mellor 2011). Abu Zeid (1993, 32) does not think Arab media research has taken account of the special function of news in developing countries, which includes the moral and social responsibility of journalists to use news in an appropriate manner, and in order to preserve national unity, it is important not to instigate ethnic or religious conflicts (Abdel Nabi 1989). Journalists generally seem to prioritize the developmental role of news, particularly with respect to preserving the moral and cultural heritage of their communities.

Arab journalists also place political news at the top of their news agenda. Their priority is news not only about local politics but, more important, about foreign policies relating to Egypt, Syria, Iraq, Lebanon, and the Palestinian territories. There is no doubt that topical political events, from kidnapping and explosions targeting American citizens in Beirut during the early 1980s, the Lockerbie bombing in 1988, and the bombing of US compounds in Saudi Arabia and Kuwait in the mid-1990s to the terrorist attacks of 9/11 in 2001, have all contributed to making Arab political news figure high on both Arab and Western transnational media agendas. It is those events that triggered debates about the much-needed political reforms in the region. The question, however, is the extent to which those events were objectively handled by media.

Objectivity in Arabic news media is bound by the attitude of journalists toward both the issue at hand and the people involved in it. The Palestinian issue serves as an example of how objectivity plays out in the public sphere (Ayish 2002, 149–50). Several, if not all, news media in the Arab countries refer to Palestinians killed by Israelis as "martyrs" while the Israelis are referred to as "aggressors" in order to keep up the morale of Palestinians in the West Bank and Gaza (Ayish 2002, 149–50). Politicians and viewers in the region were irritated by the appearance of some Israeli officials on Arab news channels, suggesting that those channels were being influenced by outside interference. One Arab newsman at the Saudi-owned Middle East Broadcasting Center (MBC) admitted that despite the neutrality sought by his station, it was quite difficult for journalists to abandon their commitment to pan-Arab issues (Ayish 2001). Arab news media were accused of applying their own code of objectivity, or what some scholars call "contextual objectivity" (El-Nawawy and Iskandar 2003), referring to the specific practices of fairness and neutrality appealing to the outlet's target audience that may be deemed subjective in another culture. Such codes of objectivity could explain why Al-Jazeera, for instance, would focus on the issue of victimization when covering the wars in Afghanistan or Iraq, compared with other international networks.

The recent Arab Spring uprisings have strengthened, rather than weakened, Arab journalists' role as activists, as many journalists do not even see any contradiction between their political involvement and their professional objectivity. One editor at the Egyptian newspaper *Al-Masry Al-Youm* defended this trend: "We are no longer hiding our political agenda. We are becoming much more upfront and clear about our political stance and our support for the revolution is becoming clearer in our editorial policy. Being the newspaper with the highest reach today, we have the tools to influence and to take part in major dialogue initiatives in the country" (quoted in Abdel-Sattar 2013, 216). It is also notable that some differences exist among the practices of outlets operating within the same country. In an analysis of the different discourses between the English-language newspaper the *National* and the Arabic-language *Al-Ittihad* (both based in the UAE), Duffy (2013) argues that the former tended to adhere to the Western principles of journalism such as impartiality and crediting sources, whether government officials or independent experts, while *Al-Ittihad* featured more photographs of the events and unaltered press releases or summaries with no credited sources; consequently, although both newspapers, based in the same country, were influenced by the same linguistic and cultural environment, each of them varied in its journalistic practices (Duffy 2013, 39–41).

Media language is also an important issue, particularly in countries like Morocco, characterized by its ethnic and linguistic diversity. Moroccan media use either modern standard Arabic (written variety) or French; the former is understood by 40 percent of the population, and the latter by only 10 percent. This makes media content inaccessible to a large portion of the population, particularly from the Amazigh communities, who have been calling for recognition of their culture and language by the Moroccan media. The country had originally declared Arabic as the official language of Morocco, and the Amazigh culture as part of the pan-Arab culture; however, King Mohammed VI created IRCAM (Royal Institute of the Amazigh Culture) in 2003 to promote Amazigh language and culture (Zaid and Ibahrine 2011, 52).

The main challenge generally facing Arab states since 2011 is how to strike a balance between reforming and liberalizing the pan-Arab media sector while downplaying similar liberalization trends in the political sphere, as will be discussed in more detail in the following section.

THE TWO FACES OF MEDIA LIBERALIZATION

Real GDP in the Arab region has continued to grow by more than 5 percent since 2011, despite the recent uprisings and thanks to the significant state spending recorded in the Gulf subregion, particularly Qatar, Saudi

Arabia, and the UAE, which accounted for more than 70 percent of that growth. The media sector, on the other hand, suffered from reduced advertising spending, particularly in Egypt, Bahrain, and Libya (Dubai Press Club 2011, 8–9). Local and pan-Arab media were generally under state control, but Arab nations also allowed a significant degree of economic liberalization across the media sector. The Arab region, in this respect, represents a unique case in which commercialization and liberalization of selected media industries have gone hand in hand with continuous state intervention and increasing self-censorship. Palestinian journalists, for instance, practice self-censorship in the Palestinian territories for fear of being subjected to punitive measures by the Israeli authorities such as detention (Nussibeh and Dickinson 2012, 105). The thriving Arab media scene is often claimed to be the result of a combination of Gulf wealth and the unifying Arabic language (IREX 2006, x–xi). Arab states confined their recent reforms to the business and education sectors, implementing Western neoliberal policies and promoting slogans about "fast-turning the production wheels" in order to accelerate the accumulation of wealth while keeping a firm grip on the cultural industries. Economic reforms were easier to implement, resulting in massive privatization programs across the region, something that also "spilled over to the communication sector with the expansion of privately-owned print media and book publishing outlets, and the launch of commercial broadcast operations inside and outside the Arab region" (Ayish 2001, 123). Arab political leaders wanted partial benefit from economic globalization—they were reluctant to simultaneously open up their cultural sphere to the same globalization forces, especially in view of warnings against the flow of American cultural products as a threat to national identity (Al-Jabri 1997). Several Arab states, such as Egypt, embraced open-market policies and competed with other nations in market liberalization and privatization, similar to the launching of several free-zone media cities in Egypt (1997), Dubai (2001), and Jordan (2001). These projects, however, continued to struggle for survival in the face of sweeping political and economic transitions (Khalil 2013).

National media reforms, on the other hand, such as those undertaken by Saudi Arabia, aimed primarily to preserve the political status quo, allowing the monarchy to expand its media reach thanks to the influence of the state-owned media presence within and outside the kingdom (Kraidy 2013). The recent uprisings in Libya led to the total breakdown of state broadcasting channels—media reforms had been completely neglected under Gadhafi's regime (Richter 2013). The broadcasting sector in the UAE contributed to the state's development plans while serving as the guardian of national identity. The UAE efforts to liberalize its media sector suggested the state's strategy to develop a sustainable media industry in the Emirates. The broadcasting sector embarked on "Emiratization" programs to ensure the recruitment of UAE nationals in this sector, while including a significant amount of national identity content in its programming (Ayish 2013). The UAE also hosts the English-language newspaper the *National*, which had more than two hundred Western journalists hired from respected outlets who contributed to the vision of the newspaper to "provide quality, must-have reading" and to help change Arab societies. The publication was led by the former editor of the British *Daily Telegraph* (Duffy 2013, 30).

It is therefore necessary to involve the state as an important factor in the analysis of the media scene in the Arab region: states, according to Guaaybess, "take part in a national destiny and political traditions; they create fluctuating ideologies like Nasserism, Arab nationalism [and] Ba'athism before finally abiding—for the vast majority of them—by the precepts of economic liberalism" (Guaaybess 2013, 6); furthermore, although private ownership of newspapers was allowed in several Arab countries, Arab governments have controlled publishing industries by using laws that differ from one country to another (see Mellor 2005, 30–33).

THE STATE AS REGULATOR

The focus of many Arab states has been on liberating the economic sphere by adopting neoliberal and capitalist values while keeping the social and political domain under state control. The expansion of private television and radio stations, the increased penetration of the Internet, and the launch of media free zones allowed the state to create a favorable business environment for media production, provided the media was not used to promote political activism through drama, talk shows, or current affairs programs. The rhetoric of the post-Arab uprisings—"fast-turning the production wheel"—was still exploited in order to enforce the idea that wealth, and not political debate, was the only avenue toward development. Arab media investments increased (particularly by the Gulf states), with several states launching free-zone media cities to encourage growth in this sector, but rigid media laws and self-censorship continued to define communication across the region. Egypt imposed an emergency law following the assassination of the former president Sadat in 1981, which was never rescinded. The 2011 Egyptian revolution was accompanied by massive protests to end the emergency law.

The Supreme Council of the Armed Forces (SCAF) did not revoke it but amended it by adding new articles in September 2011. It was partially lifted in January 2012 and finally withdrawn on May 31, 2012. A year later, the acting president, Adly Mansour, declared a new state of emergency beginning August 14, 2013, following the June popular uprising. In Jordan, journalists could be prosecuted according to the Press and Publications Law, although the Jordanian constitution guarantees citizens' freedom to express their opinion through speech, writing, photographic representation, and so on. Syria enforced emergency laws that superseded constitutional rights of free speech. Bahrain held a referendum in 2002 that supported free speech but retained Press Law No. 47, which authorized the state to prosecute journalists, therefore encouraging self-censorship. More than one hundred defamation cases in Algeria were brought to court in 2005 alone (IREX 2006).

The region still has the poorest records in terms of freedom of opinion and expression, despite the Arab uprisings and the demands for more freedom. No country ranked in the "free" category in 2012–2013, while only five countries were described as "partly free" and fourteen as "not free." Traditional media, such as print and broadcasting, remain largely controlled by government editorial directives (Freedom House 2013). Arab states' rankings were in the lower half, with Syria placed in the bottom 10 out of all 197 nations surveyed in the Freedom of the Press 2013 index (Freedom House 2013). Gains observed in Libya and Tunisia in 2011 were not accompanied by regulatory changes. Access to information had improved in 2012 in Tunisia, but the new constitution introduced further restrictions on freedom of expression. The same can be said about Egypt, where the 2012 constitution introduced new press limitations on political and cultural grounds. The Egyptian media landscape suffered from an increasing polarization following the election of the Muslim Brotherhood in June 2012—some media outlets favored the Islamist groups, while others adopted an anti-Islamist approach. The Bahraini government tightened its grip on the press following the protests in 2011 and 2012; Kuwait witnessed the shutdown of several media outlets and the arrest of some journalists who used Twitter to spread information on the demonstrations. The UAE, citing national security and social stability issues, issued the 2012 cybercrime law, which applied to a wide range of online violations. The only two states that saw some improvement were Yemen and Syria, with the former allowing private radio stations and new TV stations and the latter losing its centralized control over the media, which allowed new outlets to emerge as well as citizen journalism to increase (Freedom House 2013).

A serious challenge facing Arab journalists was the lack of ethical and legal frameworks to govern online journalism, which was a real disadvantage for online journalists who did not enjoy the protection of existing laws (Ali 2006, 48). Egypt lacked regulations that governed the Internet, and, as such, the government could arrest any social media user of Twitter or a blog, exemplified by the online activist Asmaa Mahfouz, who was arrested by the military in August 2011 on the pretext of a post to Facebook that was deemed to be incitement to violence. She was then released on bail, and the charges were later dropped (Abdulla 2013, 70). More recently, a new syndicate for online journalists was formed on March 26, 2011, in the wake of the toppling of the Hosni Mubarak regime, which caused controversy among media professionals such as the former head of the Egyptian Journalists Syndicate Makram Mohamed Ahmed. He stated that such new independent syndicates were part of a conspiracy whose aim was to weaken the Egyptian media associations instead of allowing all media professionals to unite in a single syndicate in order to address their concerns (*Al-Ahram Al-Arabi* 2013). Mahmoud Al-Dab, an Egyptian journalist, was summoned by the military prosecutor in October 2011 for criticizing the SCAF, and several other activists were sent to military trials on charges of damaging state security (Mohammed and Gunter 2012, 132).

A new syndicate for online journalists was formed in Jordan in 2012, headed by Shaker Al-Gohary, editor in chief of the online newspaper *Al-Mustaqbal Al-Arabi*. Al-Gohary said that the new syndicate was yet another step toward forming a civil coalition against the amended Press and Publications Law (Labor Watch 2012). A new committee for online journalists was set up on June 20, 2013, in Morocco: not as an independent legal entity but as part of the Journalists Syndicate. Moroccan media professionals welcomed the new legislation citing guaranteed online freedom and preventing the imprisonment of young new media users. Efforts were made to create a code for online journalists who had been calling on the government to allow funding for online outlets similar to the print media (Zaid and Ibahrine 2011, 72).

The Jordanian government, on the other hand, imposed new censorship regulations on news websites in 2013 as part of the Press and Publications Law (Sweis and Baslan 2013, 18). The spread of online news services had challenged the state's censorship regulations, pushing for more freedoms to discuss critical social problems. The Jordanian government amended its Press and Publications Law in 2010, allowing it to block offline or online content, and in 2012, several websites were barred, including the popular 7iber.com; needless to say, the law was met with fierce protests by journalists and bloggers, who saw it as a violation of their freedom of expression (Sweis and Baslan 2013, 24–66). The government also used the Information Systems Cyber Crimes Law in 2010, authorizing Internet café owners to block gambling websites and other online venues that contain sexually or religiously offensive material and to keep records of website information and browser data for a period of not less than six months (Sweis and Baslan 2013, 67). The government, therefore, had more powers to block national and international websites under the new legalization of September 2012. One Jordanian journalist commented on these legal provisions as damaging to the image of Jordan, which "[was] joining the clubs of enemies of the Internet. . . . Eventually it will be unfair to hold owners of websites accountable for readers' comments posted on their websites" (cited in Sweis and Baslan 2013, 67–68).

The government of Morocco became alerted to the power of new media following the 2011 uprisings and mass demonstrations demanding more freedom, and it began censoring and imprisoning bloggers and periodically suspending access to sites such as YouTube. The king ordered the drafting of new constitutional reforms, moving some of his power to the prime minister and declaring the status of Amazigh as an official language together with Arabic, but retained much of his power as head of the judiciary and armed forces (Abdel-Sattar 2013, 107–8).

There were only four TV channels in Iraq under Saddam Hussein's regime: two national Iraqi channels and one satellite channel in addition to "Youth TV"; citizens were banned from possessing satellite television equipment; however, after the 1991 war and with Kurds enjoying relative independence from the central movement in Baghdad, Iraq witnessed a surge in the number of Kurdish television channels—in excess of twenty outlets. The US administration dissolved the Iraqi Ministry of Information following the 2003 war and the toppling of Hussein, and several private media outlets were set up by different religious and ethnic factions, giving rise to polarized journalism based on sectarian or tribal affiliations that had divided society and induced violence against journalists; on a positive note, the diversity of voices in the media sphere suggested a more pluralist media environment (Al-Rawi and Gunter 2012, 61–66).

Not all Arab states had clear interception and access laws in the telecommunications sector, however; in Egypt, for instance, the former minister of communication in Mubarak's government passed a directive authorizing security agencies to intercept citizens' telecommunications, although subsequent constitutional amendments addressed the right of privacy in order to achieve some balance between citizens' right to privacy and national security (Khalaileh and Kisswani 2013, 19). Recent revelations about recorded calls by youth in the now banned April 6 political movement nonetheless showed continued interception in the name of national security.

MODELS OF OWNERSHIP

The six Gulf states recognized the significant role played by private media in influencing pan-Arab public opinion. Saudi Arabia, for example, established public-private partnerships to transmit news beyond its borders

(Al-Jaber and Gunter 2013, 33–34). The increase of Gulf-funded satellite channels may suggest less government ownership of these channels, but the reality was that governments could still impose local media regulations and censorship laws (Al-Jaber and Gunter 2013, 33). Some Gulf countries with the highest levels of connectivity showed very low offline activism, which refutes the causal link between information technology proliferation and militant action. State censorship in countries such as Saudi Arabia had proved effective in controlling online activism. Gulf governments were alerted to the impact of the increasing connectedness with the world via social and satellite media. This impelled them to strike a balance between connecting their states to the world through the Internet while censoring and monitoring unwanted content deemed to destabilize their societies and their cultural systems. These states often cite national security and moral protection as the underlying motives for their regulation of cyberspace and use state-of-the-art technologies. King Abdul Aziz City for Science and Technology (KACST) in Saudi Arabia, for instance, contributes to state regulation of the web by virtue of its sophisticated IT infrastructure. Bahrain also has a special unit under the Ministry of Information, responsible for monitoring and blocking websites that are deemed to threaten the kingdom's national security. The unit was set up following Decree No. 48 of 2002, which regulated online and offline printing. It was followed by another decree in 2009 that prohibited publishing material which might provoke religious hatred on the Internet (Alqudsi-Ghabra, Al-Bannai, and Al-Bahrani 2011, 47–48). Some Arab experts, moreover, called for regulating social media and online journalism, stating that a large number of people interacted via these media, some using them to insult and verbally attack public figures; conversely, the web has the advantage of offering a platform for journalism students and citizen journalists to showcase their work. Yacob Qaddori from *Al-Watan* newspaper (Bahrain) says: "Electronic media have not been used to their full potential as yet, and many of those responsible for new media come from the print sector and therefore may lack the necessary training" (Ehab 2013, 4). Arab media laws are generally restrictive and provide little or no protection for journalists, the majority of whom tend to exercise self-censorship in order to avoid punitive measures from the state (Duffy 2013, 29). In Algeria, for instance, articles 67–72 of the media law issued in 2012 state that online news should be for public interest and be subject to Algerian laws.

Howard and Hussain (2012) argue that countries with extensive cell phone usage seem to have more success in mobilizing protesters and forcing new, even if small, changes. Looking closely at the recent Arab uprisings, Howard and Hussain (2012) state that technology has played an integral role in the protests and that it should be taken into consideration when analyzing the recent upheavals. It is noteworthy that groups calling for social and political reforms existed long before the spread of the Internet or social media; however, these new forms of media have played a pivotal role in facilitating the building of contemporary and extensive networks. This technology, among other things, has provided opportunities for civil society actors to affect national politics; although social media have provided a new platform for several groups who could not otherwise voice their concerns through mainstream media channels, it is important to remember that social media served to facilitate meetings or calls for protests but did not cause the uprisings—these were possible only through sustained street protests and political activism. The Egyptian revolution was not a social media revolution, according to Al-Jazeera Online's chief, Mohamed Nanabhay, but "an Egyptian revolution. Social media and mass media were important and had multiplying effects, but people didn't protest because of Twitter" (Ostrow 2011). This technology, nevertheless, also provides new opportunities for forging stronger ties with international movements and exchanging information with them. Social media, moreover, have proved effective as suitable documentation tools for events across the Arab world, consequently sharing visible events during the so-called Arab Spring countries with their citizens and allowing them to draw lessons from ongoing incidents, not to mention the pivotal role this technology has played in changing the journalistic culture across the region.

Private ownership of broadcasting companies has recently been allowed in several Arab countries, although this sector has remained under close state scrutiny because of its potential to reach all citizens, regardless of their status or education. It has also been credited for its role in sustaining national unity and spreading the feeling of community among citizens; on the other hand, its use as a political communication instrument was also considered too dangerous to entrust to hostile hands, hence the imposition of state control (Amin 2001, 29).

There are no legal requirements for media organizations to report ownership information in Egypt, making it difficult to acquire reliable data about television ownership in the country following the revocation of the state's requirement to approve new licenses. The recent trend by businessmen to possess their own satellite channels was driven by a desire to protect themselves against potential attacks by other television stations or the press, and as such, their outlets were not necessarily meant to be profitable businesses, but rather to achieve a certain political agenda (Abdulla 2013, 64–65).

There is a mix of private and public ownership of media outlets in Morocco, including party press, which also receive government subsidies. Television, however, is still monopolized by the government, although the recent liberalization of the audiovisual sector allows for the launch of private TV channels (Zaid and Ibahrine 2011, 115). The 2004 Audiovisual Communication Law prohibited broadcasting corporations from owning more than one media outlet; the number of private radio stations, however, increased from six in 2006 to twenty-four in 2008, of which eighteen were private (Zaid and Ibahrine 2011). The government in Jordan was prevented from owning more than 30 percent of the shares in daily newspapers until 1997, but a new law rendered this provision illegal in 1998, and the government now owns more than 60 percent of the leading daily, *Al-Rai*, and 30 percent of another newspaper, *Al-Doustour*. *Al-Arab Al-Youm* and *Al-Ghad* newspapers, set up in 1997 and 2003, respectively, are the only two independent newspapers in Jordan (Sweis and Baslan 2013, 59).

The Arab print sector grew, albeit slowly, in 2010 and 2011, with the uprisings resulting in new launches, particularly in countries considerably affected by the transitions, such as *Al-Tahrir*, the now banned *Al-Horia wal Adala*, and *Al-Mesryoon* in Egypt. Arab media leaders generally foresee an increase in the use of social media as a source of news in the near future (Dubai Press Club 2011, 25). Independent or party papers have gained prominence following the uprisings, such as *Al-Masry Al-Youm* and *Youm7*. The uprisings have also resulted in an increase of new TV channels such as Al-Tahrir, Al-Hafez, and Misr 25. The latter two, however, were shut down following the toppling of the Muslim Brotherhood leadership, accused of giving strong support to the Brotherhood and Salafist parties. The year 2011 witnessed the launching of more than sixteen new channels in Egypt alone, including Capital Broadcasting Center (CBC), the Al-Nahar group of channels, and 25TV. The latter, run by young producers, relied on an interactive media concept, while CBC, owned by businessman Mohamed Al-Amin, also launched CBC2 and CBC Drama. Al-Nahar channels, previously owned by two businessmen, Alaa Al-Kahky and Walid Mostafa, relinquished the majority shares to Mohamed Al-Amin in September 2011 (Abdulla 2013, 61–62). Libya, on the other hand, witnessed the closure of several state-affiliated papers following the toppling of the Gadhafi regime. New newspapers such as *Awan* and *Assawt*, launched in the wake of the changes in the licensing laws in 2006 in Kuwait, were shut down only a few years later owing to their inability to attract enough readers and therefore advertising revenue (Dubai Press Club 2011, 28–29).

Television generally remains the most preferable medium for Arab audiences, with the number of hours spent watching TV staying unchanged between 2009 and 2012 (approximately three hours per day) (Dubai Press Club 2011, 41). It is estimated that around 660 illegal cable providers serve around one million subscribers to pay TV and other satellite packages in

Lebanon, for instance (Melki et al. 2012, 16). Reviewers, however, tend to regularly follow local news channels, according to a 2009 Nielsen survey in which sampled audiences confirmed their preference for the Lebanese Broadcasting Corporation (LBC), followed by New TV, OTV, and Future TV (Melki et al. 2012, 18–19). Newspaper readership is high in Egypt, about 46 percent of the population, compared with other countries in the Middle East, such as Saudi Arabia, where the readership is about 41 percent but is lower than that in the UAE at about 56 percent. The high readership in Egypt is not matched by high subscription rates, suggesting a free circulation of news through other media such as online. News and current affairs are the most popular topics for newspapers and magazines, although the latter are much less popular in Egypt compared with the rest of the region—around 69 percent of the Egyptian population has no preference for any magazine (Dubai Press Club 2011, 140).

THE CHALLENGE OF CITIZEN JOURNALISM

Privately owned Arab news outlets seem generally keen on engaging with their audiences, who appear to be quite reluctant to be visible in the state-controlled public sphere (Duffy 2013). New technological advances have been used by transnational outlets to fill this void. Western-subsidized media, such as the BBC Arabic Service, for instance, planned their online strategies in the late 1990s, beginning with the launch of the BBC Arabic Online in November 1999. The service was managed by Hosam Sokkari, who began his career at the Arabic Service with a popular program called *Tales of the Electronic Café* and who became the director of the entire BBC Arabic tri-media platform from 2004 until 2010. Sokkari pronounced the aim of the BBC Arabic website in an interview he gave to the Egyptian *Al-Ahram Weekly* in 2001: "Our target user was not the people who listen religiously to the BBC every day. . . . We wanted to address a new generation of Internet users emerging in the Arab world." The BBC Arabic Online proved to be a success story—it received the best news service award for the year 2000 by Arabianbusiness.com (Abdel Latif 2001). The BBCArabic.com site recently won recognition from fellow journalists in the BBC Corporation for particular online projects that raised the profile of the service. Those projects include *Hekayti* (My Story), which profiled a range of young Arab women talking about their ambitions through pictures depicting their daily lives. Other media outlets followed suit by offering their own web services after the launch of BBCArabic.com. Al-Jazeera launched Aljazeera.net in 2001 as part of the Al-Jazeera group, which provides an extensive database of news and an archive of Arabic programs. Aljazeera.net won the 2008 Arab Journalism Award, an award established in Dubai in 2004.[1] Any views published had to go through editorial approval in order to ensure "the credibility of information and that the views [were] not propaganda or incite[ment] to insult[s] or violence against religio[us] or racial groups," explains Mohamed Al-Moukhtar, acting editor of Aljazeera.net.[2] The rival channel, Al-Arabiya, based in Dubai, also launched a web service—Alarabiya.net—in 2004, after reviewing competitive sites in order to define the topics that interested young Arabs.

Newspapers such as *Al-Masry Al-Youm* recently increased their use of interactive features on their websites, introducing a *Sharek* (Participate) corner to invite comments from readers in addition to offering a live forum and social media–based live blog. During the 2011 parliamentary elections and the 2012 presidential elections, the site featured interactive maps inviting users to report election fraud cases (Abdel-Sattar 2013, 211). The expansion of technology in Arab newsrooms also meant a dramatic increase in the use of visual production, particularly videos, even on newspaper websites. Aljazeera.net made the decision to reject correspondents' reports if not accompanied by visuals; similarly, *Al-Masry Al-Youm* encouraged print journalists to produce more videos as part of its efforts to converge multimedia production within the print newsroom (Abdel-Sattar 2013, 338).

The recent Arab upheavals have also illustrated the rising role of citizen journalists, working in tandem or collusion with other journalistic traditions. An example is *Tweets from Tahrir*, a book which compiled some fifty tweets, in chronological order, from a sample of Egyptian revolutionists in Tahrir Square. The tweets were edited by Alex Nunns, a British journalist, and Nadia Idle, an Egyptian who was in Cairo during the protests. The book's online publicity material emphasizes the essential roles that activists on Twitter played in the revolution, making special note of the quality of their contributions. Bloggers also communicated information to their followers through links to mainstream news sites. Twitter was used to *retweet* coverage from the mainstream media. Mainstream journalists, on the other hand, used social media to supplement their investigations, with some receiving broken stories directly from activists (Bossio and Bebawi 2012). Digital services were also harnessed for commercial purposes. The vice-chairman of *Al-Masry Al-Youm* pointed out the profitability of the SMS service for his newspaper, although the newspaper lacked digital strategy and could not at first see the point of such a service: "I thought it was not going to bring profit. You cannot imagine how profitable it was. This was by far the most profitable [digital service] we had. I think we now have something like half a million [mobile phone] subscribers. I thought it would bring 20,000 [Egyptian] pounds a month; it is actually bringing nearly half a million pounds a month" (quoted in Abdel-Sattar 2013, 197).

Arab mainstream media depended to some extent on information from social media sites such as Facebook and YouTube during the recent uprisings because covering events in affected countries was dangerous and expensive (Ali and Fahmy 2013). Governments have continued to maintain a strong grip over traditional media, however, by attempting to infiltrate and, at times, black out what they perceive as hostile social media sites. Social media have provided a new platform for several groups who could not otherwise voice their concerns through mainstream media channels. It is important to remember that although social media have served as tools to facilitate meetings or call for protests, they have not caused the uprisings; such action can be possible only with continuous street protests and political activism. Social media have created the platform for allowing citizen journalists to be heard; traditional media have practiced their role as gatekeepers in selecting the information they want to reach wider audiences (Ali and Fahmy 2013).

Social media sites, particularly Facebook and Twitter, have provided new platforms for young Muslims to engage with their faith and with fellow Muslims across the world in what is called a virtual *umma* (nation), allowing Muslims to access a wide range of Islamic scholarship online (Janmohamed 2012). Social media have also been used by Islamic religious authorities to promote religious knowledge, such as uploading religious lectures on YouTube channels, using Twitter to tweet the Qur'an, or tweeting about Haj (pilgrimage) experiences live from Mecca (Janmohamed 2012). Social media were the main platforms in Saudi Arabia in 2012 used by those following the Saudi poet and journalist Hamza Kashgari's tweets about the Prophet Mohammed that triggered anger in the kingdom and the region at large. A Facebook group was set up calling for Kashgari's prosecution, and tens of thousands joined the group. The incident induced a fatwa by the grand mufti of Saudi Arabia, who denounced Twitter as "a platform for trading accusations and for promoting lies"; likewise, in Pakistan there were calls for Muslims to abandon Twitter and Facebook after Facebook hosted a competition to draw the Prophet (Janmohamed 2012).

Many Arab outlets embraced the new technological advances but not necessarily as an alternative public sphere, as these outlets continued to be subjected to heavy censorship and harsh state regulations. Technology, in fact, reinforced the political dimension in the analysis of Arab journalism and newsroom innovation; for instance, recent uprisings have shaped innovative decisions within online newsrooms and highlighted the political agenda within news organizations (Abdel-Sattar 2013, 347). It is therefore imperative to include the role of state, regulations, and culture in the analysis of Arab journalism.

THE GLOBAL DIMENSION OF ARAB JOURNALISM IN THE MENA REGION

Audiences in the Middle East and North Africa have been able to access journalism from media outlets based outside the region since BBC Arabic was first launched in January 1938. International radio broadcasting in Arabic remained a familiar media phenomenon in the region for over four decades, according to numerous studies suggesting the growing attraction to radio transmissions from the BBC, Radio Monte Carlo, Radio Deutsche Welle, and the Voice of America Arabic services (Ayish 1991); although these broadcasters were perceived by Arabs as outlets for political radio propaganda associated with former colonial powers, the quality of news reporting and coverage of the region's events and issues were often preferable to state-controlled media. The BBC Arabic service, the Voice of America, and Radio Monte Carlo in particular were attracting extensive listenership in the region by audiences deeply disenchanted with their own national media systems (Ayish 1991). The airing of radio talk shows, with diverse voices engaging in vigorous discussions about the region's problems, contrasted starkly with protocol-oriented state radio broadcasts, in which the scope of debate was limited to pro-government viewpoints; if foreign radio broadcasts did not effect immediate changes in the Arab media environment, they were certainly influential in promoting audience appreciation of the potential ways in which journalism could be more effective.

Pan-Arab journalism, as practiced by non-Arab media actors, went through an extraordinary phase in the early 1990s with the advent of satellite television and the web: not only did access to Western-style journalism enhance Arab audiences' understanding of what it takes to be an effective journalist, but it also raised their engagement in the emerging public sphere. A Western-style media outlook marked the rise of channels like Al-Jazeera, Al-Arabiya, and others in the news business, far removed from the rigid formats used in state-controlled media. Newscasts aired on Al-Jazeera, Al-Arabiya, Dubai TV, and so on, were no different in outlook from those carried by international broadcasters like the BBC and American and European television networks. The structure of the newscast around an anchorperson and correspondents stationed in different local and international beats was a new development for Arab audiences. The rise of sensational talk shows like Al-Jazeera's *Opposite Direction*, modeled after the American *Crossfire* show, was an important development in the region's media. The notion that a broadcast journalist was able to find more acceptance in a region where radio and television staff had long been classified as government employees was encouraging. Private ownership of broadcasting operations became another Western-style feature of media development that continued to gain positive reactions in the professional and business communities. State control, which defines broadcast media enterprises in the region, is ever present, as previously noted, but the fact that production and gatekeeping decisions are no longer made by government bureaucrats is an important development.

The growing pervasiveness of non-Arab news media in the Middle East has been triggered not only by transitions in information and communication technology but also by continued turbulence and conflicts in a region long viewed as a strategic asset for international powers. Available data suggest growing popularity for those broadcast outlets in the Arab world, where national media systems continue to be constrained by state interventions and poor funding. The presatellite television era saw broadcast rivalry in the region structured around foreign radio outlets competing with government-controlled radio operations. It was natural for Arab audiences, disenchanted with state media systems, to favor the more inclusive, professional, and diverse journalism practices those broadcasters brought to the region. In the new age of satellite television and the Internet, foreign television channels in Arabic, such as the US Alhurra, BBC Arabic, France 24, Sky News Arabia, and CNN Arabic, have to grapple with challenges emanating from more competitive outlets such as Al-Jazeera, Al-Arabiya, Al-Mayadeen, and Dubai TV. The latter seem to be using the same professional techniques and strategies associated with Western-style journalism to improve their positions on the region's changing media map. Foreign broadcast channels have been far superior to state-controlled media outlets in terms of news coverage and talk shows, but they seem to be facing challenging times competing with popular Arab channels. It is clear, however, that those international media outlets are having an enduring impact on the state of journalism in the region, regardless of the outcome that competition generates.

CONCLUSION

The above discussion shows how new media have been embraced as effective tools in the hands of local journalists to avoid restrictive state regulations associated with mainstream professional syndicates or self-censorship practices in traditional outlets. Arab journalism in the twenty-first century continues to embrace many of the traditional values of nationalism and mobilization, despite recent uprisings and the wave of liberal market developments. What contributed to the continuation of this role are region-wide regulatory policies that have not encouraged a genuine departure from traditional practices; although more investment is being put into the technology and journalism sector, this free market liberalism has not been matched by political liberalism in the public sphere; indeed, online journalism is usually characterized by its diversity of forms, freedom from mainstream media regulations, and relative delocalization (McQuail 2013, 14).

The following chapters address the consequences of the recent technological changes for Arab journalistic practices and journalists' relations to society. American and Western European journalists may see a novel form of competition embodied in "citizen journalism" and the blogosphere in the new and social media; on the other hand, Arab journalists may see in them a new way of extending their role as culture custodians while reaching out to wider audiences. It is the aim of the following chapters to assess the deployment of social media platforms in a journalistic context associated with pan-Arab media from inside the region and beyond. An assessment such as this would be an important contribution to the ongoing scholarly discussions about Arab journalistic practices, in view of the changing role of journalists in society.

NOTES

1. http://www.panarabwebawards.org/index.shtml.
2. http://www.e-msjed.com/msjed/site/details.asp?topici=953.

2

Information and Communications Transitions in the MENA Region

The 1990s were a watershed decade for communications development in the Arab world. It was in those years that the region came to experience the satellite television and the World Wide Web revolution in its inception phases. When the world was switching from digital to analog media production and distribution systems, the MENA region was not a passive bystander. The volume of investments in satellite broadcasting, mobile telephony, and the Internet, especially in the oil-rich countries of the Gulf, was quite astounding by global standards. In 2014, spending in the region, according to IDC reports, was projected to exceed $32 billion.[1] A profound belief in the power of communications to transform societies in the age of globalization was defining national and regional engagement with the sweeping digital communications revolution.

In significant ways, MENA region governments are central drivers of technological transformations, seeing them as unique opportunities for managing economic, social, and cultural transitions. Satellite television is viewed as a powerful force for taking national voices into global audiences with diverse political and cultural backgrounds. Governments came to see the burgeoning telecommunications sector, marked by huge business convergence and market entrepreneurship, as heralding a new era of economic prosperity and social integration. New web technologies were viewed as new venues for propagating political and ideological messages in an increasingly destabilized area long torn by sectarian and political conflicts. In countries like the United Arab Emirates, the government has been leading the information and communications transitions (ICT) bandwagon to ensure a competitive edge in the service sector and in the national economy at large. The UAE has been the first country in the region to apply the concept of e-government at federal and local levels. In 2014, Dubai's launch of the "smart government" initiative testified to the leading role of the state in new technology adoptions and innovations.

But governments have not been the only players in the MENA digital revolution. An emerging private sector was always eyeing media, information, and telecommunications sectors as vital to business investment. The traditional business model that showed little private-sector affinity to commercial media enterprises was giving way to new visions of commercial media as powerful contributors to national development. Toward the end of the 1980s, mostly print media had been run by private operators, while broadcasting, with the exception of the Lebanese Broadcasting Corporation (LBC), remained an exclusive state domain. The first Arab satellite television channel, the Middle East Broadcasting Center (MBC), was launched from studio facilities in London in October 1991 as a commercial broadcaster targeting audiences in the Middle East and North Africa. By the end of 2012, there were more than 900 satellite television channels with private affiliations alongside some 250 government channels in the area (ASBU 2013). The telecommunications sector has also proved to be a big lure for private investors. Traditionally a government-owned provider of wired landline telephony services, this sector has experienced major expansions with its growing engagement in the commercial delivery of paid mobile data, Internet, and multimedia content services. The private sector has also brought about huge Internet investment opportunities in the fields of e-commerce, e-services, e-learning, and others. The liberalization of the communications markets in the MENA region has clearly enabled more abundant and diversified services with greater accessibility.

Governments and private sector investors are not the only players leading technological transitions in the Arab World. The liberal winds of globalization and the recent political and social upheavals in the region have strongly asserted a significant civil society stake in those transformations. Satellite television technology has enabled average citizens' exposure to news and entertainment from countries half a world away, thus breaking up a long-standing state monopoly over television broadcasting. The proliferation of mobile telephony services has also given rise to networked societies where individuals are able to communicate in freer and more open ways with others across national frontiers. The web, with its huge social media networking potential to span the globe, is widely believed to have induced the most empowering social and political impact in the Arab world. Social media have also attracted increasing scholarly and policy attention in view of their perceived role in the recent upheavals, with some scholars and commentators seeing them as drivers of the so-called Arab Spring. This issue is highly contested in this book, with no consensus among scholars and policy makers on how social media contributed to those uprisings. On the other hand, while the MENA region's technological diffusion has been instrumental for fostering civic consciousness and market diversification, restrictive government regulations seem to have militated against genuine democratization of Arab societies.

Other stakeholders with vested interests in the Arab communications transitions include the international information technology giants, which see the MENA region as a potentially huge market for their digital communications systems. With virtually no credible competition from local players, global IT and knowledge industry heavyweights like Apple, Samsung, Microsoft, Adobe, Google, Sony, Panasonic, Blackberry, Nokia, and others have been defining the region's digital technology map. The Arab world has clearly made some headway into the knowledge industries, as evident in technology parks like Dubai Internet City and King Abdullah City for Science and Technology. But the poor presence of Arabic content on the web (3 percent) has always been a major challenge to harnessing cyberspace in social and economic development. Limited Internet access in some parts of the MENA region and shortage of Arabized software packages have always discouraged the full utilization of the Internet for content creation and dissemination. A United Nations study on the status of digital content in the Arab world (ESCWA 2012) called for initiating comprehensive digital content strategies in the region to build up national capacities and promote indigenous industries.

This chapter provides an analysis of the Arab world's communications trends and implications. The objective here is to enable readers to understand the context of ICT diffusion in which pan-Arab media social engagement takes place. In doing so, we draw on data from updated statistical reports issued by organizations like the International Telecommunications Union, the Dubai School of Government, and Arab Advisors Group. Variations in telecommunications and Internet diffusion levels across the region, among other things, are highly significant for understanding MENA audience engagements with pan-Arab media in cyberspace.

SATELLITE TELEVISION

The launch of private television in the Arab world in the early 1990s marked a significant breakthrough in the region's broadcast landscape, long monopolized by the state. From a dominantly state-controlled structure, television in the Arab world has shifted into a more diversified ownership system where private broadcasters have come to operate alongside those owned and operated by government (Ayish 2003). The

MBC was the first private television service to be launched from studio facilities in London (Ayish 1997). The MBC project was followed by scores of government satellite television launches in Egypt, the United Arab Emirates, Jordan, Saudi Arabia, Kuwait, Bahrain, Oman, Algeria, Morocco, Lebanon, Syria, and Qatar. The basic assumption at that time was that emerging satellite television technology would go a long way toward enabling MENA nations to reach out to global audiences to communicate their political and cultural views. On the other hand, satellite television was also perceived as a feature of globalization and Westernization that carried serious concerns pertaining to indigenous cultural and social values and traditions. In the Gulf region, discussions at the time came to embrace national identity and state sovereignty as the most likely casualties of globalized television broadcasting.

But apart from the social and cultural debates on satellite broadcasting in the MENA region, television, as a media operation, was experiencing substantial shifts in its formats and functions. The establishment of all-news channels and multi-themed networks brought Arab viewers, for the first time, face to face with Western-style news and entertainment. Al-Jazeera Satellite Channel (JSC) was launched in 1996 from Qatar as the first all-news Arabic channel in the region, presenting itself as a forum for "the opinion and the other opinion." The channel's critical reporting of domestic political and religious developments in several Arab countries triggered numerous diplomatic incidents, some of which led to the closure of some of its offices abroad (Da Lage 2005, 56). Miles (2003) notes that as a result of Al-Jazeera's critique of many Arab governments, Arab television was viewed by some as a virtual "political party." But Miles argues that media can surely not compensate for the lack of civil society organization and the weakness of the existing opposition. Zayani (2005) took a more critical approach to Al-Jazeera while recognizing its impressive contributions to the emerging Arab public sphere in the area. During the recent Arab upheavals, Al-Jazeera's reporting of events and issues was perceived as far less evenhanded than many had thought (Hashem 2012; Youssef 2013; Al-Basami 2013).

But Al-Jazeera is not the only leading Arabic satellite television channel to define the region's broadcast media landscape. In January 2003, Al-Arabiya satellite television channel was launched from Dubai Media City to provide Arab viewers with alternative perspectives regarding issues and events relating to the conflict in Iraq, the US-waged global "war on terror," and political reforms in the region. Lynch (2004) noted that Al-Arabiya offered a platform to liberal reformers, with a tone tempered by greater restraint and sensitivity to the concerns of major Arab states. Foreign governments also launched Arabic-speaking television channels as part of ongoing political rivalry in the region. Examples include the

US-sponsored Alhurra channel, Iran's Al-Alam channel, France 24, Russia Today, Al-Mayadeen, Al-Aan TV, and the BBC Arabic television channel. By the end of 2013, more than nine hundred satellite television channels were operating in the MENA region; the overwhelming majority of them were free-to-air channels (ASBU 2013). Free-to-air Arabic television is carried to audiences in the MENA region and beyond on satellite systems such as Arabsat, Nilesat, Yahsat, Noorsat, Turksat, Asiasat, Telestar, Eutelsat, and Hotbird (Abbassi 2013). Though those systems operate on a commercial basis, governments continue to exercise some control over their carried content. Since the start of Arab uprisings in late 2010, around seven government and private channels have been banned from transmitting over Arabsat and Nilesat systems for political or religious reasons. Among others, they included the Syrian state TV channel, the Iranian Al-Alam channel, and the London-based Al-Hiwar channel.

The rise of private/semiprivate satellite television broadcasters in the MENA region has echoed views of broadcasting as a potentially promising business investment. Emerging networks such as MBC, Al-Jazeera, the Almajd network, Orbit Showtime, the Al-Mayadeen channel, Future Television, Sky News Arabia, and the Lebanese Broadcasting Corporation (LBC) testify to the drastic changes taking place in the region's media landscape. Egypt and the United Arab Emirates have the largest number of government and private channels, which provide content ranging from news to entertainment, education, sports, and business. Private channels and networks are sustained by corporate funds, advertising, and sponsorship. Though there is no updated data on ad spending in the Arab world, pan-Arab advertising spending decreased by 12 percent in 2011 but is expected to pick up by 8.8 percent for 2015 (ZenithOptimedia 2013). In addition to government and private channels, the region's television sphere has also seen the rise of Arabic television services affiliated with foreign governments. Those include the US Alhurra channel, BBC Arabic channel, France 24 channel, Russia Today channel, and Iran's Al-Alam channel. These satellite television services broadcast around the clock with mostly news and current-affairs programming to Arab audiences in the MENA region. Some of these channels have been selected for this study's social media engagement analysis.

TELECOMMUNICATIONS: GOING MOBILE

Like satellite television, the telecommunications sector in the Arab world was for long an exclusive state concern. Prior to the 1990s, national telecommunications companies providing landline telephony and telegraphy services were owned by governments and offered services on a subscription basis. But with the advent of the information and communications transitions of the 1990s, along with the liberalization of communications markets in the region, the telecommunications sector was no longer monopolized by the state, which, however, remains the sole regulator of the sector. New entrants into the market have a mainly commercial character, competing with other private or quasi-government telecommunications service providers. Their services have come to embrace conventional landline telephony, mobile telephony, Internet communications, data, broadband and multimedia services, and mobile television. Available data suggest top telecommunications companies in the MENA region are based in Gulf countries where mobile devices and Internet technologies are most widely diffused. Leading Gulf companies like Zain, Batelco, Etisalat, Du, and Mobily are operating in national and regional telecommunications markets with wide-ranging telephony, Internet, and data services. The UAE telecommunications corporation Etisalat, for example, operates services in countries like Benin, Central African Republic, Egypt, Gabon, Ivory Coast, Niger, Nigeria, Saudi Arabia, Sudan, Tanzania, and Togo.

Despite the limited mobile telephone subscription base in the Arab world compared with other regions, the rate of growth between 2005 and 2013 was quite impressive: 4.6 times in the MENA region; 6.2 in Africa; 4.2 in Asia-Pacific; 2.8 in the CIS region; 1.4 in Europe; and 2.2 in the Americas (table 2.1). Among the Arab states, oil-rich countries have the highest telephone subscription rates per total population, which suggests greater accessibility as driven by higher investments in this sector. According to International Telecommunication Union (ITU) 2012 data, Saudi Arabia had the highest mobile subscriptions rate per total population (168 percent), followed by the United Arab Emirates (154 percent), Libya (147 percent), and Jordan (131 percent) (table 2.2). The data obviously suggest multiple subscriptions for the same individuals. But all in all, mobile telephony, especially among young users, seems to have

Table 2.1. Mobile/Cellular Subscriptions (in millions)

Region	*2005*	*2006*	*2007*	*2008*	*2009*	*2010*	*2011*	*2012*	*2013*
Africa	87	129	174	246	298	365	438	501	545
Arab States	84	125	173	213	263	310	348	374	394
Asia-Pacific	833	1,074	1,398	1,773	2,165	2,628	3,034	3,290	3,547
CIS	166	227	267	312	355	377	411	444	476
Europe	550	610	677	714	717	724	745	768	790
The Americas	459	552	649	741	809	882	952	998	1,048

Source: ITU 2013.

Table 2.2. Mobile Telephone Subscriptions per Percentage of Population in the MENA Region, 2012

Country	*Subscriptions*	*Percent*
Algeria	37,692,000	94
Bahrain	2,123,903	119
Egypt	96,798,801	119
Iraq	26,756,000	73
Jordan	8,984,252	131
Kuwait	5,100,000	122
Lebanon	3,755,169	87
Libya	9,587,000	147
Mauritania	4,023,746	110
Morocco	39,016,336	115
Oman	5,277,591	125
Palestine	3,190,233	68
Qatar	2,601,210	113
Saudi Arabia	53,012,322	168
Sudan	27,658,595	71
Syria	12,980,000	55
Tunisia	12,841,277	115
UAE	13,775,252	154

Source: ITU 2013.

achieved high penetration rates, stimulating greater Internet access and social media engagement.

In addition to a growing mobile telephony sector, the Arab telecommunications market has experienced increasing technological convergence involving audiovisual and interactive digital platforms. According to the Arab Advisors Group (Hawkes 2012), seventeen Arab countries now have 3G or 3.5G mobile networks, with mobile Internet, video calling, and mobile TV proving to be the most popular services, according to the report. Bahrain, Egypt, Iraq, Jordan, Kuwait, Lebanon, Libya, Mauritania, Morocco, Oman, Qatar, Saudi Arabia, Sudan, Syria, Tunisia, UAE, and Yemen all had 3G or 3.5G services in commercial operation by November 2011. In countries like the United Arab Emirates, the leading telecommunications service provider, Etisalat, also provides digital cable television services to subscribers. But in a region long used to free-to-air television, television subscription remains a challenge facing private telecommunications and entertainment television networks like Orbit Showtime.

THE INTERNET AND SOCIAL MEDIA

Though the Arab world had its first experience with the web in the early 1990s, the region continues to have major variations in terms of access opportunities and usage patterns. According to the ITU statistics, there were 125 million Internet users in the region in 2012, and the number was expected to rise to 141 million in 2013 (ITU 2012). But as table 2.3 suggests, the region as a whole has experienced a quantum leap in Internet access between 2005 and 2013. The number of individuals using the Internet during that period grew by 5.4 times in the MENA region, the second-highest rate in the world after Africa (8.2 times). As for individual countries, table 2.4 shows Bahrain enjoying the highest percentage (88 percent) in 2012, quadrupling in eight years, followed by Kuwait (79.18 percent), tripling in five years, and the UAE, 63 percent compared with 26.27 percent in 2005. Lebanon reached a 61.25 percent level, while Morocco registered a 55 percent level of individuals' access to the Internet. MENA countries with Internet usage percentages ranging between 35 percent and 50 percent include Egypt (44.07 percent), Jordan (41 percent), Qatar (44.30 percent), and Saudi Arabia (36 percent). The data show significant variations among the MENA countries in terms of Internet usage, which suggests variations in audiences' engagement with social media platforms.

The Dubai School of Government's Internet usage report (2013) shows online access in the region hugely enabled through laptops (63 percent) and desktop computers (49 percent) as well as through mobile phones and tab devices by all respondents. The trend toward a growing use of mobile devices to access the Internet in the Arab world seems to be in tune with global patterns in this respect. When we consider ITU data on the proliferation of mobile phones in the region, we conclude that mobility will most likely define the future of Internet engagement in the Arab world for years to come. As we find in the coming chapters, social engagement in the pan-Arab media context has been an outstanding qual-

Table 2.3. Individual Internet Users (in millions)

Region	*2005*	*2006*	*2007*	*2008*	*2009*	*2010*	*2011*	*2012*	*2013*
Africa	17	24	29	48	60	80	101	120	140
Arab States	26	36	44	55	68	90	107	124	141
Asia-Pacific	344	394	503	612	721	868	999	1,133	1,269
CIS	29	35	47	54	66	95	114	130	145
Europe	277	300	340	367	387	411	428	443	467
The Americas	316	346	385	403	424	458	502	542	582

Source: ITU 2013.

Table 2.4. Percentage of Individuals Using the Internet in the MENA Region

Country	*2005*	*2006*	*2007*	*2008*	*2009*	*2010*	*2011*	*2012*
Algeria	5.84	7.38	9.45	10.18	11.23	12.50	14.00	15.23
Bahrain	21.30	28.24	32.91	51.95	53.00	55.00	77.00	88.00
Egypt	12.75	13.66	16.03	18.01	25.69	31.42	39.83	44.07
Iraq	0.90	0.95	0.93	1.00	1.06	2.50	5.00	7.10
Jordan	12.93	13.87	20.00	23.00	26.00	27.20	34.90	41.00
Kuwait	25.93	28.79	34.80	42.00	50.80	61.40	74.20	79.18
Lebanon	10.14	15.00	18.74	22.53	30.14	43.68	52.00	61.25
Libya	3.92	4.30	4.72	9.00	10.80	14.00	14.00	N/A
Mauritania	0.67	0.98	1.43	1.87	2.28	4.00	4.50	5.37
Morocco	15.08	19.77	21.50	33.10	41.30	52.00	53.00	55.00
Oman	3.52	5.89	6.87	7.26	6.76	6.68	8.30	16.68
Palestine	1.84	3.10	4.13	4.40	16.01	18.41	21.18	24.36
Qatar	6.17	10.23	19.24	20.70	24.73	28.97	37.00	44.30
Saudi Arabia	4.68	6.38	8.00	10.23	12.71	19.46	30.00	36.00
Sudan	0.14	0.44	0.54	0.79	1.29	N/A	8.66	N/A
Syria	0.35	2.09	3.40	4.32	5.65	7.83	11.50	14.00
Tunisia	4.30	5.25	6.49	8.53	9.66	12.99	17.10	27.53
UAE	26.27	28.32	29.48	30.13	40.00	52.00	61.00	63.00

Source: ITU 2013.

ity of this mobility feature, with more Arabs going online in the past few years.

Data on web access times show daytime usages are the most common pattern in the region, with lower rates of usage during weekends and on holidays (Dubai School of Government 2013). The highest access time category was six o'clock to ten o'clock at night (30 percent), when individuals are normally outside working hours and at home or outdoors. The convenience of Internet access through mobile devices has made it possible for users to have more frequent virtual engagements. An implication of this increasing online engagement is the potential erosion of interpersonal communications in traditional family and community settings and the diminishing exposure to traditional media channels.

With respect to the use of the Internet as a source of news, the Dubai School of Government survey (2013) shows that 36 percent of respondents got their news online from news sources like media portals and blogs; 28 percent from social media networks; and 28 percent from traditional media. The data suggest a growing role of online media and social networks as credible sources of news about current events and issues in the Arab world. This finding is also consistent with worldwide trends of declining exposure to printed publications as more newspapers continue to migrate online, especially in the aftermath of the global financial crisis.

In the MENA region, the Internet is primarily used for accessing information and for social networking, and the most popular sites were found to be Facebook and Masrawy, a Cairo-based news and video portal (Dubai Press Club 2011, 143). In Lebanon, for instance, social media–savvy youth utilize such media more for chatting and social networking purposes than for political activism (Melki et al. 2012, 42). The *Arab Media Outlook* (Dubai Press Club 2011) labels youth between the ages of fifteen and thirty-four as generation Y, who constitute around 37 percent of the total population and are characterized by their preference of the Internet over television (around 62 percent of them use social media more than once a day). They are also more likely to use social media and post a video of themselves than any other age group (Dubai Press Club 2011, 19).

The *Arab Social Media Report* (Arab Social Media Influencers Summit 2015, 16–18) classifies social media users in the MENA region into five clusters: (1) social butterflies, individuals who are highly social, engage with multiple groups, and have a large circle of friends; (2) explorers, individuals who are in a constant quest for novelty and are quick to learn new features; (3) achievers, curious individuals who are eager to improve their knowledge and are on a quest for logical arguments and proofs; (4) escapists, individuals who long for sociability yet do not have a large circle of friends and who are sensitive, trusting, and even gullible at times; and (5) pragmatics, individuals using social media only when necessary and when useful, mainstreamers using the most popular channels only and residing mainly in the Levant region.

The *Arab Social Media Report* (Arab Social Media Influencers Summit 2015, 18) notes that Arab users believe social media serve as a "life enhancer," brightening up their day and adding excitement to their lives. For many young Arab individuals, being connected to social media makes them feel "alive"! Social media in the region are perceived as having numerous positive aspects that enhance the quality of life of individuals, business profitability, and governmental interaction with the public. For example, 81 percent of respondents thought social media made it easier for people to connect with each other, and 79 percent thought social media have changed the world as we know it. With regard to social media usages, 55 percent of respondents said they used social media to connect with people; 12 percent used it for gaining information, watching videos, listening to music, and sharing photos; and 8 percent used social media as an interesting way to spend time. The report also found that chatting was the most common use of social media, followed by reading others' posts. In terms of the most popular social media platforms, respondents said Facebook and WhatsApp are the most used channels in the MENA region. On average, one-third of users spend less than thirty minutes per session when using social media, and 5 percent spend more than four hours per session. More than half the users are most active on social media during evening hours, and 83 percent of them use smartphones for social media engagement.

At individual country levels, Jordan, according to the report, tops in preference for Facebook, where users accounted for 63 percent, followed by Libya and Palestine at 50 percent. It was least favored in Saudi Arabia and Lebanon, with only 24 percent each of respondents, followed by Bahrain at 26 percent. A vast majority of Facebook users—89 percent—checked in daily, with the highest usage rate in Palestine and Iraq at 99 percent each and the lowest in both Bahrain and Saudi Arabia, at 79 percent and 81 percent, respectively. The report notes that WhatsApp is the social tool most favored in the Arab world, ranked as number 1 by 41 percent. Nearly two out of five users in the Arab world said that WhatsApp is their most preferred, with the highest acceptance in Lebanon and Sudan, at 58 percent and 50 percent of total respondents, respectively. Users in Jordan least preferred it, at only 18 percent. Nearly 84 percent of the respondents had access to WhatsApp. Preference for Twitter, according to the report, was the lowest, with only 4 percent stating they turned to the social media platform and the highest preference in Saudi Arabia and the UAE at 12 percent and 8 percent, respectively, while it is lowest in Egypt at 1 percent.

The report (Arab Social Media Influencers Summit 2015) points out that preferences for Instagram were low, with only 6 percent of the total users stating that they prefer Instagram. It has the highest preference rates in the UAE, Kuwait, and Bahrain at 11 percent each. Users in each of Syria and Libya least preferred it, at only 1 percent of total users. Meanwhile, YouTube was shown to have a low preference rate, with an average 5 percent of the total users saying they prefer it, the highest being in Qatar and Bahrain at 11 percent and 9 percent, respectively. YouTube was not the preferred means for users in Syria. About subscription rates, the report showed that the highest subscription rates are in both Lebanon and Morocco, at 75 percent and 68 percent, respectively, and the lowest rates in both Syria and Palestine, at 12 percent and 15 percent, respectively. Google+, on the other hand, show preference is still very low for users in the study, with only 2 percent of the total users stating that they prefer it and with the highest rates of preference in Morocco and Lebanon at 4 percent in each. Respondents in Palestine did not cite it as a preferred means to them. Google+ has subscription rates of about 29 percent of the users of social media in the Arab world. Finally, the report indicates that LinkedIn is also one of the low-preference means for users, with only 1 percent of the total users stating it is their preferred means. LinkedIn has the highest rates of preference in the UAE and Bahrain, at 2 percent each, while users in Sudan, Libya, Egypt, Algeria, Syria, Palestine, Iraq, and Yemen do not perceive it as a preferred means of social networking.

The 2015 findings seem to be somehow consistent with results of previous social media surveys carried out by the Dubai School of Government (2012). They show that the number of Facebook users in the Arab world stood at 45,194,452 by the end of June 2012, up from 37,390,837 at the beginning of 2012, having increased by about 50 percent since the same time during the previous year. The report shows the percentage of female users remained almost static, having fluctuated slightly between 33.5 percent and 34 percent in 2011. This is still significantly lower than the global trend, where women constitute roughly half of Facebook users. Youth (between the ages of fifteen and twenty-nine) continue to make up around 70 percent of Facebook users in the Arab region, a number that has been holding steady since April 2011. The report shows Gulf Cooperation Council (GCC) countries dominating the top five Arab Facebook users as percentages of populations. The UAE remains at the top of the Arab region, followed by Kuwait, while Qatar has found its way back into the top five. Lebanon and Jordan take up the remaining spots. Recent figures indicate the rise of Arab social media users to more than 71 million (Dubai School of Government 2012), and it is estimated that by 2020, around 20 percent of the Arab labor markets will be related to the Internet and technology sector. In Egypt alone, it is estimated that broadband will help create around seven thousand direct jobs on average per year. In general, broadband helps directly create jobs related to civil works and network installation or indirectly creates jobs for businesses selling goods to those directly involved in network installation, in addition to creating jobs in new business innovation enabled by broadband adoption (Gelvanovska, Rogy, and Rossotto 2014).

The Dubai School of Government (2012) report estimated the number of active Twitter users in the Arab region by the end of June 2012 to be 2,099,706. The estimated number of tweets generated in the Arab region in March 2012 by "active users" was 172,511,590 tweets. The estimated number of daily tweets was 5,750,386 tweets per day, or 3,993 tweets a minute, or roughly 67 tweets every second. The most popular trending hashtags across the Arab region in March 2012 were #bahrain (with 2.8 million mentions in the tweets generated during this period), followed by سوريا (Arabic for Syria) with 1.5 million mentions, بحريين (Arabic for Bahrain), with 1.48 million mentions, #syria (with 1.3. million mentions), #egypt (with 900,000 mentions), and #kuwait (with 860,000 mentions). The top five Arab countries in terms of number of Twitter users are Egypt, Saudi Arabia, Kuwait, UAE, and Lebanon. For the first time, a non-GCC country besides Egypt—in this case, Lebanon—has made its way into the top five, closely ahead of the previous fifth-place-ranking country, Bahrain. The number of tweets originating in selected Arab countries in March 2012 seems highly astonishing. An interesting feature of the findings relates to tweets from Kuwait during that period (58,900,000), followed by Saudi Arabia (49,600,000), Egypt (19,530,000), and the UAE (15,500,000). Compared to Egypt, the three GCC countries have smaller populations, but two of them (Kuwait and Saudi Arabia) generated larger numbers of tweets.

The *Arab Social Media Report* (*ASMR*) (Dubai School of Government 2012) notes that the total number of LinkedIn users in the Arab world stands at 4,294,484 (as of the end of June 2012), up from 3,588,215 at the beginning of February. By the end of June 2012, the country average for LinkedIn user penetration in the Arab region was approximately 2 percent. The number of LinkedIn users in the Arab world has grown by 20 percent between February and June 2012. Similarly to Facebook, the percentage of female users is lower than that of the men, at 28 percent. This is also significantly lower than the global trend, where women constitute 43 percent of LinkedIn users. Young people (between the ages of eighteen and thirty-four) make up around 70 percent of LinkedIn users and, similarly to Facebook, seem to be the driving force behind the growth of LinkedIn. Interestingly, of this segment, university students and fresh graduates make up a much smaller percentage than young people who are more established in their careers. The percentage of female LinkedIn users is lower than that of males, at 28 percent, and is also significantly lower than the global trend, where women constitute 43 percent of LinkedIn users.

ASMR (Dubai School of Government 2012) shows that YouTube playbacks have doubled in the previous year in the Arab region. There are 167 million video views a day in the Arab region, putting the region in the number-two spot in the world (behind the United States and ahead of Brazil). Views in the region have grown by 120 percent in the previous six months. One hour of YouTube video is uploaded in the Arab region every minute. There are 90 million video views in Saudi Arabia per day (the highest number of YouTube views in the world per Internet user). Saudi Arabia leads the region with the most playbacks, followed by Egypt, Morocco, and UAE, with uploads jumping 200 percent and views increased 260 percent (Saudi Arabia); 150 percent and views increased 220 percent (Egypt); 420 percent and uploads increased 100 percent (Tunisia); 150 percent (Yemen); 140 percent and views increased 240 percent (Jordan).

The 2012 report also shows perceptions that social media played a role in empowering to influence change in community / country to be 51 percent in Kuwait; 46 percent in Egypt, Lebanon, and Oman; 43 percent in Bahrain; and 42 percent in Jordan. The percentage of respondents who felt social media connected them more to their communities was 92 percent in Saudi Arabia, 85 percent in Egypt, and 83 percent in the UAE. Those who thought social media enforced their national identity included 85 percent in Egypt, 83 percent in Bahrain, 80 percent in both Jordan and Kuwait, and 78 percent in both Oman and Saudi Arabia. The percentages of those who feel they are more of a "global citizen" today were 83 percent in Bahrain, 80 percent in Jordan, 79 percent in Egypt, and 78 percent in Lebanon. Those who thought using social media enforced their regional identity included 80 percent in Jordan, 78 percent in Egypt, 77 percent in Kuwait, and 76 percent in Oman. Those who felt using social media enforced their religious identity included 76 percent in Jordan, 75 percent in Kuwait, 74 percent in Egypt, and 73 percent in Bahrain.

Undoubtedly, social media have changed the way Arab peoples communicate. In Saudi Arabia, the majority of those who use the Internet are young (under thirty-five) males. This could be due to the availability of PCs at work and education institutions as well as in corporations, which are more accessible to men than to women. There is also a correlation between high income and education and the frequency of using electronic news sites (Al Arabi 2006, 430–31), although television is still regarded as one credible source of news, followed by radio. On the other hand, the print press is lagging behind, as will be discussed below (Al Arabi 2006, 432). Thus, in Saudi Arabia, the most fervent users of social media are youth between eighteen and thirty-four years old, and Saudis also use other forms of social media extensively, such as YouTube (Winder 2014, 2). In fact, via YouTube, Saudis watch ninety million videos per day, which is the highest rate of viewership in the world. However, Twitter remains the most important communication medium now in the Arabian kingdom, and it has undoubtedly greatly influenced the sociopolitical landscape. The usage of Twitter in the Saudi kingdom has increased by 3,000 percent in 2012, with an average of fifty million tweets posted per month. It is, again, the age groups of youth between eighteen and thirty-four that constitute the biggest demographic of Twitter users in Saudi Arabia, and women make up 45 percent of the market for Saudi Twitter accounts (Dubai Press Club 2011, 2). Among world cities, Riyadh has ranked as the tenth-largest city in terms of tweet volume, thereby profiling as the only Arab city in the top twenty metropolises.

INFORMATION AND COMMUNICATION TECHNOLOGY REGULATION

Generally speaking, it is clear that the diffusion of digital technologies in the Arab world was not accompanied by relevant regulations. As elsewhere, technology always predates policy making. This situation has created problems in the way those technological systems have been deployed. Not only has this trend made most regulatory frameworks highly reactive, but it has also rendered them terribly inadequate. For governments, control remains the prime feature of all regulations, which means that a good number of social, political, cultural, and economic concerns are most likely to be compromised. In national media regulations, priority has been given to issues like state security, political stability, social cohesion, and cultural identity. While some Arab countries have evolved technology-specific regulations to address issues arising from the diffusion of satellite television, telecommunications, and the Internet, others have used old regulations such as press and publications laws to deal with emerging technologies. An important implication of those approaches has been the obfuscation of the peculiar features of those technology-specific issues that need to be addressed on new legal and ethical grounds.

In the area of satellite television, national regulatory frameworks have defined how broadcasters handle different issues and events through prime or secondary regulations. All satellite television channels in the Arab world are either regulated through legislation or through cabinet decisions that define their technical features, functions, content policies, and relations with audiences. Since government-affiliated channels operate within national broadcast structures, they are subject to specific radio and television regulations that come under audiovisual or broadcast laws. Examples include audiovisual laws in Lebanon (1994), Jordan (2002), Kuwait (2007), Saudi Arabia (2012), Morocco (2005), Algeria (2012), and Egypt (2008). The Saudi General Authority for Audio and Visual Media applies the following standards to reinforce audiovisual regulations (Saadi 2013):

1. Reinforcing the religious, social, and cultural values of the kingdom;
2. Ensuring that the public is provided with a high-quality collection of entertainment;
3. Setting up flexible and clear mechanisms for licensing the audiovisual media;
4. Transmission, in a way, which keeps abreast of the advanced commercial and technological trends;
5. Ensuring that equal opportunities are provided in the markets and securing fair competition in the area of the General Authority's activity;
6. Supporting the development of audiovisual media transmission and content in the kingdom; and
7. Supporting and implementing the objectives of the kingdom's media policy and national plans through audiovisual media transmission and content.

But the big challenge facing governments has resulted from transnational and transborder television transmissions, where national states have no control over the flow of political or cultural content into their territories. The best collective action Arab states could take dates back to 2008, when Arab information ministers issued a "Satellite Television Charter." Article 6 of the charter calls, among other things, for respecting human dignity and the rights of others' satellite television contents; respecting individual privacy and abstaining from any violations in any way; avoiding inciting hatred based on ethnic, color, racial, or religious discrimination; prohibiting materials that would incite violence and terrorism and differentiating between them and the resistance of occupation; considering the professional ethical codes in conducting dialogues, respecting the right to respond for concerned parties; protecting children and youngsters against all that would abuse their physical, mental, and ethical growth or would incite corruption of their manners; complying with the religious and ethical values of Arab society and maintaining its family ties and social integrity; and refraining from insulting God, revealed religions, prophets, religious sects, and religious symbols and banning any materials that include obscene scenes or pornography (Arab League 2008).

In the telecommunications sector, specialized authorities or agencies operating under special government mandates regulate all telecommunications service providers. Telecommunications regulatory authorities or commissions set technical standards for facilities and equipment, allocate spectrum and technical resources, provide licenses to service providers, and ensure service quality to users across the geographical areas of coverage. With the telecommunications service providers increasingly turning into audiovisual and interactive content providers in the MENA region, media content regulations pertaining as applied to radio, television, and cable systems have been enforced on the telecommunications sector. The trend toward greater convergence in the telecommunications market, including the use of social media, has driven much of the regulation in the Arab region. In the United Arab Emirates, for example, the Telecommunications Regulatory Authority (TRA) policies on the use of Instagram emphasize issues like morality and proper conduct, harassment and defamation, privacy, and IT security (TRA 2013). In countries like Saudi Arabia, Kuwait, Lebanon, Jordan, and Bahrain, telecommunications service providers have also set standards for using social media networks.

In cyberspace, some MENA countries have evolved their national online or cyber communication laws that incriminate a range of activities relating to state security, individual privacy, intellectual property rights, religious values, and cultural traditions. Examples include the Saudi Anti-Cyber Crime Law of 2007, the UAE cybercrime law of 2012, Jordan's website law of 2013, and Syria's e-publishing law of 2010. More or less, those laws seem to echo legislations applied on real-world communication practices. Penalties for violators range from fines to imprisonment and shutting down online sites. Those laws and others share one important feature: cyberspace should be taken as seriously as physical space, something that could have a profound, chilling effect on those who envision the Internet as a source of empowerment for free speech. But, of course, there is a positive side to those regulations in that they serve as a powerful deterrent of potential abuses relating to children, human trafficking, drug trafficking, and terrorism.

IMPLICATIONS FOR SOCIETY AND THE STATE

It is clear that the information and communication transitions of the new millennium have had varying effects on societies in the MENA region. Oil-rich countries of the Gulf have been at the forefront of communications development, with billions of dollars invested in the information and telecommunications sector. The role of media convergence in economic development has never been more realized in most of those countries where notions of knowledge, society, and economy are being promoted to define national development strategies. On the other hand, countries with fewer resources or those going through civil wars seem to have less impressive information and telecommunications features, as evident in lower Internet access and telephony subscription rates. They are most likely to be deprived of the bounties of the knowledge economy gained from new technology investments. The data in this chapter shows significant variations among MENA region nations in the ITC front; however, all Arab states seem to have developed positive expectations about those digital transitions. Since the 1990s, liberal market orientations have been instrumental in eroding the long-time state monopoly of the information and telecommunications sector. In the first decade of the new millennium, the leading players in the information and telecommunications market are not governments but commercial companies who have found huge profit-making opportunities in emerging media convergence markets.

Though it may be too early to spell out the implications of new technologies for society and the state in the Arab world, it is clear that digital communications are creating critical discussions about their implications for social and political relations in the region. The privatization of broadcasting and digital communications has raised concerns about the potential effects of commercial interests on the quality of social and cultural contents. In the 1990s, debates about the perceived negative effects of satellite television on Arabic language and Islamic values and traditions had only accentuated public suspicions about this. In the GCC region, one of the collective responses addressing such cultural and religious concerns was evident in the 2008 Doha declaration on the negative effects of satellite television on local cultural values. Those concerns were also addressed through the launch of television channels with focused indigenous cultural content to "counter" incoming regional and global flows of television. Examples include the launch of Almajd television network in Saudi Arabia and a host of cultural- and heritage-centered channels in other countries. The goal of those initiatives was to provide Arab audiences, especially the young, with alternative television programs with relevant content. The big challenge faced by such TV launches was how to cope with around-the-clock transmissions in human and technical terms, a reminder of the region's early television experiences of the 1960s and 1970s, when program imports seemed to have been the only alternative to sustaining daily transmissions.

Political concerns on the part of governments over the flow of transnational political television into their territories were highly visible. The fact that Arab audiences were able to watch multiple channels with diverse political contents was quite irritating for many governments who had enjoyed years of single-channel transmissions in their countries. Al-Jazeera channel in particular was a source of irritation for a few governments who perceived the channel to be promoting a political and cultural agenda in the region. In the first decade of the new millennium, JSC was seen as the voice of grassroots concerns in a region long subjected to political repression. But in the aftermath of the recent Arab upheavals, Al-Jazeera performance came under fire for its perceived siding with the Muslim Brotherhood in Egypt, Libya, Syria, and other countries. Such perception gave rise to massive migration of JSC staff to rival channels, especially the Beirut-based Al-Mayadeen channel. But, as noted earlier, there is little that governments could do to eliminate the negative effects of transnational political channels beyond jamming of transmissions or calling for compliance with some ethical principles.

But the information and communications revolution of the twenty-first century has not been only about political controls and commercial profiteering. It has also been about cultural and political expression and grassroots empowerment. The so-called Arab Spring experience has suggested a central role for satellite television and the web in promoting transformations in areas with serious political, social, and economic woes. At best, social media in particular have been recognized as vital for coordination and mobilization in the recent Arab upheavals. In significant ways, social media provided alternative platforms for expressing social, cultural, and political discontent and dissent in countries like Tunisia, Egypt, Syria, Morocco, Libya, and Bahrain, where transitions have been marked by massive civil protests and bloody conflicts. Alongside social media, satellite television has also been a major player in those transitions, with channels like Al-Jazeera and Al-Arabiya serving as arenas for pro- and antigovernment voices. On the cultural front, both social media and satellite television channels have functioned as powerful outlets for cultural expression and social development. But all in all, the role of satellite television and the web in Arab world social, political, cultural, and economic transitions has been shrouded in much hype that bordered on conceptions of those communications as magical wands that could create real change. The fact of the matter is that those media played only a supportive role in the fight against political oppression, social injustice, and economic inequality.

NOTE

1. IDC (International Data Corporation), "Middle East IT Spending to Exceed $32 Billion in 2014," December 11, 2013, accessed December 12, 2014, http://www.idc.com/getdoc.jsp?containerId=prAE24514713.

3

Digital Transitions

Social media have steadily found their way into international newsrooms over the past few years, with some remarkable success. BBC News set up a social media department in 2005, for instance, to process user-generated content (UGC), and CNN started a similar initiative called iReport in 2006 (Bruna 2013). Ten years ago, social media were met with some skepticism as being trivial tools with no potential for any impact. One example was Dan Rather's comments regarding bloggers who talked about "leaked memos" that confirmed President George W. Bush had received favorable treatment in the Air National Guard in the 1970s. Rather referred to bloggers as "those sitting in their pyjamas writing what they think," but a few years later, they were proved right, and Rather had to resign in 2005 (*Economist* 2011). The growth of blogs soared shortly after, with many newspapers and news channels hiring bloggers and inviting readers to contribute comments. The Huffington Post was launched in May 2005, based on blog posts from volunteers and celebrities (*Economist* 2011), as journalists began to regard social media as an adjunct to traditional media. Crowdsourcing, in terms of obtaining information from large sections of online users, could bring in a range of new information, but the challenge was always its veracity. Social media platforms enabled audiences to respond to natural disasters, evident in the case of the *South-East Asia Earthquake and Tsunami Blog* (*SEA-EAT*), which chronicled the disaster and helped raise funds for its victims (Ekine 2009), and *Katrina Struck New Orleans* blog in 2005; however, one enduring issue in social media reporting is that not all circulated information is truthful: one example is the incorrect report about the Boston Marathon bombing—which originated from social media—where speed seemed to have trumped accuracy (Dingman 2013). The "Find Boston Bombers" campaign on the Reddit site mistakenly identified a missing Brown University student as a suspect, and the rumor quickly spread on social media sites. The reason for broadcasting or publishing unsubstantiated news may be the desire for an exclusive story scoop.

This chapter addresses the pan-Arab journalism sector by describing new developments in applying digital technology in newsrooms, whether print, online, or radio broadcasts. The chapter reviews and analyzes technology integration trends in the region's journalism sector, the different applications arising from this development, and how social media have changed the way Arab journalists communicate with their audiences. One important shift in the MENA reportage arena has been the rise of citizen journalism, in which audiences interact and contribute to news content, such as the coverage of the 2010 Iraq election. This chapter also provides an outline of the uses of social media in Arab journalism, focusing on how these have disrupted traditional news values in pan-Arab outlets, as well as discussing the rise of vernaculars online—the most favored linguistic code, especially among young Arab audiences.

A study commissioned by AnaZahra.com, a portal for Arab women created by Abu Dhabi Media Company (ADMC), confirmed that the Internet had become a breathing space for Arab women, with 34 percent of the surveyed Arab females stating that they spent at least ten hours a week online, surfing the Internet—the highest figure in the Gulf states. For Saudi journalist Badria Al-Bishr, social and news media provide a safe haven for Arab women: "The vast space of social media, tucked away from censors' control, [has] displayed the rebirth of the social consciousness of young women who want to express their basic needs" (France 24 2011). There are barriers, on the other hand, to women's full utilization of those media; Al-Saggaf (2011) classifies them as environmental and personal: the former refers to cultural constraints, the latter to the technical skills needed to access these media. Women in Gulf societies see a new tool for empowerment in social and new media—reality testifies to persistent inequalities in the work domain, family laws, and political participation; among the most popular women's websites is *Sayidaty*, a Saudi-funded electronic magazine, which claimed more than 1.5 million users in 2013, according to Google Analytics (Middle East Publishers Association 2013). *Sayidaty* is also one of the largest women's electronic publications circulating in the region and has demonstrated its success on social media platforms with more than 1.6 million fans on Facebook, 170,000 Twitter followers, and 12.5 million viewers of its videos on YouTube, not to mention 600,000 downloads through iPads and smartphones (Middle East Publishers Association 2013). Looking at the Arab region as a whole, Twitter is the most used medium in Saudi Arabia (about 38 percent), followed by Egypt (30 percent). An interesting observation is that media professionals constitute 62 percent of all Arab users as shown in figure 3.1. (El Ahmad 2012).

The rising number of Internet users has prompted Arab media, both pan-Arab and local, to establish a foothold on the World Wide Web. Regarding the newspaper sector, the Lebanese *Al-Hayat* began to publish an edition on CD-ROM in 1995, and in the same year, it launched its electronic archive. The Kuwaiti *Al-Qabas* also released its content on CD-ROM in 1996, as did the Lebanese *Al-Nahar* and *Al-Safir* in 1997. A new electronic newspaper was launched in 2000, *aljarida.com*, followed by *elaph.com* in 2001 (Ali 2006, 42–43). The MENA region had an abundance of online forums by 2013, such as Maktoob, Planet Arabia, Naseej, Ayan, and Arab Fiesta, and several online newspapers such as *Elaph, Jarida, Bab*, and *Etijahat* (Al-Faysal 2006, 216). The Lebanese online newspaper *Al-Khabar* was launched in 2006; it quickly became popular and gained a large market share, thus becoming the top-ranking online newspaper in Lebanon, ahead of long-established newspapers such as *Annahar* (Melki et al. 2012, 74). Noteworthy is that none of the Arab online newspapers or magazines charged for their online content, not to mention the viewers' unwillingness to pay for it (Dubai Press Club 2011, 37).

There are three key categories of coexisting social media sites in the region: first, international sites, such as Facebook, that have managed to gain the largest popularity due to their strong brand names and early entry into the market; second, international players, such as Twitter, that

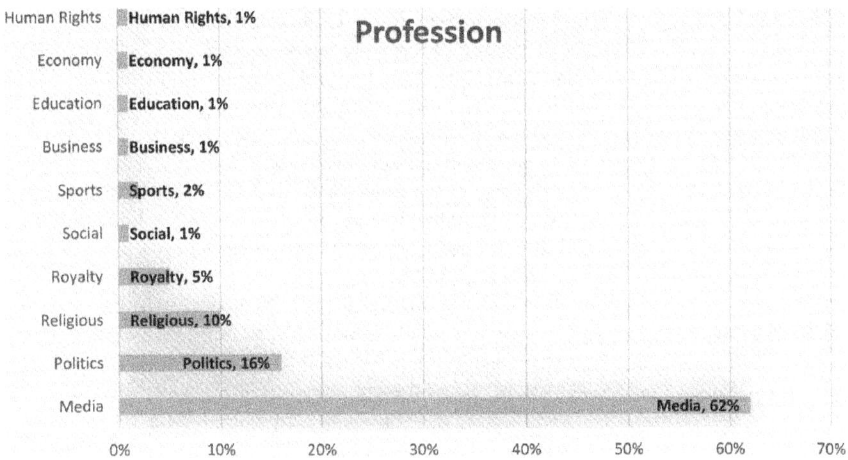

Figure 3.1. Arab Twitter Users Divided by Profession
Source: El Ahmad 2012.

have recently introduced an Arabic interface which is expected to grow in popularity over the next five years (Internet penetration has increased in the larger Arabic-speaking markets such as Egypt and Saudi Arabia as awareness grows); and third, local companies such as Maktoob, Jeeran, and UAE Women's Network have expanded their user bases, despite strong competition from international players. Companies offering additional services to social media, such as Maktoob, have performed particularly well and have the potential for significant growth. The most popular websites in the Arab region in the news and media sectors are Maktoob (owned by Yahoo!) and Arabia.msn, according to the Alexa site, followed by Al-Arabiya (see table 3.1).

The most popular social media sites in Arabic, in terms of their online presence, their ability to integrate their content with social media tools, and the number of likes and subscribers, according to a *Forbes* article from

Table 3.1. Popular News Sites in the Arab Region, 2012

Website	*Description*
maktoob.yahoo.com	Online community, discussion forums in English and Arabic, and free bilingual web-based e-mail
arabia.msn.com	A Middle East version of the worldwide portal MSN.com. Offers news, entertainment, sports, weather, games, and classifieds
alarabiya.net	Arabic-language news network. Breaking news and features along with videos, photo galleries, and "More In Focus" sections on major news topics (Arabic, English, Persian, and Urdu)
bayt.com	The leading job site in the Gulf and Middle East
gulfnews.com	Online version of the daily newspaper
aawsat.com	A pan-Arab daily, launched in London in 1978
alhayat.com	Pan-Arab independent daily published from London
arabianbusiness.com	Middle East business and industry news with daily updated financial and market news and views
khaleejtimes.com	A global face of the newspaper on the Internet; also provides many interactive features exclusive to the online edition
mubasher.info	Real-time reports from stock markets throughout the region in English and Arabic
zawya.com	Provides free regional business and finance coverage
arabnews.com	English-language daily newspaper covering local and regional news plus Islam, business, and sports
sana.sy	Offers news about the country, the Middle East, and the daily life of Syrian people; reports in Arabic, English, and French
albawaba.com	Portal for Middle Eastern news and information

Source: *Forbes Middle East* website, http://www.forbesmiddleeast.com/view.php?list=44466.

2012, was topped by the Emirati newspaper *Al-Bayan* (with more than a quarter of a million "likes" on Facebook), followed by the Kuwaiti *Rai* newspaper, the Egyptian *Al-Youm Al-Sabei* (or *Youm7*), the Egyptian *Al-Ahram*, and the Lebanese *Daily Star*. Other outlets in the top list of sites included the Emirates-based *Khaleej Times* and the *National* as well as *Al-Ittihad*, the *Jordan Times*, the Kuwaiti *Anbaa*, the Palestinian *Al-Quds*, and the Qatari *Al-Sharq*.

Online media websites in Morocco did not necessarily provide novel content but mostly a copy of what was already available offline; for instance, a 2010 survey of eighteen Arabic- and French-language newspapers and magazines, a major TV channel, and radio stations in Morocco found that the online content of those outlets was either updated from the print version or an archive service with some basic information such as stock exchange or weather forecasts (Zaid and Ibahrine 2011, 23). Moroccan journalists typically used e-mail as a tool to send their articles and images in real time and to receive feedback from their editors. The Internet was also used for information gathering, although Moroccan journalists were usually skeptical about the reliability of online information (Zaid and Ibahrine 2011, 49). Egyptian journalists saw the strength of social media resting in the abundance of sources they provided for journalists in verifying the information they received. They cited the example of the altered photograph of former president Hosni Mubarak, heading world leaders at the Middle East peace talks in Sharm-el-Sheikh in 2010, whereas the original photograph showed Obama leading the way; as one journalist commented: "There are so many sources now to contend with, and it makes the job of the journalist a lot more difficult and a lot more important" (Abdulla 2013, 43).

Electronic media in the Palestinian territories began during the Al-Aqsa Intifada in 2000, with the aim of advocating Palestinians' rights and avoiding Israeli censorship. Such sites aimed to shed light on the Palestinians' suffering and to reach out to the largest audience (Talahma 2012, 47–49). *Ammon News* in Jordan, the first news website in the country in 2006, became the most popular with Jordanians. The news website called *Jfranews.com* managed to become the sixth-most-visited website in Jordan in 2013, with over 2.6 million Facebook users (Sweis and Baslan 2013, 18). Another successful outlet was Al-Balad, an online radio service that went on the air in 2005 as the only community radio channel focusing on social and cultural topics (18–19). In 2008, Jordan also had its Arabic version of Twitter, WatWet, which claimed to have 25,000 users, but it was closed down in 2011 because it could not compete with Twitter (34). Twitter is useful for voicing views and opinions about social problems. The initiative #Fadfed (or "chat"), set up by the NGO Leaders of Tomorrow, invited audiences to comment on sociocultural topics (36). A video posted on YouTube in 2011 revealed the physical punishment received by a Jordanian pupil, Ahmad Al-Saket, in a Jordanian classroom. This was later reported by several print outlets, demanding an investigation after numerous tweets had protested against the use of corporal punishment in schools (37). More than 80 percent of Jordanian journalists sampled in an opinion poll in 2010 believed that new media had enhanced press freedom in Jordan, although there were still concerns about user-generated content (UGC) and its ethical challenge (41). There are several websites and blogs in Jordan, such as 7iber.com, which provide training for citizen journalists. The launching of a new independent TV channel, ATV, was proposed in 2007, to be jointly owned by *Al-Ghad*, the royal family, the government, and a number of media experts; however, the channel was not launched until 2008, when the two hundred employees arranged a sit-in to protest the delay (60). *Al-Ghad*, described as the most interactive website in Jordan, was ranked among the strongest fifty websites in the region in 2010 (63).

Several outlets in the United Arab Emirates declared their mission to focus on raising journalistic standards in the area, such as the Abu Dhabi–based *National*, an English-language newspaper which had more than two hundred Western journalists hired from respected outlets. They all contributed to the vision of the newspaper to "provide quality, must-have reading" and to help change Arab societies. The outlet was led by the former editor of the British *Daily Telegraph* (Duffy 2013, 30). Al-Jazeera English, launched in Doha in 2006 with financial support from the emir of Qatar, expanded its news and social media functions by dividing them into three departments: the Internet, mobile, and social media (Bruna 2013). The number of staff in the social media department increased from eight in 2010 to around twenty in 2011 (Bruna 2013). The Al-Jazeera English website won an Online Journalism Award from the Online News Association (ONA) for its coverage of the Egyptian revolution, bearing in mind that more than 70 percent of the traffic to its website originated from social media (Bruna 2013).

DISRUPTING TRADITIONAL NEWS VALUES

New and social media have provided unprecedented opportunities for Arab journalists to interact with their audiences, thus contributing to breaking up the traditional one-way communication model through which journalists used to communicate their views while audiences had little chance of responding or commenting on what was being presented. Interactivity embedded in this new model, however, was problematic for Arab journalists, explained Samar Karam from Deutsche Welle Arabic:

"Interactivity is a challenge, because it forces us to think constantly about developing our content" (interview, April 2014). Karam also suggested that this new interaction had helped confront traditional Arab news values in which political hard news used to dominate: "Audiences now like soft news more than hard news. People want an attractive image and a catchy headline without necessarily thinking what is behind this news story which they read, share or comment on and they don't even verify it. They have become [an] uncritical audience." Social media for Karam have helped provide what she called "fast-food journalism. Easy, quick news consumed fast but . . . not necessarily healthy food [for thought]." The new role of the Arab journalist, according to Karam, was to "add some seriousness to make audiences think" (interview, April 2014).

This is a radical departure from traditional news standards that tended to focus on political news. A number of historical factors lie behind the prioritization of political news in Arab media: postindependence Arab states felt the need to focus on issues of nationalism and pan-Arabism rather than on critical (investigative) journalism that addressed domestic affairs—a difficult task to tackle under authoritarian rule. Other factors included the turbulent political and economic situation in the region, which made political news a default priority; the fact that the state still controlled news media allowed government officials to steer the news agenda (Ayish 2001). Jones (2002) saw a correlation between political and sexual repression, on the one hand, and downplaying the entertainment function of the news, on the other: when the authoritarian pressure was lifted, people tended to show great interest in sensational news (crime, sex, domestic scandals). The degree of tabloidization of the press can therefore be regarded as a measurement of the liberalization of society (172).

One of the journalists at the Al-Arabiya channel said that local news about social affairs is usually prioritized in Western media because Western societies have different sets of problems while a state of denial seems to define Arab media handling of social problems; besides, European audiences are rather apathetic to news about killings and violence in the Arab region: "Western media are more locally-oriented. . . . They can have the story of a missing child as the main headline. . . . For them 20 killed in Iraq can be packaged in a short news item. . . . They care about social issues like sexual abuse or paedophiles . . . these are the issues that we usually ignore although they plague us as well . . . but we've chosen to turn a blind eye to them" (cited in Mellor 2011, 97).

An attempt to appeal to the fast-growing audience on social media sites, however, has inspired Arab news media to shift the news order, prioritizing soft news on certain platforms, particularly Facebook. The Al-Arabiya network, for one, noticed the audience's interest in soft news, including entertainment, according to Sultan Batawi, head of the social media unit: "The Facebook audience want more visuals and entertaining news. If we put a photo of a mosque and people praying on the occasion of Ramadan, people interact with us and share the image; but if we add a visual and item about a murder case, they usually do not interact. We upload more features on Facebook. People like it when we post a question and ask for their comments. They are also willing to move across platforms if we guide them via different hyperlinks." Twitter seems to cater to a different audience: "Twitter is for [a] professional audience [that] seeks to find news quickly, and they are less willing to follow external links. Twitter is like a big alley, where you hear the salesman, café customers, and everyone talking. But Facebook is like one residential bloc where residents are having a conversation among themselves" (interview, May 2014).

This does not mean that hard-core political news is a bygone product; on the contrary, news consumption has become a trendy habit in the Arab region in contrast to other world regions, argues Sultan Batawi of Al-Arabiya; for instance, in the United States, a survey by the Pew Research Center (2012) shows that there has been continuous decline in the number of young Americans under the age of thirty who consume news, and this trend has been ongoing since 2008. Only 24 percent of this age bracket enjoys following the news, compared to nearly double that figure among older generations. Arab youth, in contrast, are avid consumers of news online or offline: "In the old days, news used to be for the older generation, while people in my generation focused on gaming. Now, the new generation cares much about the news. A seventeen-year-old wants to appear well informed about what is happening around [him or her]. [This group is] already on social media platforms watching Al-Arabiya news and playing games simultaneously," Batawi pointed out (interview, May 2014).

Interest is not only in news about the region but also about Arab communities in Europe, for users of Arabic-speaking outlets subsidized by Western institutions such as Deutsche Welle Arabic: "One of the most popular topics for our audience on social media is Arab and Muslim communities in Germany. Most Facebook audience come from Egypt, followed by Morocco, while Twitter's audience comes primarily from Saudi Arabia. The majority of our audiences are not based in Europe," says Samar Karam from Deutsche Welle Arabic. Social media helped brand Deutsche Welle among this cohort of audiences who follow the network on social media platforms looking particularly for German views on recent developments in the Middle East. Karam added:

> We use social media to know the trend among the audience in the countries we want to reach. The most popular news is science news. [Arab] people

> think of Germany as a country of progress and science and they expect us to talk about scientific progress. We found such news gets a lot of likes and shares, so we post this type of news more often. Political news is still a must, although audiences are also interested in social topics posted by our correspondents such as the issue of circumcision. People come to us because they are attracted to the German view on Middle Eastern affairs, and our German press review is a very popular item to follow on social media. We often see great attention [being paid] to German foreign policy toward the Middle East (interview, April 2014).

Audiences also like to follow tourism news about Germany: "When we post an image of a German town, users' comments pour in and they tend to share it. . . . I think social media helped brand our name as Deutsche Welle. We have instant user statistics online and we have a loyal audience who regularly comment on all our stories, and we sometimes take their suggestions on board," added Karam.

Social media such as Facebook and Twitter, therefore, are changing the way people communicate in Saudi Arabia, for example, where youth specifically use Twitter to voice their social concerns, particularly with traditional media such as television and print media being under strict censorship (Winder 2014, 2). Comments made on social media are likely to be in native vernaculars, whether Lebanese, Egyptian, Saudi, or Moroccan, and there are distinct lexical and syntactical differences among these dialects. Some comments are also made in written standard Arabic (*fusha*), but because social media are characterized as more informal platforms, most of the comments, especially on Facebook, are in the vernacular, argues Sultan Batawi of Al-Arabiya. This is a notable departure from the conventional code of news in the Arab region, where journalists may be seen to form their own discourse community, favoring the written form of Modern Standard Arabic (MSA), or "*fusha*," as the main language of news and current affairs programs. The code of journalistic ethics approved by the Council of Arab Information Ministries even calls for Arab journalists to act as guardians of the classical language and the literary heritage of the Arab nation (Hafez 2002, 242). Previous analyses of the use of MSA in the news found that the use of the vernacular in hard news is rather rare (Ennaji 1995). Newspapers usually use the written form of language, reserving the vernacular for humorous or sarcastic commentaries and caricatures. The media's role, then, was to convert these vernacular phrases into classical Arabic when reporting on a speech; hence, the language marks the difference in social hierarchy and authority in society and emphasizes the news media's role in upholding this difference and in "guarding classical Arabic from the impurity of the vernacular." The Arabic language in general has a status (*makāna*), and it has managed to survive throughout the ages, although at times it was at risk of being alienated (Mejdell 2008,

111); nonetheless, a number of journalists see *fusha* as a complication in reaching the hearts and minds of audiences, therefore ignoring the important communication role of vernaculars. One journalist at BBC Arabic, for instance, said that written Arabic is "a big obstacle. It does not allow fluent self-expression when we're worried about verb inflection in *fusha*. I think we have a language complex, and this makes us evaluate journalists according to their language competence" (interview, June 2007). Another journalist at Al-Arabiya expressed a similar view:

> Our news will never reach people's hearts because we speak one language and write in another. . . . We will always have the language problem. . . . Everybody holds onto the written language because of the Qur'an, thinking that we'd be abandoning the Qur'an if we abandon the written language. Indonesians are Muslims and they can read the Qur'an but they use another language in their media. I think you'd never reach the lower classes unless you speak their language . . . otherwise people will always feel that the news is distanced from them. . . . Until we do something about this issue, we will always have this gap. When you write an e-mail or a letter in English, you do not think twice, you just write your thoughts, but if you need to write a letter in *fusha*, you have to think a lot before writing one sentence (interview, October 2007).

The following section discusses the rise of vernaculars on social media sites in light of the current status of the Arabic written language online.

THE RISE OF VERNACULARS ONLINE

The Arabic language lies in seventh position in the list of top ten languages used on the Internet, according to Internet World Stats, with about 19 percent by the Arab population. This position is considered as an incentive for future growth of the digital media industry in the region. Arabic, however, is not always the most preferred language online, as revealed by a recent survey among three thousand Arabs from twenty-two countries—the picture varies from one country to another; consequently, while Arabic is the preferred linguistic code for about 61 percent of the users in Egypt, 67 percent in Iraq, 71 percent in Libya, 81 percent in Yemen, and 75 percent in Palestine, the language is notably abandoned in other Arab countries, where the preferred online linguistic code is either English or French. English, for instance, is used by about 72 percent of the users in Lebanon, 62 percent in Bahrain, and 66 percent in the Emirates, while French is the preferred language code for about 57 percent of users in Algeria, 62 percent in Morocco, and 76 percent in Tunisia ("Arab Social Media Outlook" 2014, 12). The Saudi users are more or less equally divided between Arabic and English, with 49 percent of users in Saudi Arabia preferring Arabic and 39 percent preferring English, while in Oman, 46 percent prefer to use English. Arabic articles in Wikipedia, moreover, constitute only 0.9 percent of the total of 31 million articles ("Arab Social Media Outlook" 2014).

The Arabic-speaking users on the Internet increased by 2,500 percent during the first decade of this millennium; with this growth, the importance of the Arabic language also grew, but this rise in the number of users has to be matched by an increase in digital content in Arabic, which is about 3 percent of all online content. The soaring popularity of the Internet as a main information source, particularly among the 40 percent of the Arab population whose ages range between fifteen and thirty-five, has made it imperative to invest in Arabic material on the Internet rather than rely on English-language material. This is why Google launched "Arabic Web Days" to boost Arabic web content and localize websites. Another initiative is Taghreedat, which started in Doha and moved to Abu Dhabi, dependent on 2,500 volunteers to localize popular web platforms such as TED and *Wikipedia* (Khalaf 2013). Arabic is the fastest-growing language on social media, according to the French company Semiocast (2011), particularly Twitter, which saw an increase of 2,000 percent in just one year; of the 180 million tweets published in October 2011, more than 2 million were in Arabic, leaping from the figure recorded in October 2010 of approximately 99,000. Arabic consequently now accounts for 1 percent of the tweets (see figure 3.2). Semiocast analyzed a sample of more than

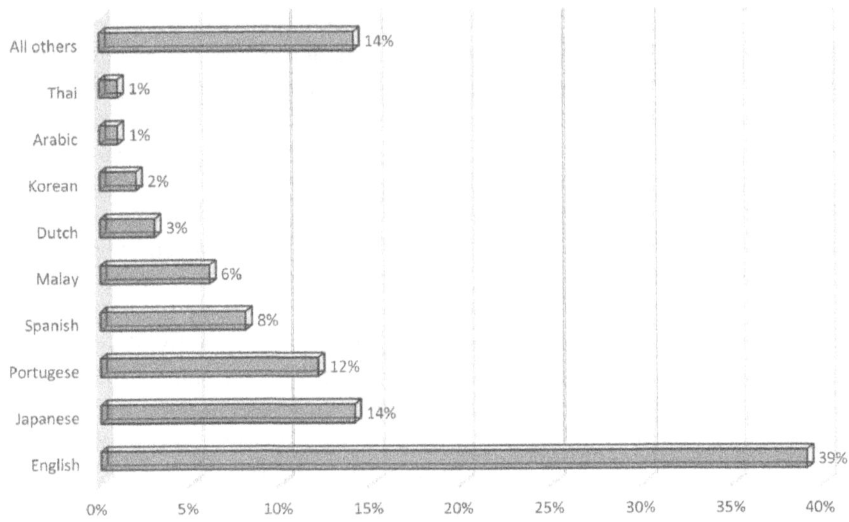

Figure 3.2. Top Languages on Twitter
Source: Semiocast 2011.

five billion tweets in 2010–2011 to reveal the top ten languages used, and Arabic was the eighth most used.

Experts lamented the low number of Arabic websites, particularly when compared with the number of sites in other languages. The number of Arabic sites in 2010–2011 was around 5.3 million, according to the *Arab Knowledge Report* 2010/2011 (Arab Thought Foundation 2011, 57–58). An Egyptian study among youths between fifteen and thirty-five years of age, moreover, warned against the emergence of a parallel language used by youths on the Internet, which could threaten written Arabic. The youths seem to have a unique culture and language online that reflects their rebellion against social order. Others blame the youths for attempting to escape from a physical world society into virtual communities of their own creation (Gomaa 2007). A problematic feature of the Arabic language on the Internet is the use of Arabizi, which is a language developed by integrating numbers and Latin characters when writing in Arabic by using the numbers 7, 3, and 2 to replace difficult Arabic alphabetical symbols (nonexistent in most European languages) when they transcribe the text into Latinized alphabets: Arabizi is claimed to have created a fracture of Arabic content (Khalaf 2013). The *Arab Knowledge Report* 2010/2011 also warns against the use of Arabizi in view of findings that nearly 70 percent of Egyptian blogs use Arabic but the majority of them confuse colloquial and Modern Standard Arabic (Arab Thought Foundation 2011, 57–58). Mobile users also adopt the Latin alphabet and numerals when sending text messages, which, according to the report, could threaten the Arabic language culture in the long term.

It is difficult to avoid using the vernacular on social media, on the other hand, given that the main purpose of networking with peers and others is in a code that is convenient for users. Blogging, for instance, is an expression of personal views and thoughts and thus it requires "more relaxed presentation than that which we would expect in a piece of Arabic writing which traditionally requires Modern Standard Arabic" (Ramsay 2012, 50). Online communication can indeed incorporate elements of oral and written expressions, thereby blurring the lines between speech and writing, and it is therefore not surprising that many bloggers often mix the vernacular with the written variety of Arabic in their posts (Ramsay 2012). Analyzing a sample of such blogs by Egyptian activists, Ramsay (2012, 84) concludes that activist bloggers tend to use the vernacular in their blogs or a mix of the oral and written varieties. The written variety is used particularly in educational blogs, which means the probability of using this variety increases if the purpose is pedagogical.

Sultan Batawi, head of the social media unit at Al-Arabiya network, commented on the need to adjust the language on social media platforms—he preferred the use of vernaculars: "I think the first rule in media is to communicate with audiences in a language they can relate to and understand. If we use very classical words like they do in newspapers, we may not be able to reach our audiences. Sometimes audiences comment in vernacular, and at times in simplified *fusha*. We use popular proverbs in [the] vernacular, so audiences can relate to them. On Facebook, we can post a picture and invite comments and usually we add a caption in [the] vernacular. On social media, we may still follow the TV agenda, but we have to adapt it to the mood and age of our online audience" (interview, May 2014).

The ease of posting comments in the vernacular, on the other hand, may have negative implications on the mode of online debate: "Anyone of any educational background can write anything on social media sites, so whether they master written Arabic or not, they can now post a comment on social media," argues Zahi Alwai (interview, May 2014); indeed, obscene language and name-calling are not unusual either in social media or on the Internet. A recent study found that uncivilized comments online were common and could lead to polarization of views surrounding an issue (Anderson et al. 2014). Users may focus on corresponding messages about that issue in particular while discrediting irrelevant ones, which means they end up enforcing their preexisting views and extending online polarization. Arab users, argue social media editors such as Sultan Batawi of Al-Arabiya, are inclined to use indecent language to demean or insult those with opposing views, using their own vernaculars when commenting on a Facebook post or a story online. It is then that such editors apply rigorous moderation policies on their online sites. It may not be feasible, however, to filter words in all available Arab vernaculars; therefore, this moderation may not be an optimal solution. In addition, the likely threat is the polarization of debate on these platforms.

The challenge for some journalists is to understand tweets or Facebook posts written in different Arabic vernaculars from their native dialect; for instance, Samar Karam of Deutsche Welle Arabic commented: "Sometimes their comments are in dialect, and it is difficult to understand all the comments, so, for example, I did not understand posts written in Moroccan dialect. We tend to select some comments from our sites on Facebook and Twitter, and I usually select comments in the written variety of Arabic or in educated colloquial. We think our average users are well educated, and this is the cohort we want to reach anyway." Fatima Reda at *Al-Hayat* newspaper also found it difficult to understand posts written in certain vernaculars, but more important, she pointed out the need to filter insults and comments made in obscene language: "People tend to insult on the web or on social media sites, it is a pity that they do not engage in a constructive debate as it is easy to insult [in dialect]. Comments tend to be fired against writers and columnists. If one writer criticizes something, you will see many readers insult him or her on social media sites. We have one site in English and another in Arabic. Comments made on the English site are usually constructive, but those made on the Arabic site are obscene. [It is odd because] the English section includes English translations of the same Arabic articles," according to Reda. She cited the example of the Facebook group regarding Syrian female refugees (which will be discussed in chapter 7): "Many people on the Syrian refugees' site used obscene language against the site administrator instead of engaging in a temperate discussion about this topic," said Reda. Abdel Bari Atwan of *Al-Rai Al-Youm* agreed with this view: "Some people abuse social media sites by disseminating incorrect news about assassinations of famous figures, fake scandals, or firing insults at others. Some intelligence systems also use these sites to influence public opinion against their enemies. In fact the majority of comments on the internet are indecent," Atwan claimed. "Arab audiences," Sultan Batawi of Al-Arabiya continued, "will use any platform until they abuse it: they join Facebook, Google+, and any similar platform so that they can shout."

CONCLUSION

There is no doubt that rising access to the Internet at large and the spread of social media in the Arab region have triggered contradictory responses by Arab governments. Many of the current Arab states have expressed their commitment to political as well as economic reforms while keeping a firm grip on the cultural industries. Economic reforms have been easier to implement, and they have spilled over to the media sector, with private media ownership being allowed in several Arab states. The challenge, however, was to apply open-door policies by embracing economic globalization while keeping the cultural heritage intact. Several Arab commentators and scholars (cited in Mellor 2014) also warned against the threatening impact of the flow of American cultural output on the native identity and the vulnerability of Arab youth, who may be easy prey to fast-paced cultural globalization. Media, then, have been regarded as a double-edged sword: they can be utilized as a mobilization tool to win public opinion but can also be harnessed as a powerful instrument to undermine the ideological foundations of Arab societies and states. The war on terror rhetoric has provided more reasons for the Arab states to wield more control over media industries, on the pretext of protecting their nations from terrorism; even after the recent uprisings, Arab states still stressed the social responsibility of media not to agitate public opinion for the sake of national unity.

The following chapters provide a closer look at the various layers of changes across pan-Arab newsrooms, paying particular attention to the rising phenomenon of citizen journalism and the challenges facing the traditional gatekeeper roles of Arab journalists.

4

Social Media Traffic Trends

As noted earlier, pan-Arab media organizations see social media not only as credible drivers of conventional print and broadcast content but also as a platform for enhancing more interactive audience engagements. Before the Web 2.0 revolution that gave rise to social networks, pan-Arab media organizations like the Middle East Broadcasting Center (MBC), Al-Jazeera, the Voice of America, and the BBC Arabic Radio had relied on conventional market research tools as well as on direct audience feedback to keep abreast of how their services were faring in the Middle East and North Africa (MENA) region and beyond.[1] Recently, social media platforms have shifted pan-Arab media audience attention from traditional survey-based market research to social media analytics, drawing on direct interactive conversations involving both their outbound traffic and user-generated content (UGC). By harnessing social space to enhance communications with their audiences, pan-Arab media have been able to keep themselves informed of how those publics are thinking about their traditional media content. Inspired primarily by social, technological, and political transitions in the region, pan-Arab conversations in cyberspace suggest significant shifts in conventional paradigms about media effects and public opinion building. Audiences are no longer captive publics targeted by one-way messages from centralized media sources. Social media have hugely empowered audiences to claim a share in how media content is constructed and consumed in virtual space (Hanna, Rohm, and Crittenden 2011).

The incorporation of social practices into pan-Arab media operations falls within the broad notion of communications convergence, a process that enables the bringing together of multiple digital media into single operational platforms (Jenkins 2006). In the evolving convergence-induced models of media industries, the website or portal turns into an incubator of a mix of print, audio, visual, and other forms of media that work in sync to fulfill specific communication strategies for the organization. In the convergence-based business models of media operations, traditional media outlets are gradually coming under the roof of centralized online platforms that enable users' exposure to the different media under one digital umbrella. Social media units serve as central components of the emerging converging media environment as they enable audiences' UGC to shape social conversations in cyberspace.

The integration of social media into conventional media operations in the MENA region seems to have gained increasing visibility in recent years. And one inspiring example is the BBC Arabic *Talking Point*, or *Nuqtat Hiwar, G710,* and *(I-Witness) Ana Shahid* radio and TV shows, which harness audience-generated feedbacks to drive the programs (Abdel-Sattar et al. 2012). Launched on March 26, 2003, *Nuqtat Hiwar* (presented in more focus in chapter 7) is a TV and radio phone-in show broadcast on BBC Arabic Service. The first edition of *Nuqtat Hiwar* presented listeners' views on the war in Iraq. The program goes live five days a week, with the first part broadcast on radio and television from 15:06 till 15:57 GMT while the second part is broadcast only on radio from 16:06 till 16:30 GMT. *Talking Point* reaches its audience through numerous communication channels. The program has a Facebook fan page and a Twitter account (Abdel-Sattar et al. 2012). Dialogue among Arab audiences in the Middle East regions and diasporas is made possible through skillful moderation by the program presenters, who contest arguments and aggregate UGC to support some claims arising in the show. *Nuqtat Hiwar* uses a wide range of social media tools in the conversations, such as Skype, SMS, e-mail, Facebook, Twitter, and Instagram. The program ideas are crowdsourced on Facebook and Twitter to alert viewers and listeners about the upcoming episodes and motivate their participation. A review of *Nuqtat Hiwar*'s episodes in August 2014 shows the following questions being addressed: (1) What drives highly educated and skilled Arab youth to join Jihadi groups? (2) How do conditions look in Sanaa (Yemen) after tensions arose between Huthis and government forces? (3) How could British Muslims counter extremism? (4) How ready are the Israelis and Palestinians in Gaza to hammer out a peace agreement? (5) What do you think of Syria as the most dangerous place for journalists to work?

Another example of social media integration into pan-Arab media functions is Al-Jazeera's Sharek (sharek.aljazeera.net), or "Share." The citizen journalism platform, modeled after CNN's iReport, was first launched in 2008 and has claimed more than seventy thousand video uploads from across the MENA region. Marc Lynch points out in the *Economist* (2011) that the staff in Al-Jazeera's Arabic and English newsrooms went through intense social media training only one month before the outbreak of the Arab Spring upheavals. The training, a culmination of a two-year initiative to make better use of social media throughout Al-Jazeera, was prompted by rising audience interest in seeking information online during the three-week Gaza war of 2008–2009. According to Lynch (*Economist* 2011), the Al-Jazeera move meant convincing journalists that social media are not a threat but "the biggest assets you can have." Instead of flying a reporter somewhere to cover a story, Al-Jazeera can draw on networks of trusted volunteers whose credibility is already established.

This chapter draws on sample analytics to describe and analyze how ten pan-Arab media organizations harness social media to expand their reach, brand their names and products, and enhance audience engagement with their contents. The discussion draws on analysis of multiple time-frame outbound content generated by ten pan-Arab media organizations on two social media platforms: Facebook and Twitter. The analysis is informed by data generated through systematic firsthand observations of both Facebook and Twitter by the authors in addition to data acquired from one of the leading social media analytics companies, Simply Measured, over a frame of two weeks for the ten pan-Arab media organizations covered by the study. Though the use of social space by pan-Arab media organizations goes beyond these two platforms to embrace YouTube, LinkedIn, Instagram, and others, the volume of data generated from those outlets would be too huge to manage in a single chapter. The objective here is not to investigate internal social media practices within the target organizations, as this has already been covered in other parts of this book through observations and interviews; it is rather to discuss and analyze a sample of outbound pan-Arab media-originated social media traffic in terms of topic, format, objective, geographical scope, and orientation. Examples of how social media are integrated into pan-Arab media news operations are also added to give more relevance to the discussion. Based on interviews and observations, social media contents are managed in pan-Arab media by specialized social media departments to ensure sustainablity in content flow, conversation moderation, and audience interactivity. Social media departments operate according to clearly defined policies that set the standards for work practices in cyberspace for both the institutions and the professionals.[2]

The ten pan-Arab media organizations surveyed in this study harness social media tools to achieve objectives relevant to typical online media operations like self-branding, promoting programs and contents, communicating news (including breaking news) to users, and crowdsourcing (Mijatović 2013). The basic model of social media integration shared by all ten pan-Arab media includes the establishment of a website/portal that serves as a central hub for a variety of online communications such as news posts, commentaries, video screenings, social media feeds, and user feedback. In most of the ten pan-Arab media covered by the study, the online hub is the central space for converging media outlets and making them accessible to users. All pan-Arab media outlets covered by the study have established social media units that function as part of broader news and program operations and information technology facilities to ensure the highest possible user engagement. Specialists manage social media units with training in information technology and media functions. For example, Sky News Arabia has placed the ability to "sense and respond" to viewers via social media as a critical component of increasing viewer-to-viewer engagement and gaining extended market reach (Brandwatch 2013). According to the channel's management, social media present one of the best means for understanding viewer behavior and interests and for better understanding how they perceive Sky News Arabia reporters and stories (Brandwatch 2013).

PAN-ARAB MEDIA OUTLETS COVERED BY THE STUDY

The following section provides an overview of the ten pan-Arab media organizations covered by this study.

Al Jazeera Channel: http://www.aljazeera.net/portal

Al Jazeera Arabic satellite channel was launched from Doha, Qatar, in 1996 with the declared mission of promoting "opinion and the other opinion" (El-Nawawy and Iskandar 2003). Funded by the Qatari government, the channel became part of a global network of six television channels and a news website. The channel gained worldwide attention in the aftermath of the US invasions of both Afghanistan (2001) and Iraq (2003). In the first decade of the twenty-first century, the Index on Censorship praised the network for circumventing censorship and contributing to the free exchange of information in the Arab world, and the Webby Awards nominated JSC website as one of the five best news websites, along with BBC News, *National Geographic*, and the Smoking Gun (*New World Encyclopedia* n.d.). At the height of the so-called Arab Spring upheavals, Al-Jazeera found itself at the center of heated controversies regarding its news coverage of issues and events. In those uprisings, Al-Jazeera was playing a proactive role in promoting political transitions in countries like Egypt, Libya, Tunisia, Syria, Morocco, and Bahrain. The channel's perceived sympathy for the Muslim Brotherhood was seen as critically diminishing for its reputation as an independent media outlet in the Middle

East. Across the MENA region, Al-Jazeera has been a major user of social media in its communications with audiences (*Economist* 2015).

Al-Arabiya Channel: http://www.alarabiya.net

This twenty-four-hour television channel was launched in Dubai in January 2003 on the eve of the Anglo-American invasion of Iraq. MBC, Lebanon's Hariri Group and other investors from Saudi Arabia, Kuwait, and other Gulf states are major stakeholders in the channel. As part of what some call the "Saudi media empire" (Sakr 2006), Al-Arabiya has offered a platform to liberal reformers with a tone tempered by greater restraint and sensitivity to the concerns of major Arab states, notes Lynch (2004). On the eve of its launch, speculation floated about the channel being created to counterbalance Al-Jazeera's pro–Muslim Brotherhood stance. Those perceptions proved to be highly credible a decade later as both channels engaged in carrying two different narratives of the so-called Arab Spring events in the MENA region. In 2014, Al-Arabiya had a new television service, Al-Hadath, with a focus on news developments and analysis. The channel has a social media department with extensive cyber activities across multiple platforms.

Al-Mayadeen Channel: http://www.almayadeen.net

Al-Mayadeen is a Beirut-based pan-Arab satellite television channel launched on June 11, 2012, "to represent reality as is." The channel is part of Al-Mayadeen Satellite Media Network, which also houses a production company, a radio station, a website, an advertising company, and other media-related projects. Though the ownership of the channel remains enigmatic, Al-Mayadeen is perceived to have risen to prominence in the context of political and social upheavals in the region in general and in Syria in particular. A good number of its staff, including its manager, Ghassan Bin Jiddo, had for years worked for Al-Jazeera channel but left the Qatari television service over what they perceived as its skewed reporting of Syrian news. Since its launch in 2012, the channel has demonstrated sympathies for the Syrian government, Iran, the Lebanese Hezbollah Party, the Palestinian Hamas movement, and Egypt's El-Sisi-led government. Al-Mayadeen uses social media to enhance its content reach, engage audiences, and promote its brand (*Economist* 2015).

BBC Arabic Channel: http://www.bbc.co.uk/arabic

BBC Arabic Television is a news channel broadcasting to the Middle East as part of the British Broadcasting Corporation, which is funded by the British Foreign Office. The Arabic radio service dates back to January

1938, while the television channel was launched on March 11, 2008. Run by the BBC World Service, the channel was established eight years after the failure of a joint BBC-Orbit Communications venture (a subsidiary of the Saudi Arabian Mawarid Holding) to launch an Arabic television channel. On April 21, 1996, the channel was "pulled off the air" following an episode of *Panorama* that was critical of the Saudi Arabian government (Ayish 2003). Many of the staff who had worked for the Orbit–BBC Arabic Television service migrated to Al-Jazeera channel; but over the past few years, BBC Arabic Television managed to attract good Arab media talent with profound interest in new media applications. BBC Arabic, as noted earlier in the book, is a major user of social space to enhance its content reach and achieve higher audience engagement.

CNN Arabic: http://arabic.cnn.com

CNN Arabic is a news website launched in Dubai Media City on January 19, 2002, as part of the US CNN network. The website provides international news "from an Arab perspective," with continuous updates on regional and international developments. The CNN Arabic website, managed by veteran Jordanian journalist Caroline Faraj, consists of a number of sections, including world news, Middle East, science and technology, business, entertainment, and sports, in addition to special reports and videos. The website reflects debates on social media like Facebook, blogs, and Twitter. The video section features stories from politics, technology, business, culture, and arts. In early 2014, CNN relaunched its Arabic website with the objective of "making news more social" (Hamid 2014).

Alhurra Channel: http://www.alhurra.com

The US government launched the Alhurra channel, "the Free One" in Arabic, in 2004 in the aftermath of the war in Iraq. According to its website, Alhurra's mission is to provide "objective, accurate and relevant news and information" to its audience while seeking to "support democratic values" and "expand the spectrum of ideas, opinions, and perspectives" available in the region's media."[3] The channel is operated by the nonprofit corporation Middle East Broadcasting Networks, Inc. (MBN), which, in turn, is financed by the US government's Broadcasting Board of Governors (BBG). The BBG serves as oversight and as a firewall to protect the professional independence and integrity of the broadcasters. The channel broadcasts news and current affairs programming to audiences in the Middle East and North Africa. Alhurra harnesses social media tools to engage with pan-Arab audiences and to promote its content.

Sky News Arabia Channel: http://www.skynewsarabia.com/web/home

Sky News Arabia was launched in May 2012 as an Arabic news and current affairs channel broadcasting mainly in the Middle East and North Africa. Based in Abu Dhabi's twofour54 media zone, the channel is a joint venture between UK-based BSkyB and Abu Dhabi Media Investment Corporation (ADMIC). Sky News Arabia uses BSkyB's Sky News brand and has a network of bureaus across the MENA region, along with offices in London and Washington, DC, in addition to sharing access to Sky News's wider international network. Since its launch, Sky News Arabia has been known for its strong virtual presence on almost all main social media platforms. The channel has a social media department with an integrated newsroom social traffic system.

***Al-Hayat* Newspaper: http://alhayat.com**

Al-Hayat is a leading London-based daily pan-Arab newspaper with a circulation exceeding 200,000. *Al-Hayat* is considered by some as the newspaper of record for the Arab diaspora and the preferred venue for liberal intellectuals who wish to express themselves to a large public.[4] The newspaper "is regarded as by far and away the best and most intensely read Arab newspaper," according to a 1997 article in the *New York Times*. A 2005 *New York Times* article described *Al-Hayat* as a "decidedly Arab nationalist paper."[5] The paper has been known for its pro-West and pro-Saudi orientations with balanced and open views regarding other regional questions. The paper draws on numerous veteran Arab journalists such as Jehad Al-Khazen, Jamal Khashoggi, and Hazem Saghieh. It prints in London, New York, Frankfurt, Dubai, Riyadh, Jeddah, Dammam, Beirut, and Cairo and has offices in London, Paris, Washington, New York, Moscow, Riyadh, Jeddah, Beirut, Cairo, Baghdad, Dubai, Amman, and Damascus. *Al-Hayat* publishes multiple editions like *Al-Hayat Politics*, *Al-Hayat Culture*, *Al-Hayat Saudi*, *Al-Hayat Egypt*, and most recently, *Al-Hayat Gulf*.

***Asharq Al-Awsat* Newspaper: http://www.aawsat.com**

Asharq Al-Awsat is part of the Saudi Company for Publishing and Distribution, owned by Faisal bin Salman, a member of the Saudi royal family. Like *Al-Hayat*, *Asharq Al-Awsat* has often been seen as a voice for Saudi policies and perspectives (Boyd 2001). Launched in London in 1978 and printed in twelve locations internationally, the paper is described as "the leading Arab daily newspaper" and calls itself "the premier pan-Arab daily newspaper."[6] *Asharq Al-Awsat* covers events via a network of bureaus and correspondents throughout the Arab world, Europe, the United States, and Asia. The paper also has copyright syndications with the *Washington Post*, *Los Angeles Times*, *New York Times*, and *Global Viewpoint*, permitting it to publish Arabic translations of columnists such as Thomas Friedman and David Ignatius.

France 24 Channel: http://www.france24.com/ar

France 24 is an international news and current affairs television channel based in Paris. Its stated mission is to "cover international current events from a French perspective and to convey French values throughout the world."[7] France 24 Arabic TV was established in 2005, though it began transmission in late 2006. Since 2008, the French government has owned the channel, which thrives on France's strong relations with the Arab world in the past few decades. Its priority is to build a news market and attract Arab viewers (Ziani, Fahmy, and Elareshi 2014). According to Seib (2010), France 24 was designed to help spread French political values, paying attention to the less well-covered parts of the world and encouraging public debates. The channel has an impressive social media presence with activities across multiple platforms.

THE PAN-ARAB MEDIA SOCIAL MEDIA LANDSCAPE

We notice that all pan-Arab media organizations included in this study have varying forms of social media engagement as part of their overall media operations. As figure 4.1 shows, though all pan-Arab media outlets share their use of social media tools such as Facebook and Twitter, they vary in terms of usage of other platforms such as Google+, YouTube, and LinkedIn. Some pan-Arab media websites also have live broadcasts, Instagram tools, and syndicated news feeds. All ten pan-Arab media outlets have developed their own iOS or Android-based applications to help users gain faster and more convenient access to their online content. Analysis shows users may access a variety of media services available on their websites, including live broadcasts. Since this study is limited to Facebook and Twitter social media platforms, there is no ready data on how the other social tools are being used by both media organizations and audiences for daily engagement. Of course, as noted in the introduction of this book, the issue here is not simply about pan-Arab media establishing social media accounts but rather about how they harness them to sustain user engagement and interactivity. In some parts of the region,

Media Outlet	Facebook	Twitter	Instagram	Google+	LinkedIn	YouTube	RSS	LIVE	APPS	OTHER
Al Jazeera	√	√	x	√	x	√	√	√	√	√
Al Arabiya	√	√	√	√	x	√	√	√	√	√
Al Mayadeen	√	√	√	√	x	√	√	√	√	√
BBC Arabic TV	√	√	√	√	x	√	√	√	√	√
CNN Arabic	√	√	x	√	x	√	√	x	√	√
Al Hurra	√	√	x	x	x	√	x	√	√	√
Skynews Arabia	√	√	x	√	√	√	x	√	√	√
Al Hayat	√	√	x	√	√	√	x	x	√	√
Asharq Alwsat	√	√	x	√	√	x	√	x	√	√
France 24	√	√	x	√	x	√	√	√	√	√

Figure 4.1. Pan-Arab Media Social Media Presence

user engagement, as we will see in chapter 6, seems to be undermined by poor telecommunications infrastructures and strict state censorship.

GROWTH TRENDS

Data generated in this chapter is derived from multiple time frames to show levels of growth in social media traffic generated by the pan-Arab media organizations covered by this study. From April 1 to August 31, 2014, we found a rather steady growth of social media features such as Facebook "likes," tweets, retweets, and followers. Al-Jazeera and Al-Arabiya channels topped the sample study outlets in terms of total likes and growth rates (over one million increase in five months), followed by Alhurra, Sky News Arabia, and Al-Mayadeen channels. As newcomers to the social media world, both *Asharq Al-Awsat* and *Al-Hayat* newspapers scored the lowest number of Facebook likes (fewer than 200,000; see table 4.1). While those figures suggest how popular pan-Arab media are getting in the social media sphere, they may not imply any form of audience loyalty when it comes to engagement. In chapter 6, a qualitative analysis of user-generated content relating to stories posted by those media on Facebook shows a good part of the audience engagement was in fact bordering on critical reactions to pan-Arab media outbound traffic.

Table 4.1. Facebook Likes (April–August 2014)

	Cumulative Likes				
Organization	*April*	*May*	*June*	*July*	*August*
BBC Arabic	2,635,134	2,700,000	2,961,723	3,191,955	3,299,060
CNN Arabic	604,497	621,000	644,993	665,612	685,167
Sky News Arabia	3,503,838	3,700,000	4,056,285	4,303,896	4,467,491
Al-Jazeera	7,074,172	7,400,000	7,749,564	8,170,938	8,542,457
Al-Arabiya	7,002,288	7,400,000	7,852,121	8,270,244	8,620,998
Al-Mayadeen	1,708,853	1,884,556	2,037,449	2,229,893	2,402,314
Alhurra	3,832,871	4,027,839	4,221,761	4,486,049	4,659,339
Asharq Al-Awsat	180,721	181,000	182,882	184,603	186,823
Al-Hayat	150,802	153,000	155,008	157,415	159,752
France 24	2,230,185	2,336,632	2,346,202	2,372,350	2,397,184

The five-month (April 1 to August 31, 2014) monitoring of Facebook traffic relevant to the ten pan-Arab media also showed steady growth in the number of posts. Data on monthly posts show Sky News Arabia leading in terms of the volume (12,350), followed by CNN Arabic (7,780), Al-Arabiya (7,100), Al-Jazeera (5,930), and Al-Mayadeen (4,250). Alhurra scored the lowest number of posts during the five-month period (280). Data from Simply Measured Analytics for the August 8–22 frame show different types of formats being posted on Facebook by the ten pan-Arab media outlets. CNN Arabic came first in terms of link-based posts (557), followed by Al-Mayadeen (369), Al-Jazeera (344), and France 24 (258). Sky News Arabia scored the highest number of posts occurring in multimedia formats (pictures and video) (830), followed by Al-Arabiya (357), Al-Jazeera (202), and *Al-Hayat Politics* (185). The highest number of status posts was created by Sky News Arabia (387), followed by Al-Arabiya (337) and CNN Arabic (49). It is clear that Sky News Arabia was leading the other pan-Arab media outlets in terms of the number of posts created during the analysis period, while Alhurra was lagging behind in Facebook traffic. The fact that channels like CNN Arabic and Al-Mayadeen scored rather high in terms of their link-based posts showed their clear interest in driving traffic to their websites. On the other hand, both Sky News Arabia and Al-Arabiya's focus on multimedia suggested their perception of the power of visual communications in the emerging convergence environment. By posting a picture, a video, or a cartoon, those channels seem to give more consideration to reinforcing attitudes and values among target audiences than to simply enhancing their awareness.

Data on the type of posts initiated by pan-Arab media (August 8–22, 2014) show that 82.71 percent of BBC posts were links and 17.28 percent were multimedia, while Al-Mayadeen had 86.82 percent of its posts as links, followed by *Asharq Al-Awsat* (73.94 percent) and CNN Arabic (49.91 percent). Multimedia posts were used by Sky News Arabia (97.87 percent), followed by Al-Arabiya (84.59 percent), *Al-Hayat* (82.23 percent), and Alhurra (34.66 percent). The highest percentage of posts as status was associated with Alhurra (62.66 percent) and Al-Jazeera (38.16 percent). The high percentage of multimedia posts by Sky News Arabia and Al-Arabiya channels suggests strong perceptions of the centrality of visual content for audience engagement. The high percentage of posts occurring as links in some pan-Arab media Facebook pages also shows interest in driving traffic to other websites or resources of relevance to the channels.

Data on tweeting shows most of the ten pan-Arab media services achieving steady growth during the five-month time frame of the analysis (figure 4.2). Those included BBC Arabic (40,000 to 44,300 tweets), CNN Arabic (47,400 to 52,600 tweets), Al-Arabiya (74,600 to 80,100 tweets), *Asharq Al-Awsat* (51,400 to 60,900 tweets); *Al-Hayat Politics* (65,700 to 75,200 tweets); and France 24 (76,600 to 82,900 tweets). Fluctuations in tweeting activities were noted with respect to Sky News Arabia (59,800 to 47,500 tweets) and Al-Jazeera (19,100 to 13,220 tweets). It is difficult at this point to explain such irregularities in tweeting traffic by both Sky News Arabia and Al-Jazeera since this might require a more direct observation of the two broadcasters' social media work practices, which is not part of

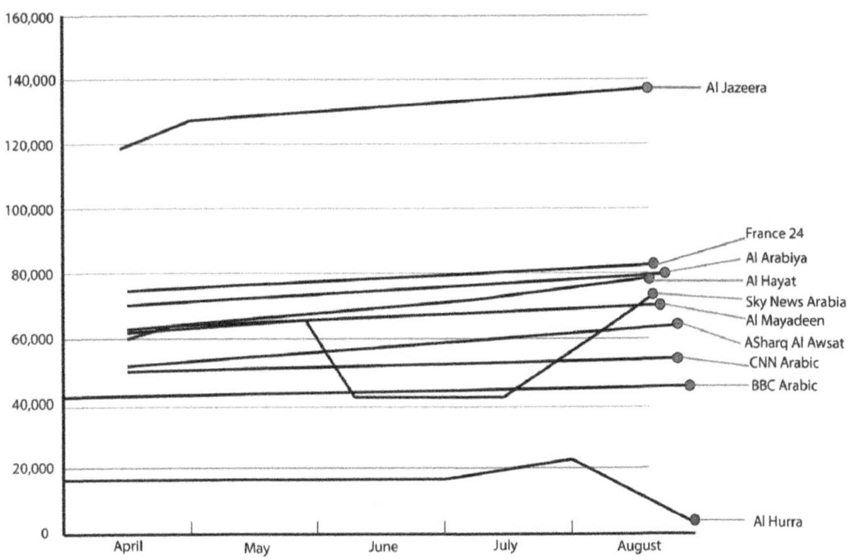

Figure 4.2. Growth of Pan-Arab Media Tweets (April–August 2014)

this study. Technical or staff shortage problems might have caused those issues in both channels.

SOCIAL MEDIA USAGE PATTERNS

Social media staff in media institutions are typically gatekeepers who follow selective approaches to handling their initiated posts and tweets. Their information ecosystem incorporates multisourced news carried by their websites or broadcast/print media and/or ideas they initiate to generate audience engagement. We believe an investigation of the nature of posts and tweets initiated by pan-Arab media organizations would provide more insightful information on their news and information agendas in the age of cyberspace communications. This gatekeeping process in the social world of the Internet, however, has its own complications given the undefined parameters of information traffic. The use of social media–based information as news has always been a contested issue in media organizations around the world, including the Middle East. One BBC Arabic journalist notes that verifying material to ensure its suitability for broadcasting can be an elaborate process (*Economist* 2011). Checking snippets of information posted on Twitter is more difficult. Tweets can be a useful way to gauge the public mood about an issue and are now often incorporated into news coverage as digital "vox pops." As the BBC journalists comment, "Many journalists use Twitter to solicit leads, find sources, or ask for information. But Twitter is a public forum where anyone can say anything. By providing more raw material than ever from which to distil the news, social media have both done away with editors and shown up the need for them" (*Economist* 2011).

A content analysis of Facebook posts and tweets appearing on the ten pan-Arab media accounts during May 2014 reveals data about geographical scope and topic. As the analysis shows, the majority of Facebook posts concerned local events and issues in the region's states, such as violence, civil conflict, economic developments, political unrest, and social/scientific events. Al-Jazeera, Alhurra, Al-Arabiya, and Sky News Arabia's Facebook posts concerned stories about local Arab developments in Egypt, Syria, Iraq, Qatar, Sudan, Lebanon, Libya, Morocco, and Algeria. In May 2014, those countries were experiencing major developments ranging from civil wars to political upheavals and economic hardships. *Al-Hayat* newspaper had major posts about transitions in Egypt, civil war in Syria and Iraq, and Saudi efforts to support Egypt's emerging government of Abdel Fattah El-Sisi. Yemen was also a major story in pan-Arab media Facebook postings, with ongoing military conflicts involving

Huthis, Al-Qaeda, and South Yemen. It should be noted that regional issues and events involved news about Turkey, Iran, Israel, and Southeast Asia, while international news postings addressed US-European engagement with the Middle East and the fight against terrorism in addition to US relations with Egypt, Libya, and Iran. The dominance of local news in pan-Arab media Facebook posts reflects interest in the region's local developments as highly relevant for engaging audiences in their social media activities. Proximity here defines how much audiences are likely to engage in online communications pertaining to their localities compared with those dealing with remote geographical areas and regions.

The same patterns defining the scope of Facebook posts seem to apply to pan-Arab media tweets. The May 2014 analysis shows that local issues and events dominated news tweets by media outlets with leading hashtags appearing in most of the Twitter conversations. Hashtags for Egypt's El-Sisi, the Muslim Brotherhood, Syria, ISIS, Bahrain unrest, Iran's nuclear claims, former Iraqi prime minister Nouri Al-Maliki, Libya's civil war, and Gaza conditions were related to tweeted stories by the ten pan-Arab media covered in this study. Explicit references to emerging hashtags in the conversations suggested how keen pan-Arab media were on engaging users in the discussion of issues pertaining to their localities. Alhurra, Al-Jazeera, CNN Arabic, and Al-Arabiya led Twitter conversations with tweets on local events and issues. International issues relating to US and European engagement with the region's developments in Syria, Iraq, Libya, Yemen, and Egypt also made good showings in tweets initiated by the ten pan-Arab media organizations. BBC Arabic, *Asharq Al-Awsat*, and France 24 scored the highest number of tweets on international events and issues. As in Facebook, regional events and issues like Iran's nuclear program and Turkey's political unrest were scoring low in Twitter conversations.

In a region long defined by political and military conflicts, it seems rather normal to see the social media sphere buzzing with heated political discussions and news. The content analysis of Facebook topics posted in May 2014 shows political/military conflicts dominating Facebook traffic by pan-Arab media organizations. The situations in Egypt, Syria, Iraq, Libya, Algeria, Bahrain, and Lebanon came to dominate Facebook posts and user-generated content during the same period. Political topics defined over 90 percent of Al-Mayadeen channel's posts and over 80 percent of posts by *Al-Hayat Politics* and Alhurra and Sky News Arabia channels. Al-Jazeera had over 75 percent of its posts about political events and issues. Traditionally, politics has been an enduring feature of the region's national and international news media, and engaging users in political discussions of issues bearing on their lives has always been an exciting topic of research (Ayish 2002). Most of the pan-Arab media outlets covered by the study seem to hold strong views about the role of social media in bringing about political changes in the region in view of the so-called Arab Spring experience. On their parts, Arab audiences also seem to find a lot of fulfillment in engaging in political discussions online as a means of expressing themselves more freely in a generally inhibitive national media environment. In the MENA region, politics has been a major taboo, and social media have come to be huge contributors to breaking those taboos.

In addition to politics, social and cultural issues relating to religious beliefs and traditions have also been resonating in social media spheres. The issue of sectarianism revolving around some divergent Sunni-Shi'ite beliefs was ranking high in social media posts by pan-Arab broadcasters and print media during the study period. All ten pan-Arab media outlets produced varying content formats on sectarianism such as talk shows, news reports, or commentaries, and their posts and tweets were highly reflective of those coverage patterns. But, as we will see in chapter 6, pan-Arab media focus on those issues was also giving rise to heated social media conversations that only deepened existing rifts between social and political factions. The true and genuine meaning of Islam was the prime casualty of those sensational debates as driven by conflicting political agendas in different directions. Science and technology topics were receiving good attention in posts by CNN Arabic, BBC Arabic, Al-Arabiya, *Asharq Al-Awsat*, and Sky News Arabia outlets. Posts and tweets initiated by those media often linked users to video reports, stories, or other websites for more details on topics such as renewable energy, water desalination, mobile telephony, and online innovations.

Economic news was significantly visible in posts and tweets by Sky News Arabia, *Asharq Al-Awsat*, France 24, and BBC Arabic. Most of the news feeds connected users to media content in the forms of video reports, talk shows, feature stories, and interviews. Most of the economic news postings and tweets were related to developments in the Gulf Cooperation Council (GCC) region where megaprojects and investments are launched. Egyptian efforts to revitalize the economy through support from Saudi Arabia, the United Arab Emirates, and Kuwait were also visible in Facebook posts. But again, for Twitter feeds, economic news, like that of science, technology, and the environment, was less frequent than political and military news. Twitter has been best known as a tool of reporting crisis and breaking news to keep users posted on developments. Political and military news generally thrives on fast dissemination while news about economic development, science, and technology is less urgent and may be delayed for hours without losing its value.

MOST FAVORED TOPICS POSTED BY PAN-ARAB MEDIA

Drawing on a two-week sample (August 8–22, 2014), we used Simply Measured social media analytics to generate data on most favored topics carried by pan-Arab media Facebook accounts. The results of the analysis show wide variations among the ten pan-Arab media organizations in terms of how their audiences perceive their posts. As will be discussed in chapter 6, users' engagement with pan-Arab media seems to be largely defined by their ability to access the conversations online and communicate their ideas to a global audience. Signing up as followers of pan-Arab media Facebook and Twitter pages is in no way indicative of any sense of loyalty on the part of those users. For example, while Al-Jazeera had the story about Turkish prime minister Erdoğan's victory in the elections as the number one story for audiences, comments incorporated a mixture of negative and positive reactions that reflected users' divergent political attitudes on Turkey and Erdoğan. Another example was the situation in Gaza as a high-ranking topic on Al-Jazeera's Facebook agenda that attracted a good number of mixed reactions from users. In general, those Gaza reactions were very assertive in hailing the steadfastness and resistance of the Gaza people against what was perceived as a "barbaric Israeli onslaught" while very few comments blamed Hamas for the miserable conditions of civilian populations in the besieged Gaza Strip.

On the other hand, Gaza was ranking low on Al-Arabiya and other pan-Arab media channels, barely occurring as one of the most favored topics for those media. Al-Arabiya's most favored Facebook engagement concerned a photo of an elephant in Africa trying to jump over a small car used by tourists, something that turned out to be an advertisement for a German automaker. There was one story on Gaza and another on ISIS terrorists fighting in northern Iraq. The same thing applied to CNN Arabic posts on the US Missouri riots and Egyptian reactions to those events in addition to the brutal beheading of a US journalist in Syria. Sky News Arabia had the most balanced postings, with diverse topics ranging from the Ferguson riots to Egyptian squabbles with international human rights organizations, Turkey's elections, and Bill Gates's and Mark Zuckerberg's participation in the Ice Bucket Challenge. BBC Arabic's most favored topics carried features similar to those of Sky News Arabia, with postings on Erdoğan's victory in Turkey, Egypt's tensions with human rights groups, a UK-based campaign to support Gaza victims, and the awarding of an international prize to an Iranian female mathematician.

Since the ranking of topics carried by the ten pan-Arab media organizations is generally more a function of users' political and cultural preferences than of media editorial choice, one should not overlook the fact that media themselves sometimes do intervene in this process, at least in defining the initial discussions in social space. Social media posts are generally related to media content pan-Arab media carried in their traditional communication channels, and in this sense, the agenda-setting function of the media continues to play out well in the social media world despite the fact that user-generated content does significantly affect cyber conversations.

CONCLUSION

It is clear that all pan-Arab media organizations covered by the study were active users of the two leading social media platforms: Facebook and Twitter. If the ultimate goal of pan-Arab mass communications since the 1990s and before had been developed around building up some public opinions among the region's populations relevant to their diverse political and ideological orientations, social media have made that mission most possible. In the past, traditional regional media such as BBC Arabic radio, the Voice of America, Radio Cairo, and Radio Monte Carlo had little success in engaging Arab populations in their news agendas. Lacking reliable audience data and state censorship had always militated against the development of solid engagement strategies with the region's audiences. In the age of social media, pan-Arab communications have made audience engagement most possible and measurable. The proliferation of new information and communications technologies among the region's populations have only enhanced pan-Arab media organizations' reach to audiences to engage them in global conversations on issues of high relevance to the Middle East. The steady flow of social media traffic from pan-Arab media organizations testified to the determination of those media to make social platforms an integral part of their communications. The establishment of social media units and recruitment of social media specialists by all pan-Arab media outlets covered by the study suggest that those operations are serious in going social not only for institutional development, but for survival as well. As elsewhere, social media have become the new frontier for the marketing not only of goods and services but of ideas and values as well.

Since our knowledge about social media's role in marketing and communications continues to be quite fragmented, more research is needed to grasp the full picture of how social venues are being harnessed by pan-Arab media to achieve audience engagement. A more longitudinal investigation of pan-Arab media usage of a wider range of social tools could yield more insightful results on where this emerging sector is heading. But as these study findings suggest, social media is here to stay as part of pan-Arab media operations. We are likely to see more expansions in social media integration into overall pan-Arab media operations controlled by ideologically and politically divergent nations that are resolved to push forward their ideas and policies in a constantly destabilized yet strategically important region. MENA's experience with the so-called Arab Spring uprisings shows that people's voices do matter in shaping the Middle East's future. Hence, engaging Arab populations with new ideas for constructive transitions is of paramount importance to nations in the region and beyond. Harnessing the social tools of the information and communications revolutions has proved the most effective way to achieve that goal.

NOTES

1. Market research outfits like the Dubai-based Pan-Arab Research Center (PARC) used to provide much of the audience research data needed by national and international media and advertisers.
2. Many of those social media policies have not been publicized, and their circulation remains limited to internal staff for observance.
3. See http://www.alhurra.com/info/english/112.html.
4. See https://en.wikipedia.org/wiki/Al-Hayat.
5. See Yousif Ibrahim, "Al Hayat: A Journalistic Noah's Ark," *New York Times*, January 15, 1997, and Hassan M. Fattah, "Spreading the Word: Who's Who in the Arab Media," *New York Times*, February 6, 2005.
6. See http://www.asharq-e.com/aboutus.asp.
7. France 24 Arabic identifies itself as a media platform for international news drawing on a multiperspective French viewpoint. See more at http://www.dailymotion.com/france24arabic.

5

How Journalists Use Social Media

Social space is not an exclusive institutional concern limited to pan-Arab media organizations. Professional media practitioners in a wide range of transnational communications functions are also active users of social media platforms. Though this study shows that pan-Arab media journalists surveyed vary in their usages of both Facebook and Twitter as the prime two social media platforms, the overall picture suggests that professionals' use of those platforms is a function of social media policies enforced in those organizations. While media outlets like Al-Jazeera and Al-Mayadeen seem to give much room to their journalists to use social media to promote their own ideological opinions (which are not contravening those championed by both channels, anyway), others seem to have more restrictive policies in place. Some journalists even have no personal social media accounts and would work only through their TV-show accounts to engage audiences or promote those shows. Though the study does not address the social media platforms, apart from Facebook and Twitter, used by pan-Arab journalists, it is clear that most Arab journalists seem to see social media as yet another communications frontier with empowering engagement.

The chapter shows that some of the pan-Arab media journalists have built up extensive followings at regional and international levels mainly because of the positions they advocate and the ideas they disseminate. Others, who have opted to use social media to promote their shows, seem keener on avoiding critical political issues by limiting discussions to their nonpolitical media segments in sports and culture. Another group of journalists have chosen to keep off the social media arena either for personal reasons or in compliance with established social media policies that discourage personal engagement with social media platforms, especially in culturally and politically sensitive issues. This chapter describes and analyzes patterns of social media usage by twenty-six journalists working for the ten pan-Arab media organizations covered by the study. Journalists were randomly selected from a pool of one hundred media persons working for those organizations with social media activities. The analysis addresses journalists' personal/official Facebook and Twitter accounts in quantitative terms to illustrate the number of followers, the topics of traffic, the use of visuals, and the nature of tweets/posts over a five-month period (April 1 to August 31, 2014). The quantitative analysis is supplemented by a qualitative analysis of the content originating at the journalists' accounts.

JOURNALISTS AND SOCIAL MEDIA: A GLOBAL OVERVIEW

Around the world, journalists' use of social media in their work has generated extensive interest among researchers. Some discussions have addressed the issue of social media as empowering tools that journalists can harness to express personal opinions that they could not air on their government or corporate media channels. Generally speaking, all international media seem to encourage their professional journalists to have their own personal social media engagements. However, guidelines set by those media seem to put major strings on how those journalists may address events and issues in the context of established professional standards and practices.

Despite growing skepticism about the role online in promoting democratization and free expression (Morozov 2012), discussions of social media around the world noted that new technologies have also turned more empowering for individual journalists seeking to communicate with their audiences in a more direct way. It was noted that journalists dealing with social media in their work are guided not only by general organizational and editorial norms applicable to all staff but also by specific social media guidelines that spell out duties and responsibilities in cyberspace. Around the world, media organizations have formulated social media policies to define the boundaries of interactive communications their professional staff could engage in without compromising the fundamental professional standards of their journalistic practices.[1] While most of those guidelines seem to recognize the centrality of social platforms for media organizations, they also echo cautious concerns regarding possible abuses of those networks in a manner that could be detrimental to their standing. Questions raised by those guidelines generally address issues relating to individual journalists expressing personal opinions in social spaces, publicizing internal issues pertaining to the organization, handling matters relating to competitors, and reporting information from unverifiable sources.

Most of the social media guidelines we accessed emphasize objectivity, transparency, credibility, and observance of the organization's editorial orientation. For example, Agence France-Presse (AFP) social media guidelines require that journalists may have separate social media accounts as personal outlets while maintaining an institutional account as AFP journalists. Journalists are advised to avoid vulgarity or overopinionated comments and not to post information they come across without going through the central wire service. The Associated Press encourages all its journalists to have accounts on social networks with mandatory identification of themselves as AP staff. According to the guidelines, AP employees must refrain from declaring their views on contentious public issues in any public forum and must not take part in organized action in support of causes or movements. The *Washington Post* guidelines state that *Post* journalists must refrain from writing, tweeting, or posting anything—including photographs or video—that could be perceived as reflecting political, racial, sexist, religious, or other bias or favoritism. Journalists are instructed when posting content online to ask themselves: Would this posting make a reader question my ability to do my job objectively and professionally (whether you are a reporter, an editor, a developer or a producer)? If so, the journalist should not post it. BBC guidelines state that the personal use of the Internet by BBC staff must be tempered by an awareness of the potential conflicts that may arise. They also require a clear division between "BBC" pages and "personal" pages. On social networking sites, BBC journalists should be mindful that the information they disclose does not bring the BBC into disrepute. The BBC's new rules require journalists to file a story and tweet simultaneously instead of tweeting before submitting a story. According to a report from the *Guardian*, the rules apply to all the company's correspondents. The BBC's updated social media rules came a day after Sky News instructed its writers not to retweet anything from rival organizations or outside a particular reporter's beat. That means a Sky News journalist covering, say, national politics couldn't tweet about his or her favorite soccer club on a personal account. Sky News cited similar reasons for its new Twitter policies, while adding that content retweeted from other news outlets have not been vetted by the company's own internal editorial process.

In the Middle East, the case of CNN journalist Octavia Nasr, who was dismissed from her job for writing personal views about a Lebanese Shiite scholar, has generated mixed reactions relating to editorial control and journalists' personal independence (Walker 2010). CNN's Roland Martin was suspended in February 2012 in response to a series of controversial tweets he sent during the Super Bowl. Many gay rights organizations took offense to Martin's comments about soccer star David Beckham's H&M commercial and a New England Patriots player's pink jumpsuit. Established social media policies across the region's media landscape seem to discourage what may amount to be a political or ideological professional journalist's propagation of some ideas regarding issues he or she is supposed to handle with objectivity or with consideration of some political, cultural, or social issues.[2] In January 2015, veteran CNN journalist Jim Clancy made a series of controversial tweets about Israel and the Charlie Hebdo shooting that led him to quit the network after thirty-four years of work.

But social media empowerment for journalists is not only political or social but professional. Social media tools for professional journalists that enable aggregation, online search, content sharing, tracing virtual conversations on topics of interest, and crowdsourcing have been developed and are quite common in the media business (Palumbo 2014). Grabowicz (2014) notes that for journalists and news organizations, social networks provide an opportunity for connecting with people, distributing news stories, and complementing news coverage with feeds from social media. He cites examples of journalists' use of social media when reporters can join the networks, converse with people, and showcase their stories, thus developing personal brands for their work. For news organizations, according to Grabowicz (2014), social networks can alert people to important news stories the news organization has published or post other items of interest to its followers. Social networks are great for generating conversations among people about stories. Many news media have found that the volume of reader comments on a story posted on Facebook can exceed comments posted on the news organization's website. Journalists also can use social networks like Facebook to find sources for stories.

Falkow (2014) reports the findings of an Indiana University School of Journalism report based on online interviews with 1,080 US journalists. The study found out that the majority of journalists use microblogging on Twitter to engage with their audiences (53.8 percent), followed by blogs (23.6 percent), crowdsourcing (20.2 percent), professional networks (10.6 percent), and citizen blogs. The report shows 78 percent of journalists checking social media for breaking news, 56.2 percent using it to find additional information about a topic, 54.1 percent to find sources for stories, and 40 percent of US journalists saying that social media are very important to their work. On the other hand, over 80 percent say that social media does help to promote their work, and almost 70 percent say because of social media they are more engaged with their audiences. In addition, 62 percent say that social media allows them to do faster reporting of news.

PAN-ARAB JOURNALISTS' SOCIAL MEDIA PROFILES: AN OVERVIEW

The twenty-six journalists covered by the study have been randomly selected from a pool of one hundred journalists with social media relevance to the ten pan-Arab media organizations discussed in chapter 4. They include:

- *Faisal Al-Kasim*: a British-Syrian anchor and television talk show presenter based at the Al-Jazeera Arabic channel. He hosts the controversial weekly show *Opposite Direction* and contributes substantially to social media conversations on issues relating to regional politics. Al-Kasim's Facebook and Twitter accounts are: https://www.facebook.com/falkasim and https://twitter.com/kasimf.
- *Khadija Ben Ghana*: An Algerian television presenter with Al-Jazeera in Doha. She has presented a range of talk shows in addition to prime-time newscasts on the Arabic channel. She is also active on social media and has her own website. Ben Ghana's Facebook and Twitter accounts are: https://www.facebook.com/khdyjtbn and https://twitter.com/khadijabenguen.
- *Ali Al-Dfiri*: A Saudi program anchor and talk show presenter on Al-Jazeera channel. He has presented the *In Depth* talk show on Al-Jazeera and contributes to the Qatari *Al-Watan* newspaper. Al-Dfiri's Facebook and Twitter accounts are: https://www.facebook.com/Ali.Dfiri and https://twitter.com/AliAldafiri.
- *Samir Farah*: BBC Arabic editor and presenter of the social media–rich talk show *Nuqtat Hiwar*. Farah's Facebook page is: https://twitter.com/SamFarahBBC.
- *Nour Eddine Zorgui*: A Moroccan-born BBC Arabic editor and presenter of the social media–rich talk show *Nuqtat Hiwar*. Zorgui's Facebook account is: https://www.facebook.com/noureddinezorgui.
- *Rasha Qandeel*: An Egyptian-born BBC Arabic anchor and presenter of several talk shows, including the social media–rich *Nuqtat Hiwar*. Qandeel's social media accounts are: https://www.facebook.com/RashaQandeelBBC and https://twitter.com/RashaQandeelBBC.
- *Taleb Kanaan*: A Lebanese-born anchor and talk show presenter at Al-Arabiya channel in Dubai. Kanaan's Facebook and Twitter accounts are: https://www.facebook.com/Taleb.fanpage and https://twitter.com/TalebKan.
- *Rima Maktabi*: A Lebanese-born TV reporter and presenter who had previously worked as host of CNN's show *Inside the Middle East*. Maktabi's Facebook and Twitter accounts are: https://www.face

book.com/pages/RIMA-MAKTABI/8186642569 and https://twitter.com/rimamaktabi.

- *Lutfi Al-Zoabi*: A Jordanian-born sports newscaster at Al-Arabiya channel in Dubai. Al-Zoabi's Facebook and Twitter accounts are: https://www.facebook.com/lutfi.alzoabi and https://twitter.com/lutfialzoabi.
- *Zina Yazji*: A Syrian-born television anchor and talk show presenter at Sky News Arabia. She had worked at Dubai Television before joining Sky News Arabia in early 2014. Yazji's Facebook account is: https://www.facebook.com/pages/Zina-Yazji-56998635889.
- *Mohannad Al-Khatib*: A Jordanian-born newscaster and television show presenter at Sky News Arabia in Abu Dhabi. His show, *Hiwar Al-Laylah*, features interviews with different personalities on mostly political issues. His Facebook and Twitter accounts which are dedicated to his show are: https://www.facebook.com/hiwarskynewsarabia and https://twitter.com/HiwarSky.
- *Hamad Al-Mahmud*: A Saudi-born head of Sky News Arabia's Riyadh bureau. Al-Mahmud's Twitter account is: https://twitter.com/hamadalmahmud.
- *Ghassan Bin Jiddo*: A Tunisian-born journalist who manages the Beirut-based Al-Mayadeen channel. He had previously worked at the Al-Jazeera channel before leaving in early 2012 to establish the Al-Mayadeen channel. Bin Jiddo's Facebook account is: https://www.facebook.com/pages/116487605104318.
- *Sami Kleib*: A Lebanese-born television journalist who had worked at Al-Jazeera channel before joining Al-Mayadeen channel in early 2012. Kleib's Facebook account is: https://www.facebook.com/samikleib.
- *Lina Zahreddine*: A Lebanese anchor and talk show presenter who had worked for Al-Jazeera before joining Al-Mayadeen channel in early 2012. Zahreddine's Facebook account is: https://www.facebook.com/LinaZahredine.
- *Caroline Faraj*: A Jordanian journalist who joined CNN as head of the CNN Arabic bureau in Dubai n 2002. Faraj's Twitter account is: https://twitter.com/cfaraj.
- *Jamal Khashoggi*: A Saudi journalist and commentator with long professional experience in several Saudi newspapers, including *Al-Hayat*. Khashoggi's Facebook and Twitter accounts are: https://www.facebook.com/jamal.khashoggi and https://twitter.com/JKhashoggi.
- *Khaled Al-Dakheel*: A Saudi journalist and commentator working for the London-based *Al-Hayat* newspaper. Al-Dakheel's Twitter account is: https://twitter.com/kdriyadh.

- *Amjad Rasmi*: A Jordanian-born cartoonist working for *Asharq Al-Awsat* newspaper. Rasmi's Facebook account is: https://www.facebook.com/AmjadRasmiFans.
- *Salman Aldosary*: A Saudi journalist working for *Asharq Al-Awsat* newspaper. Aldosary's Twitter account is: https://twitter.com/SalmanAldosary.
- *Mohammed Fahad Al-Harthi*: A Saudi journalist and commentator with extensive experience in numerous publications, including *Arab News* and *Al-Iqtisadi* magazine. Al-Harthi's Twitter account is: https://twitter.com/mfalharthi.
- *Rafik Sahali*: An Algerian-born television presenter and talk show host working for the Arabic Service of France 24. Sahali's Facebook account is: https://www.facebook.com/pages/Rafik-sahali/153807361394574.
- *Toufic Gebran*: A Lebanese-born television presenter who hosts the *I-Tech* show on Alhurra channel. Gebran's Facebook account for his show is: https://www.facebook.com/itechshow.
- *Hussein Jaradi, Michael Ghandour*, and *Mohamed Ali Haidari*: The three journalists alternate in hosting the *Free Hour* talk show on Alhurra channel. The show's Facebook account is: https://www.facebook.com/freehour.
- *Taoufik Mjaied*: A Tunisian-born television newscaster and presenter who hosts the *Niqash* talk show on France 24. Mjaied's Facebook account for the show is: https://www.facebook.com/debat.f24.ar.
- *Jehad Al-Khazen*: A veteran Lebanese journalist and commentator working for *Al-Hayat* newspaper. Al-Khazen's Twitter account is: https://twitter.com/JihadelKhazen.

PAN-ARAB JOURNALISTS' SOCIAL MEDIA USAGE PATTERNS

A survey of the social presence of the twenty-six media professionals selected for the study shows variations in their presence across social media platforms. While few of them have maintained accounts in both Facebook and Twitter (Faisal Al-Kasim, Khadija Ben Ghana, Taleb Kanaan), others have kept only one account of their own in either one of the two social media platforms. On the other hand, it was found that some media professionals were contributing to social media conversations not as owners but as users of accounts that carry names of the shows they host. Examples include presenters of TV shows from Alhurra and Sky News Arabia. Furthermore, it was noted that while some journalists were keen to observe their media employers' guidelines pertaining to engagement in sensitive political and cultural issues, others working for channels like

Al-Jazeera and Al-Mayadeen demonstrated conspicuous political and ideological inclinations in their social engagements to reflect their own personal opinions. The cases of Faisal Al-Kasim of Al-Jazeera channel and Ghassan Bin Jiddo of Al-Mayadeen channel are worth consideration. For both channels, social space is just another frontier for the political and ideological fight waged in conventional media spaces. As we discuss the two cases in detail in this chapter, this conduct may be posing critical problems for the future of social media as empowering tools for independent journalism in the Arab world. Social media could be most powerful when they echo the professional orientations of journalists as they deal with emerging issues of a complicated political or ideological nature. This type of association between media organizations and ideologically biased journalists could have some detrimental effects on their reputation in the future. As chapter 6 shows, the whole issue of social media is about engagement, and the fact that audiences are increasingly becoming part of media-initiated conversations carries much significance for the future development of journalism in this part of the world.

Data generated by the Simply Measured social media firm show pan-Arab media journalists enjoying varying levels of follows and tweets, hence varying levels of Klout scores[3] that reflect their divergent standing in the social world of the Internet. Faisal Al-Kasim of Al-Jazeera channel had the highest Klout score on Twitter (71.6), followed by Salman Al-Dossary of *Asharq Al-Awsat* (69.9), Ali Al-Dfiri of Al-Jazeera (67.6), and Khadija Ben Ghana, also of Al-Jazeera (61.8). Generally speaking, all surveyed pan-Arab journalists with Twitter accounts, except for one (Amjad Rasmi of *Asharq Al-Awsat*) had a 40-plus Klout score, which is the global average for media influencers. The findings suggest the dominance of Al-Jazeera journalists in audience engagement and tweeting traffic as compared with other pan-Arab media professionals covered in this study. The fact that Al-Jazeera journalists are able to advocate specific political stands that fall in synch with the channel's media policies seem to have bolstered their standing as media influencers.

Pan-Arab media journalists who aspire to become more "professional" and less "ideological" score lower on the Klout index, which means they are generating less sensational and controversial traffic, which normally triggers lower engagement. According to the analysis of Twitter traffic generated by fifteen pan-Arab media journalists covered in this study, the Klout score was not always proportionate to the volume of traffic initiated by individual journalists (see table 5.1). For example, Faisal Al-Kasim of Al-Jazeera had 42,876 tweets by late August 2014, which far exceeded the average tweet volume of his followers (762), who had an average Klout score of 17, far below the world average of 40. The same thing applies to Salman Al-Dossary of *Asharq Al-Awsat*, whose tweets totaled 29,819,

Table 5.1. Pan-Arab Media Journalists' Twitter Usage and Klout

No.	*Journalist*	*Organization*	*Followers*	*Audience Followers*	*Tweets*	*Audience Tweets*	*Klout Score*	*Audience Klout Score*
1	Ali Al-Dfiri	Al-Jazeera	479,957	537	23,127	762	67.6	18.9
2	Amjad Rasmi	*Asharq Al-Awsat*	313	8,633	805	3,321	35.6	28.6
3	Faisal Al-Kasim	Al-Jazeera	1,689,795	208	42,876	279	71.6	17.0
4	Hamad Al-Mahmud	Sky News Arabia	1,135	4,949	3,386	3,845	49.1	24.1
5	Mohammed Al-Harthi	*Asharq Al-Awsat*	13,166	2,926	683	1,967	54.4	21.2
6	Jehad Al-Khazen	*Al-Hayat*	7,020	1,833	571	2,643	41.1	20.1
7	Khaled Al-Dakheel	*Al-Hayat*	97,469	2,256	7,082	1,822	61.8	22.6
8	Khadijah Ben Ghana	Al-Jazeera	48,940	736	5,502	1,946	62.8	21.3
9	Nour Eddine Zorgui	BBC Arabic	6,471	3,912	8,549	2,323	51.3	19.5
10	Rima Maktabi	Al-Arabiya	393,970	529	5,864	215	61.0	16.6
11	Salman Al-Dossary	*Asharq Al-Awsat*	74,831	1,523	29,819	8,478	69.9	23.4
12	Samir Farah	BBC Arabic	5,209	2,044	856	3,208	46.1	19.4
13	Taleb Kanaan	Al-Arabiya	141,348	296	6,327	651	48.0	14.5
14	Zina Yazji	Sky News Arabia	40,486	1,063	17,211	2,012	52.8	19.7
15	Mohannad Al-Khatib (*Hiwar* show)	Sky News Arabia	3,086	1,691	754	2,197	43.0	18.1

while average tweets of his followers totaled 8,478 with an average Klout score of 23.4. Ali Al-Dfiri had 23,127 tweets, while the average number of tweets initiated by his followers was 762, giving rise to an average Klout score of 18.9. Nour Eddine Zorgui of BBC Arabic had 8,549 tweets, while average tweets by his followers totaled 2,323 with an average Klout score of 19.5. One journalist who had an audience average number of tweets that exceeded his own average is Hamad Al-Mahmud (3,386 and 3,845, respectively) with an audience average Klout score of 24.1. Other journalists outnumbered by their average audience tweets included Mohammed Al-Harthi (683 and 1,967, respectively); Amjad Rasmi (805 and 3,321, respectively) and Jehad Al-Khazen (571 and 2,643, respectively). Those journalists enjoy high standing among audiences with active social media profiles.

Pan-Arab journalists' Facebook fans covered by this study have varied in their follower base, with Faisal Al-Kasim taking the lead with an over five million lifetime fan record since late August 2014. Al-Kasim had over 1,100 posts on Facebook[4] from April to August 2014, all dealing with political issues and events relating to the situation in the Middle East in general and Syria in particular. As in his tweets, Al-Kasim's Facebook postings reflected his clear political stands against current Arab political governments in general and the Bashar Al-Assad regime in Syria in particular. Al-Kasim's posts explicitly condemned Syrian government-driven violence and called for an end to dictatorship in that country. As we will see in chapter 6, the fact that Al-Kasim engaged in social conversations as a party to the conflict more than as a broadcast journalist commenting on the situation was bound to generate highly critical and sensational comments from followers and fans. He was viewed more like a political figure making political statements than a journalist making fair commentaries about the evolving conditions in Syria and the Middle East. Khadija Ben Ghana of Al-Jazeera had the same Facebook standing in terms of fans and posts. Her fans exceeded 4 million toward the end of August 2014, while her posts in the period from April to August 2014 totaled 2,850. Her posts covered subjects relating to Palestine, Syria, Egypt, Lebanon, Algeria, Turkey, and other nations in the Middle East and had a visible Islamist tone. Her Facebook account was partially used to drive traffic to her personal page (http://www.khadija-bengana.net).

The politicized use of Facebook for expressing personal political/ideological inclinations was not confined to Al-Jazeera journalists. Al-Mayadeen journalists covered in this study had no Twitter accounts, and Facebook was the only social media platform they used to communicate with audiences on issues and events in the region. Lina Zahreddine of Al-Mayadeen, with 13,677 fans and 100 posts in the April–August time frame, was promoting the central theme of Al-Mayadeen about the resistance front, often termed as the resilience front, in which Syria is a centerpiece. Posts by Ghassan Bin Jiddo and those of Sami Kleib, though quite few compared with the torrential traffic from Faisal Al-Kasim and other Al-Jazeera journalists, seem to propagate narratives of Syria, Iran, and Hezbollah about the changing conditions of the Middle East. The theme of a conspiracy being hatched in the West and in the moderate Arab camp against Iran, Syria, and Hezbollah is quite visible in all traffic originating from the three journalists on Facebook. In August 2014, most of the postings hosted by Al-Mayadeen journalists were defined by the rise of ISIS as a force to be reckoned with in the Middle East and how its threat should be countered by all nations, including Syria and Iran.

Other journalists followed a highly moderated ideological approach to social media conversations to demonstrate their professional practices in cyberspace. Some have chosen to do their social media work through specific shows, such as all Alhurra journalists who focused their social media space on promoting their programs and engaging with their audiences on issues relevant to those programs. The same pattern applies to France 24's Taoufik Mjaied, who presents the *Niqash* show. Other journalists promoted their own writings and sought to enhance traffic to their media organization's websites through links. Those included BBC Arabic and Alhurra journalists, who were noted for their active crowdsourcing on Twitter and Facebook. Their goal was mainly to cultivate more audiences to engage with their central news portals and hence reinforce their standing online. By sticking to their organizational context and engaging with audiences on issues relevant to what they do on their shows or write in their articles, those journalists seem to have complied by social media guidelines adopted at their organizations. They also present themselves as less politicized and biased so as to gain more credibility among audiences. But as we will see in chapter 6, the credibility of the individual journalists does not derive solely from what they post or tweet but rather from how they handle engagements with followers and fans in critical issues of the day. This is exactly social media's cutting edge compared with conventional media operations. In the social media world, journalists are not unidirectional communicators who follow one-way traffic to a captive audience; they are partners in a global conversation shared by the millions of people around the MENA region.

Journalists covered in this study used varied forms of communications in their Facebook posts. The findings of the five-month analysis for the twenty-six journalists show that they had 15,749 posts on Facebook and that 48.8 percent of them were links, 33.1 percent were text, and 18.1 percent were multimedia (see table 5.2). The fact that the majority of posts were links suggests that journalists were using Facebook primarily to drive traffic to their media websites or portals. Nour Eddine Zorgui of

Table 5.2. Pan-Arab Journalists' Facebook Activities (April–August 2014)

					Type of Posts						
No.	*Name*	*Media Outlet*	*No. of Posts*	*Fans*	*Links*	*%*	*Status*	*%*	*MM**	*%*	*Total*
1	Amjad Rasmi	*Asharq Al-Awsat*	30	9,251	0	0	0	0	30	100	100
2	Faisal Al-Kasim	Al-Jazeera	3,780	5,252,915	1,125	30.3	2,428	65.4	244	6.5	3,707
3	Khadija Ben Ghana	Al-Jazeera	7,480	4,256,116	2,847	38.0	2,323	31.0	2,311	30.8	7,481
4	*Free Hour*	Alhurra	140	845,030	0	0	134	92.4	11	7.5	145
5	Lina Zahreddine	Al-Mayadeen	100	13,677	0	0	63	57.7	46	42.2	109
6	*Neqash*	France 24	70	135,368	0	0	73	100	0	0	73
7	Rasha Qandeel	BBC Arabic	180	10,808	34	17.8	105	54.9	52	27.2	191
8	Taleb Kanaan	Al-Arabiya	30	34,227	0	0	0	0	33	100	33
9	Ali Al-Dfiri	Al-Jazeera	50	51,754	55	100	0	0	0	0	55
10	Nour Eddine Zorgui	BBC Arabic	3,380	1,754	3,343	98.7	41	1.2	0	0	3,384
11	Mohannad Al-Khatib	Sky News Arabia	50	6,233	0	0	32	100	0	0	32
12	Caroline Faraj (Facebook Private)	CNN Arabic	57		25	40.3	4	6.4	33	53.2	62
13	Ghassan Bin Jiddo	Al-Mayadeen	20	11,840	5	21.7	2	8.6	16	69.5	23
14	Sami Kleib	Al-Mayadeen	520	141,737	264	50	191	36.2	72	13.6	527
Total					7,698	48.8	5,203	33.1	2,848	18.1	15,749

* Multimedia

BBC Arabic, for example, had the majority of his posts as links to divert audiences to the central BBC Arabic website for full news accounts and commentaries. This feature of posts was quite clear in traffic originated by journalists like Faisal Al-Kasim, Khadija Ben Ghana, and Ali Al-Dfiri (all from Al-Jazeera). Ben Ghana in particular was using links to drive traffic to her personal page. Status constituted 33.1 percent of total postings in the case of journalists such as Faisal Al-Kasim, Khadija Ben Ghana, the Alhurra *Free Hour* team, Lina Zahreddine (Al-Mayadeen), France 24's *Niqash* talk show, and Mohannad Al-Khatib (Sky News Arabia). Those journalists sought to promote their own programs through postings reflecting the changing status of their evolving traffic themes. The use of multimedia was lowest for total posts (18.1 percent) from all journalists with Facebook accounts. Topping the list for this category were journalists like Khadija Ben Ghana (Al-Jazeera); Lina Zahreddine and Ghassan Bin Jiddo (Al-Mayadeen); Taleb Kanaan (Al-Arabiya channel), and Caroline Faraj (CNN Arabic).

Although the scope of the study does not include how pan-Arab media journalists use social media as a professional journalistic tool in news search, gathering, writing, and production, available data show that very few of them subscribe to the professional network LinkedIn to communicate with peer professionals in the region and around the world. We noticed that journalists subscribing to LinkedIn include Mohammed Al-Harthi (*Asharq Al-Awsat*), Rima Maktabi (Al-Arabiya channel), Rasha Qandeel (BBC Arabic), Mohannad Al-Khatib (Sky News Arabia), Caroline Faraj (CNN Arabic), Samir Farah (BBC Arabic), and Amjad Rasmi (*Asharq Al-Awsat*). It is clear that journalists not affiliated with professional networks like LinkedIn are working for advocacy channels like Al-Jazeera and Al-Mayadeen. In those channels, there seems to be a conviction that social media are to be harnessed for engaging the largest number of mass rather than specialized audiences in the profession. The issue may have to do with journalists' self-conceptions about the role of the journalist as a professional versus his or her role as an advocate. We should keep in mind also that those journalists with LinkedIn accounts work for media organizations with guidelines that discourage the expression of personal opinions on social media networks.

PATTERNS OF SOCIAL MEDIA USAGE

The analysis shows that, all in all, pan-Arab media journalists were using both Twitter and Facebook to achieve four distinctive objectives:

1. *Crowdsourcing*: hunting for ideas from audiences to enrich their programs

2. *Driving traffic* to their own or their organizations' central websites or portals
3. *Sharing links* with audiences on issues not directly addressed by employer organizations
4. *Commenting* on developments in the region and around the world

Crowdsourcing Ideas in Social Media

Pan-Arab media journalists with talk show programs were shown to be active in soliciting ideas from audiences via social media on topics addressed by those shows. Facebook was more frequently used to carry out this crowdsourcing function in programs aired by BBC Arabic television shows like *Nuqtat Hiwar* (*Talking Point*). Most of the posts from the presenters of the program, Nour Eddine Zorgui, Samir Farah, and Rasha Qandeel, dealt with forthcoming episodes. They normally posed questions to seek out feedback from audiences around the region. As noted in chapter 4, *Talking Point* addresses issues ranging from politics to education, medicine to religion, and culture to military conflicts in the Middle East and North Africa. Social media, including Facebook and Twitter, are used not only to trigger feedback from audiences online but also to engage audiences in the live broadcast. In other programs such as Alhurra's *Free Hour*, questions are posted on the show's Facebook wall to generate answers from audiences regarding the issues at hand. Some of those audience comments are used by presenters as evidence of public opinion regarding the topics being discussed or to provide new insights into how those issues should be handled by the presenter. As chapter 4 shows, the practice of crowdsourcing by pan-Arab media marks a shift in how audiences are viewed in the emerging new media landscape. They are perceived more as central stakeholders in the news-making process, which they could define in significant ways. Crowdsourcing has also been used by Faisal Al-Kasim for his weekly *Opposite Direction* show, by Sami Kleib (Al-Mayadeen) for his weekly *Game of Nations* show, and by Mohannad Al-Khatib for his *Hiwar Al-Layla* talk show on the Sky News Arabia channel. Through audience feedback on Facebook and Twitter, broadcasters are able to "feel out" the public opinion orientations regarding issues addressed by their programs. In most cases, audiences do not respond with specific answers to questions posed on social media but rather with an avalanche of ideas marked by highly sensational contents. The same case applies to Zina Yazji of Sky News Arabia, who posts quotes from her interviewees made on her show *Frankly with Zina*.

Driving Traffic to Media Websites/Portals

This study shows that pan-Arab journalists used social media to enhance visibility and exposure to their mother media organization websites, their own websites, and their media contributions in other media outlets. Khadija Ben Ghana of the Al-Jazeera channel makes most of her postings and tweets link to her website or that of Al-Jazeera. The same feature of usage applies to posts and tweets by Sami Kleib of Al-Mayadeen (who refers audiences to his columns in *Al-Akhbar* newspaper); Jamal Khashoggi of *Asharq Al-Awsat*; Nour Eddine Zorgui of BBC Arabic; Lina Zahreddine of Al-Mayadeen; Caroline Faraj of CNN Arabic; Ali Al-Dfiri of Al-Jazeera, who posts links to his column in the *Al-Watan* newspaper; and Jehad Al-Khazen, who posts links to his articles in *Al-Hayat*. The objective of this traffic diversion is to make content accessible to audiences and enhance their engagement.

Sharing Links with Audiences on Issues Not Directly

A good number of pan-Arab journalists use Facebook and Twitter to share information with audiences beyond their immediate professional realms. These include links on subjects relating to human interest, sports, science and technology, climate change, education, innovation, human development, and morality. In those cases, audiences are diverted to information resources in text, audio, graphic, or video formats appearing on other websites or portals and produced by journalists/creative talent not related to the employed organization.

Commenting on Developments in the Region and around the World

Some journalists generated narratives with strong political/ideological features as an expression of their own personal convictions regarding issues and events in the region and around the world. This online behavior is typical of advocacy journalism as a defining feature of the region's media development. Faisal Al-Kasim, Khadija Ben Ghana, and Ali Al-Dfiri make those statements in varying fashions via explicit or implicit ways to show their personal views and opinions on the issues at hand. Faisal Al-Kasim in particular has been noted for his alignment with Syrian antigovernment opposition, and most of his tweets and posts speak to that position. Of course, his positions never stray off the overall editorial path of Al-Jazeera channel in supporting Syrian opposition against the Assad regime in Damascus. The same thing applies to both Khadija Ben Ghana and Ali Al-Dfiri, whose selection of topics for audience engagement reflects a specific political and ideological line that is harmonious with that of Al-Jazeera. On the other hand, the same ideological features of Facebook posts and tweets are visible in traffic generated by Al-Mayadeen journalists. The theme of "front of resistance or resilience" that defines Al-Mayadeen channel is visible in traffic appearing on social media accounts for Ghassan Bin Jiddo, Sami Kleib, and Lina Zahreddine. The general narrative reflects opposition to the Muslim Brotherhood and the Gulf states' position on Syria, which, along with Iran and Hezbollah, are viewed as the guardians of Arab resistance and steadfastness.

Topics addressed by journalists covered by the study reflected not only their own professional/political priorities but those of the audiences as well. The findings of the analysis show those pan-Arab journalists' Facebook posts have varied according to their individual professional and ideological orientations. Of course, audiences defined the scope and reach of those posts originally initiated by journalists. As we note in chapter 6, audience engagement with posts and tweets in no way suggests positive endorsement of the social content initiated by the journalist. In many cases, it involves serious, hostile attitudes that could be detrimental to the standing of those journalists as independent voices of truth.

It was natural that events in Gaza in July and August 2014 were bound to attract good audience attention. Amjad Rasmi's cartoon on Gaza scored the highest engagement, and so did postings on the same subject by Khadija Ben Ghana, Lina Zahreddine, and Sami Kleib. Three other issues were competing with the Gaza news at the time that also won first rank in terms of audience engagement: the victory of Tayyip Erdoğan in Turkey's presidential elections, the formation of the Iraqi government that replaced that of Nouri Al-Maliki, and the deteriorating situation in Libya. Faisal Al-Kasim's picture post on the Zaatari refugee camp for Syrian refugees in Jordan attracted the highest engagement, and so did Khadija Ben Ghana's posted picture of a Palestinian girl in Gaza during the Israeli attack. It is interesting to note that picture posts were quite common as they generated the highest levels of engagement. The least attractive posts were those composed of text, as in the cases of Mohannad Al-Khatib (Sky News Arabia), Taleb Kanaan (Al-Arabiya channel), and Nour Eddine Zorgui and Rasha Qandeel of BBC Arabic.

CONCLUSION

It is clear that the twenty-six journalists covered by the study had some form of engagement with social media at personal and professional levels. The volume of traffic originating from those pan-Arab journalists shows how increasingly integrated social media were becoming in their journalistic practices. But while we could generally describe all twenty-six journalists as active social media users, the patterns of usage seem to vary according to social media guidelines defining their work at media organizations. All in all, two categories of social media users have been identified: the advocacy journalism users and the professional journalism users. The first category is inclusive of journalists working for Al-Jazeera and Al-Mayadeen channels, where clear political and ideological inclinations are being promoted. The second category embraces journalists working for media channels with social media policies that discourage expression of personal opinions and emphasize professional standards in dealing with social space. This does not suggest that media in the first category have no guidelines for social media work. They actually do, but at the same time, journalists' engagement with audiences as voices of the same ideology of the organization does not seem to be discouraged.

The study found that pan-Arab media journalists use social media in four distinctive ways: crowdsourcing ideas from audiences to enrich their programs; driving traffic to their own or their organizations' central websites/portals; sharing links with audiences on issues not directly addressed by employer organizations; and commenting on developments in the region and around the world. It was found that journalists working for the two ideologically oriented channels, Al-Jazeera and Al-Mayadeen, were most active in using social media in the four areas with noticeable emphasis on the advocacy feature of the social media traffic. It was also found that journalists had varying levels of engagement with audiences as based on their Facebook posts. Al-Jazeera's journalists were at the forefront in terms of engagement, mainly because the topics about which they posted were highly controversial and were bound to generate highly sensational feedback. On the other hand, journalists in other media were receiving lower engagement due to the less dramatic nature of their posted topics, which were in mostly text formats.

NOTES

1. See a sample of international social media guidelines for journalists at http://www.kellyfincham.com/international-social-media-guidelines-for-journalists/123.
2. Most social media guidelines instituted by pan-Arab media organizations are not publicly circulated outside the organization and are meant to serve as frames of reference for individual journalists who happen to deal with social networks.
3. The Klout score is a number 1–100 that represents your influence. The more influential you are, the higher your Klout score.

4. A Facebook status is an update feature that allows users to discuss their thoughts, whereabouts, or important information with their friends. Similar to a tweet on the social networking site Twitter, a status is usually short and generally gives information without going into too much detail. When a status is updated, it posts on the user's personal "wall," as well as in the news feeds of the user's friends. Statuses can be updated from a web browser, from a mobile site, or through text message. See http://whatis.techtarget.com/search/query?q=facebook+status.

6

Audience Engagement

The general consensus among scholars is that the engagement of media organizations and professionals with their audiences represents an outstanding emerging feature of mass communication scholarship (Livingstone 1999; Harrison and Barthel 2009). In traditional mass communications models, media effects were conceived in the context of unidirectional flows of content to what looked like a captive audience (Strauss 1991). In those traditions, researchers were looking for explicit and implicit impacts of media messages on audiences' knowledge, attitudes, and behaviors. Traditional Western theories and models of communication effects were developed around notions of agenda setting, two-way flows of information, cultivation, knowledge gap, and the diffusion of innovations (Bryant and Beth 2009). At a more critical level, media effects theories took on forms such as media imperialism, colonialism, and hegemony. The basic common denominator for all those theoretical models is a conception of media as powerful influencers of mass audiences who seem too helpless to stand up to those media (Katz 1987).

In the age of social media and the Internet, the dominant paradigm of communications effects has experienced major shifts in how audiences are perceived in the communication process. Audiences are no longer the passive receivers of messages from mighty communicators who could shape their knowledge and attitudes according to their agendas (Livingstone 2004). They are rather turning into more powerful partners in the communication process almost at par with traditional media organizations and practitioners. Thanks to Web 2.0 technologies, audiences are contributing to local and global conversations in social space on issues of relevance to their personal living experiences as well as to their communities. This empowerment function has been most visible in how audiences engage with others on social media platforms using a wide range of formats within an increasingly interactive and visually rich process of communication.

This chapter discusses how social media—namely, Twitter and Facebook—gave rise to enhanced pan-Arab media engagement with audiences in the MENA region and around the world. Drawing on data generated by a five-month analysis of social media usage patterns and a two-week engagement analysis by Simply Measured of those media outlets and journalists with audiences, the chapter aims to demonstrate how social platforms are enhancing pan-Arab media reach with audiences and also how those audiences are enabled to be active partners in the emerging cyber communications landscape. Analysis is based on data generated by systematic observations of social media traffic as well as by Simply Measured analytics for the ten media outlets and twenty-six journalists covered by the study.

PAN-ARAB MEDIA IN SOCIAL SPACE: A NEW FRONTIER IN AUDIENCE ENGAGEMENT

Before the advent of social media to the MENA region, pan-Arab media like the Voice of America, BBC Radio, and other transnational radio broadcasters and satellite television channels of the 1990s drew on market research and individualized viewers' feedback to bring their programs into closer alignment with audience needs and preferences. Across the region, annual and semiannual audience surveys were presented primarily as pieces of evidence to either support media organizations' popularity claims, to attract advertisers' attention, or to introduce new developments in program contents and formats. Data generated from such audience engagement methods reflected exposure patterns to radio and television transmissions in addition to program preferences and criticisms. It was a mediated form of feedback traffic between media organizations and audiences conducted on a seasonal basis and for specific purposes. As one scholar noted, much of the market research conducted on broadcasters' popularity was meant to convince advertisers and decision makers of the efficacy of dropping or maintaining specific program contents or funding/not funding them (Eickelman and Anderson 1999). In significant ways, data used in those analyses lacked meaningful relevance to audience perspectives or personal viewpoints not only about the quality of contents or formats delivered by broadcasters and print media but also about the issues embedded in those contents. Since audiences were conceived as more captive recipients of messages developed by a media organization, their views about programs were generally placed in a back-burner position in media planning and development.

The introduction of social media into the conventional mass communications sector has revolutionized the way audiences are perceived by media organizations. Audiences are no longer captive receivers of unidirectional messages aiming to effect some change in their knowledge, attitudes, or behaviors. They are seen more as active participants in the communication process; their personal and political views in social media conversations are gaining greater recognition. Audiences are empowered to go beyond reacting to specific program contents and formats into expressing opinions about how issues are handled by the media organization and how those issues play out in the general context of social, political, cultural, and economic conditions of the MENA region. A Facebook or Twitter link to a television, radio, or newspaper story would less likely generate reactions about the quality of the format and the relevance of the content, but it would create a social buzz about the political, cultural, or ideological implications of that issue for society and the state. By elevating social discussions to a political or ideological level, audiences are increasingly turning into active participants in a more democratized communication process. The original content that triggers social media conversations would be reduced to a mere single element of a more comprehensive narrative in which hundreds of thousands, if not millions, could engage. In this case, the central driver of conversations is no longer the single story or program but the media organization and its political and professional standing in the eyes of the audience.

Around the world, audience engagement in social media has been hailed as marking the end of the dominant paradigm in mass communication and the rise of an empowered audience. Yet as much as this development has offered both media organizations and audiences opportunities for interaction and engagement, it has also presented serious challenges relating to how media handle critical audience traffic in cyberspace. Goode (2009) calls for a research agenda that investigates new forms of gatekeeping and agenda-setting power within social news and citizen journalism networks. Drawing on the example of three sites, Goode (2009) highlights the importance of both formal and informal status differentials and of the software "code" structuring embedded in the new modes of news production. Skoler (2009) notes that the problem with mainstream media isn't that "we lost our business model. We have lost our value. We are not as important to the lives of our audiences as we once were. Social media are the route back to a connection with the audience." Lee (2012) notes that recent events from the crisis in the Middle East to the earthquake and tsunami disaster in Japan have demonstrated that social media are changing the way individuals consume and share news.

PAN-ARAB MEDIA AUDIENCE ENGAGEMENT: PRELIMINARY FINDINGS

This section of the chapter draws on a two-week sample analysis of outbound traffic engagement made available by the social media analytics company Simply Measured.[1] Data generated by the analysis show different levels of engagement represented by Facebook "likes" and Twitter followers, being followed, and being retweeted from April 1 to August 31, 2014. Figure 6.1 shows a steady growth of fans for the ten pan-Arab media on Facebook with channels, such as Al-Jazeera and Al-Arabiya approaching the nine million mark toward the end of August 2014. Sky News Arabia started with a little less than six million likes in April 2014, diving into a low of less than four million in May before picking up and taking a steady rise into August. It is yet unclear why that decline occurred in a network with a solid social media track record. CNN Arabic experienced good but slow growth, and its base of fans was kept at a point below the one million mark. Both *Asharq Al-Awsat* and *Al-Hayat Political* remained

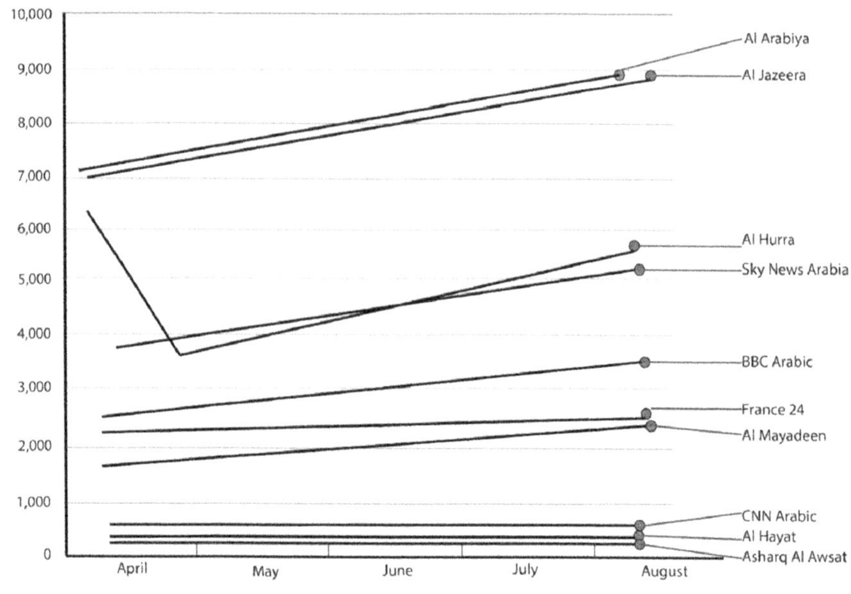

Figure 6.1. Growth of Facebook Fans for Pan-Arab Media (May–August 2014)

at the lowest level of fewer than 200,000 fans. BBC Arabic, although it did not match the Al-Jazeera and Al-Arabiya fan growth over the five-month period, was also going through impressive expansions in its audience network, with over three million fans by the end of August 2014.

To better understand the quality of audience engagement affected by pan-Arab media outlets on Facebook, statistics about fans may not yield significant results. Hence, it is necessary to investigate the contents of audience interactions in the conversations triggered by pan-Arab media in social space. To shed light on this qualitative dimension, the authors have analyzed samples of audience inputs into conversations generated by pan-Arab media posts on different developments. The prime question addressed in this analysis relates to what sorts of conversation pan-Arab media trigger on Facebook through audience engagement. In other words, what is the quality of audience feedback to the traffic generated on Facebook by pan-Arab media outlets? The analysis covers audience engagement with the top five posts initiated by the ten pan-Arab media outlets. The authors investigated features such as tone of reaction, mode of approach, and type of position adopted toward the issues at hand.

Study data show that top posts by the ten pan-Arab media outlets more or less reflect the professional and political parameters defining gatekeeping practices at the ten pan-Arab media organizations covered by the study. For example, Al-Jazeera had more focus on Gaza and Turkey while Al-Mayadeen gave more attention to Gaza and to the ongoing conflict in Syria. France 24 seemed more concerned with European news, and so did CNN Arabic with its focus on the Ferguson, Missouri, riots and Egypt's statements on those events. Alhurra demonstrated more balance in its top posts, which addressed issues in Gaza, Iraq, technology, and the Suez Canal project. The BBC Arabic focus was more diversified, with top posts on issues relating to Turkey, Egypt, Gaza, and Iran. Both *Asharq Al-Awsat* and *Al-Hayat Political* posts concerned issues in the region and beyond. Of course, what counts here is not the type of topic posted on Facebook but rather the levels of engagement generated on the part of audiences. In other words, it is the type of narrative in Facebook conversations that needs to be examined to define the quality of engagement in cyberspace.

Findings show that top posts triggered varied levels of comments by audiences. France 24 was able to generate extensive buzz among audiences on stories about the robbery of a Saudi prince in Paris, the discovery of a gold treasure in Paris, and the impact on European farmers of the European economic embargo on Russia. Sky News Arabia's most extensive commentaries were generated by stories about the Ferguson riots, Erdoğan's presidential victory, and Muslim Brotherhood–related developments in Egypt. Al-Jazeera's most extensive engagements came in connection with stories about Turkey's presidential elections and the war on Gaza, while Al-Arabiya's were stimulated by stories on ISIS massacres in Iraq, Gaza events, and an African elephant falling on a small car. Both *Asharq Al-Awsat*'s and *Al-Hayat Political*'s top posts generated commentaries on ISIS in Iraq and the Gaza crisis.

PAN-ARAB MEDIA TOP POST ENGAGEMENTS ON FACEBOOK

BBC Arabic: During the two-week period of August 8–22, BBC Arabic, according to Simply Measured's analytics, generated 159 posts with a total of 252,398 engagements at the rate of 1,587.4 engagements per post. During that period, BBC Arabic posts attracted 19,603 comments, 219,957 likes, and 18,838 shares. The top post on Erdoğan's victory in Turkey's presidential elections generated 9,732 likes and 2,658 shares. Fans conveyed their congratulations to the Turkish leader on his victory, hailing him as a Muslim leader in the Middle East and an Ottoman caliph of the twenty-first century. On the other hand, the conversation also drew critical remarks from those who saw Erdoğan as a camouflaged Muslim Brotherhood leader with a terroristic face. In general, the conversation in this post was structured around the personality of the Turkish leader both as a savior for Muslims and as a disaster for the future of the Middle East. One could easily sense the same narrative in debates involving Muslim Brotherhood and secular people, where the issue is framed as a conflict between theocracy and secularism. The post triggered 978 comments addressing the issue from both perspectives, which reflected the two theocratic-secularist features of political debates in the post–Arab Spring era. The same bipolarity was also expressed in the second and third top posts on the Human Rights Watch report regarding events in Egypt in August 2013. The posts, which attracted 6,416 likes and 2,835 shares, also drew 1,364 comments from audiences. Critics of the Human Rights Watch report, as reflected in the overwhelming majority of comments, referred to American atrocities in Iraq and Israeli killings of Palestinians that went unnoticed by international organizations. Some commentators charged that Human Rights Watch and other international organizations have hidden agendas that are detrimental to Arab national interests. The BBC Arabic post on British fund-raising for Gaza victims drew 3,040 likes and 884 shares in addition to 116 comments. Critical remarks were directed at Arab countries that failed to deliver support to Gaza during the crisis. They praised British civil society assistance to Palestinians as "more honorable" than that of Arab countries. Once again, the narrative of the conversations moved along the same lines of the top three posts: Arab secularism versus Hamas-related religious ideology.

Asharq Al-Awsat: This newspaper initiated 278 posts, with 1,978 engagements at the rate of 7.1 engagements per post. Comments triggered by all posts totaled 224, with 1,620 likes and 134 shares. The top post showed an Azidi elder standing near a temple in Mosul, Iraq. The post attracted thirteen comments and twenty-eight likes but no shares. Almost all comments were critical of the Azidi sect as a community of infidels who should not be left alone worshipping their own god. The comments reflected a clear religious fundamentalism with no room for accommodation and inclusiveness. The second top post showed a picture of Hamas fighters in one tunnel, drawing thirty likes and two shares. The two comments on the Hamas picture were divided between one that supported Hamas and another that blamed the Palestinian organization for making civilians suffer. The third post was also about Azidis in Iraq; it drew twenty-three likes and no comments, while the fourth post was a cartoon by Amjad Rasmi on the challenges of forming a new Iraqi government. The post drew twenty-three likes, one share, and one comment critical of Saudi Arabia. It is clear that *Asharq Al-Awsat* did not generate extensive conversations on its Facebook page despite the controversial nature of the issues being discussed. This fact may be explained by low audience engagement in social media platforms that the paper has to work hard to enhance.

Al-Jazeera channel: During the two-week study period, Al-Jazeera channel had 593 posts with 2. 7 million engagements at the rate of 4,582 engagements per post. Simply Measured data show that the top post about Erdoğan's victory in the Turkish presidential elections generated 56,660 likes, 8,462 shares, and 6,003 comments. All comments were supportive of Erdoğan, who was described as a historic figure who deserves to lead the Muslim nations into victory. It is clear that all comments were positive probably because of some possible filtering at the central website. The second top comment was about Egypt and the United States' cover-up of Israeli violations of international law. The post drew 32,818 likes, 14,075 shares, 47,881 total engagements, and 988 comments, which were highly critical of Egyptian president Abdel Fattah El-Sisi. It is clear that the narrative of the conversation was shaped by the broader debate in the area about the Muslim Brotherhood and secular politics in the MENA region. Critical comments of the cartoon were far fewer than those praising it. The third top post was similar to the second, a cartoon presenting El-Sisi as giving hand to Israel. The post attracted 29,342 likes, 7,420 shares, 38,854 total engagements, and 2,078 comments. Reactions to the cartoon generally ranged between those who accused El-Sisi of being an Israeli and Western agent and those who think of him as a genuine Egyptian hero who will restore past Egyptian glories. Another cartoon in the fourth top post showed Arabs staring at Palestinians who were drowning in seas of blood under the watch of an Israeli soldier. The cartoon drew 26,574 likes, 9,257 shares, 36,539 total engagements, and 708 comments. The cartoon triggered waves of criticism of Arab leaders who were presented as "collaborators" in the Gaza crisis. On the other hand, there were comments critical of Qatar and Al-Jazeera. It is obvious that the same spirit of sensationalism common in Al-Jazeera channel's programs was well manifested in its Facebook postings. Their goal was "to stir up still Arab waters" through triggering debates on issues of political relevance to Qatar.

Sky News Arabia: This channel had 135 posts during the analysis period, generating 864,881 engagements, 793,075 likes, and 232,252 shares. The top post on Missouri riots triggered 5,474 likes, 1,324 shares, 7,134 engagements, and 375 comments. The conversation on the Missouri events was defined by critical remarks of the US government's handling of the riots. Some commentators wished those riots would lead to America's destruction, and others foresaw the end of America. The narrative suggested some sort of vengeance against the United States, which commentators claimed was condoning Arab regimes' suppression of opponents in their countries. It was noticeable that commentators did not strike back at one another because, all in all, the trend of the conversation was sharply anti-American. The second top post concerned the arrest of "cells" in Egypt who sought to sabotage power facilities across the country. The post generated 4,136 likes, 2,354 shares, 6,840 engagements, and 525 comments. The conversation was marked by critical remarks about the Muslim Brotherhood (MB), which was blamed by most of the commentators for the alleged sabotage attempts. MB was accused of being a traitor organization seeking to destroy Egypt, and there were calls on police to be tough with the group. The third top post was about Erdoğan's victory in Turkey's presidential elections. It attracted 5,406 likes, 208 shares, 6,080 engagements, and 470 comments. The conversation was marked by huge support for the Turkish leader while few reactions were critical of his policies and doubted his future leadership. The fourth top post included pictures of violent clashes in the Libyan capital of Tripoli. The post triggered 4,874 likes, 545 shares, 5,805 engagements, and 375 comments. Most of the comments expressed sympathy with the Libyan nation while few others engaged in what looked like an exchange between Muslim Brotherhood supporters and their opponents.

Al-Arabiya channel: Al-Arabiya initiated 710 posts with 2,970,479 engagements, 218,350 comments, 2,646,905 likes, and 105,224 shares. The top post on an African elephant crashing on a small, sturdy car (looks like a commercial) triggered 31,356 likes, 9,838 shares, and 1,254 comments. The interesting thing is that almost all comments had nothing to do with the elephant on the Volkswagen car. Exchanges flared up on issues relating to Egypt, Gaza, and the Muslim Brotherhood. The second post related to Dubai's banning of the entry of the leader of a devil-worshipping group into the country. The post generated 30,333 engagements, 16,844 likes, 3,855 shares, and 12,179 comments. The conversation on this issue was marked by disgust on the part of most commentators, some of whom wished the man would fall into the hands of ISIS. The third post, on ISIS taking vengeance on an Azidi town, triggered 25,813 engagements, 18,066 likes, 3,145 shares, and 6,416 comments. The overwhelming majority of comments were highly critical of ISIS, labeling it as a criminal, brutal, and un-Muslim terror group. The fourth post, on Palestinians searching for victims under the Gaza rubble, generated 25,316 engagements, 23,490 likes, 988 shares, and 818 comments, which all were sympathetic to Palestinians in the Gaza Strip. No comments critical of Hamas appeared in the conversation.

Al-Mayadeen channel: During the study period, Al-Mayadeen channel had 425 posts generating 1,177,338 engagements, 37,789 comments, 1,099,051 likes, and 40,498 shares. The top post, on Syrian army control of a new town near Damascus, generated 25,673 likes, 453 shares, and 1,063 comments. The majority of comments spoke lyrically of the Syrian army while few were critical of the Syrian government as oppressive and brutal. The second top post, on a global campaign to support Gaza, triggered 16,928 likes, 2,371 shares, and 250 comments. The general narrative of the conversation was marked by mixed views of the situation in Gaza as both "suicidal" and "sacrificial." The third top post quotes Israeli newspaper reports about the launching of sixty missiles from Gaza on that day. The post triggered 14,374 likes, 344 shares, and 305 comments, which were all praising Palestinian fighters for their steadfastness and heroism. The fourth top post quoted Israeli sources as saying that total Israeli losses in the Gaza war were sixty-four military personnel and three civilians. Again, comments glorified Palestinian fighters in that military conflict.

Al-Hayat Political: Data show that *Al-Hayat Political* had 212 posts with 2,071 engagements, 143 comments, 1,678 likes, and 250 shares. *Al-Hayat Political*'s top post was on the picture circulating online about alleged Azidi refugees in North Iraq, which proved to be an old picture of Kurds evicted into mountainous areas by Saddam Hussein's army in the late 1980s. The picture attracted forty-two engagements, thirty-four likes, four shares, and four comments, which were all sympathetic to the refugees' plight. The second top post, on a Palestinian boy standing against a devastated house in Gaza, triggered thirty-four engagements and thirty-eight likes but no shares or comments. It seems *Al-Hayat* followers were not keen on getting news about Gaza from the newspaper. The third and fourth top posts, on Azidis as a neglected sect put under the spotlight by ISIS, attracted fifty-seven engagements, fifty-one likes, five shares, and two comments; one of them called for national unity in Iraq while the other was about Palestine.

CNN Arabic: During the period of the study, CNN Arabic had 778 posts, which generated 19,602 engagements, 15,185 likes, 3,832 comments, and 2,585 shares. The top post, on the United States rebuffing Egyptian statements on the Missouri riots, generated 286 engagements, 153 likes, 51 shares, and 80 comments. The conversation on the issue was marked by three lines of thinking: those who thought of the United States as a racist nation that discriminates against its citizens, those who said that Egypt is right in its statements about violence in Missouri, and those who thought that both America and Egypt are two oppressive nations. The second top post, on the governor of Missouri deploying the National Guard, attracted thirty-six engagements, sixty-four likes, twenty-eight shares, and two comments that were condemning the way riots are handled in the United States. The third post, on Middle East oil and gas reserves, generated eighty-three engagements, forty-eight likes, thirty shares, and five comments, which expressed rage at the United States for "exploiting Arab natural resources." The fourth topic was about the awarding of an honorary doctoral degree to Saudi king Abdullah by Al-Azhar University. The post generated seventy-eight engagements, twenty-two likes, five shares, and fifty-six comments. Most of the comments were sarcastic about the degree conferral.

Alhurra channel: Alhurra had only twenty-eight posts during the study period, but the engagements generated totaled 141,183 with 122,593 likes, 3,182 shares, and 15,408 comments. The top post of Alhurra channel, on a new phone application that increases the likelihood of giving birth to a male baby, generated 11,544 engagements, 11,192 likes, 268 shares, and 124 comments. The conversation on this subject triggered views about fatalism, disbelief, and passivity. The second top post, on the future of Iraq in view of Al-Maliki's rejection of government change, generated 11,389 engagements, 8,279 likes, 118 shares, and 2,994 comments. More or less, the conversation generated by the topic reflected the overall Iraq debates in the wider public sphere: Al-Maliki as an Iranian puppet with a sectarian agenda and Sunni Arabs as allies of terror groups. The third post concerns a Palestinian girl who transformed Gaza miseries into creative works of art. The post attracted 10,482 engagements, 9,819 likes, 520 shares, and 145 comments. The post generated generally positive comments that glorified Gaza people and their steadfastness. The fourth top post by Alhurra, on Cairo negotiations over Gaza, attracted 10,090 engagements, 9,754 likes, 88 shares, and 258 comments. Most of the comments were critical of Arab leaders for not backing up Palestinians, while a few blamed Palestinians for putting themselves in that debacle.

France 24: France 24 posted 272 items, generating 372,325 engagements, 23,017 comments, 317,101 likes, and 32,107 shares. The top post, on the robbery of a Saudi prince in Paris, generated 5,654 engagements, 4,612 likes, 499 shares, and 553 comments. The conversation on that post was defined by critical reactions to Saudi royalty "for squandering wealth." The second post, on a French Christian holiday, drew 2,691 engagements, 2,289 likes, 50 shares, and 359 comments, which were defined by a majority of voices glorifying Islam as the greatest religion and a minority who respected Christian traditions and interfaith coexistence. The third post was on a gold treasure found in France that attracted 1,603 engagements, 1,489 likes, 86 shares, and 32 comments, which were generally sarcastic about the way the people handled the find. The fourth post dealt with European Union allocation of 125 million euros in assistance to farmers affected by the embargo on Russia. The post attracted 1,580 engagements, 1,670 likes, 86 shares, and 34 comments, which were sarcastic about the measures, calling on Russia to cut off gas supplies to Europe.

PAN-ARAB JOURNALISTS' TOP POST ENGAGEMENTS ON FACEBOOK

Individual pan-Arab journalists covered by the study have generated interesting conversations on their Facebook pages. The following section reviews engagement analytics for individual journalists during the two-week period of the study as provided by Simply Measured, a social media analytics firm (table 6.1).

Pan-Arab journalists with Facebook accounts had varying interactions with audiences, as based on post-generated engagements, likes, shares, and comments. It was clear that Al-Jazeera's Faisal Al-Kasim stands at the forefront of pan-Arab media influencers. Al-Kasim, with over five million Facebook fans at the time, was creating the most exciting and thrilling buzz through his controversial posts. During the two-week period of the study, Al-Kasim initiated 378 posts, which triggered 4,525,712 engagements, 4,122,776 likes, 207,971 shares, and 194,965 comments. His top post, on the Zaatari refugee camp in Jordan, the largest in the Middle East, triggered 85,630 likes, 7,759 shares, and 5,033 comments. The conversation tackled the misery of Syrian refugees in Jordan with critical remarks of how they are treated in the kingdom, giving way to exchanges with some Jordanians who thought the refugee burden was too heavy to be borne by Jordan alone. The next top post was a cartoon on Erdoğan's 52 percent victory compared to the 95-plus percent victories claimed by both Bashar Al-Assad and Abdel Fattah El-Sisi. The cartoon post generated 90,814 engagements, 73,715 likes, 15,873 shares, and 1,332 comments

Table 6.1. Pan-Arab Journalists' Facebook Engagement (August 8–22, 2014)

No.	*Name*	*Outlet*	*No. of Posts*	*Engagements*	*Likes*	*Shares*	*Comments*
1	Amjad Rasmi	*Asharq Al-Awsat*	3	832	773	40	19
2	Faisal Al-Kasim	Al-Jazeera	378	4,525,712	4,122,776	207,971	194,965
3	Khadija Ben Ghana	Al-Jazeera	748	1,829,867	1,391,886	189,202	248,779
4	*Free Hour*	Alhurra	14	5,943	4,726	63	1,154
5	Lina Zahreddine	Al-Mayadeen	10	3,271	2,762	276	370
6	*Neqash*	France 24	7	1,543	1,025	28	490
7	Rasha Qandeel	BBC Arabic	18	210	170	1	39
8	Taleb Kanaan	Al-Arabiya	3	120	106	1	13
9	Ali Al-Dfiri	Al-Jazeera	5	1,399	1,187	148	64
10	Nour Eddine Zorgui	BBC Arabic	338	239	225	3	11
11	Sami Kleib	Al-Mayadeen	26	41,753	1,854	35,491	4,408

that were very complimentary for Turkey and critical for Arab governments. Al-Kasim's superiority in levels of engagement is explained by his stated political views regarding events and issues in the Middle East and his being a party to the ongoing conflicts. The other journalists seemed to abide by their social media policy guidelines, keeping to the topics and issues of relevance to their employers' agenda rather than to their own.

Khadija Ben Ghana of Al-Jazeera also demonstrated solid engagement on Facebook, with 748 posts generating 1,829,867 engagements, 1,391,886 likes, 189,202 shares, and 248,779 comments. Ben Ghana's posts dealt mostly with human and religious issues, and few of them covered national or regional politics. The other pan-Arab journalists with Facebook accounts had lower engagements compared with those of Al-Jazeera. Sami Kleib of Al-Mayadeen triggered 41,753 engagements, followed by Alhurra's *Free Hour* team (5,943 engagements), Al-Mayadeen's Lina Zahreddine (3,271 engagements), Al-Jazeera's Ali Al-Dfiri (1,399 engagements), and Amjad Rasmi of *Asharq Al-Awsat* (832 engagements).

PAN-ARAB MEDIA TWITTER ENGAGEMENT

As noted in chapter 5, pan-Arab media use of Twitter as a communication platform with audiences was growing at a steady pace from April to August 2014, with notable increases in tweeting traffic and numbers of followers. Channels like Al-Jazeera, Al-Arabiya, Sky News Arabia, CNN Arabic, and France 24 were leading in terms of followers' size and tweet volume (see table 6.2). Again, both Al-Jazeera and Al-Arabiya outlets seem to be leading in terms of the volume of followers, followed by CNN Arabic, France 24, and Sky News Arabia. In terms of August tweets, Al-Jazeera, France 24, and Al-Arabiya were at the forefront with 134,000 tweets for Al-Jazeera, 84,900 for France 24, and 80,200 for Al-Arabiya. Both *Asharq Al-Awsat* and *Al-Hayat Political* showed steady growth in the number of tweets from 51,400 in April to 64,400 (for *Asharq Al-Awsat*) and from 65,700 to 80,200 for *Al-Hayat Political* during the same period. It was also noted that most pan-Arab media outlets were not following large numbers of tweeters online. For example, BBC Arabic followed 117 in April, and the number rose to 176 in August, while CNN Arabic followed 175 in April, and the number dropped to 171 in August. Both *Asharq Al-Awsat* and *Al-Hayat* newspapers followed the lowest number of tweeters (nine and ten, respectively), while France 24 was following 1,054 tweeters in August. The low number of tweeters followed by pan-Arab media suggests low dependency on Twitter as a source of news and information and the platform's heavy use as a tool of communicating ideas with users. France 24's large following base suggests how the French channel

Table 6.2. Pan-Arab Media Tweets and Followers (April–August 2014)

		BBC	*CNN*	*SKY*	*JSC*	*ARBYA*	*MYDN*	*HURRA*	*ASH'ST*	*HAYAT*	*FRANCE*
April	Tweets	40K	47.4K	59.8K	19.1K	74.6K	61.9K	17.27K	51.4K	65.7K	76.6K
	Following	117	175	178	0	29	16	10	9	10	1,048
	Followed	616K	2M	686.5K	3.95M	3.4M	132.9K	19.3K	460.1K	240.3K	1.1M
May	Tweets	41.5K	49.2K	63.1K	126K	75.7K	64.3K	17.9K	54.9K	69.5K	78.6K
	Following	121	170	177	14	29	16	10	9	10	1,051
	Followed	677K	2.13K	741K	4.03M	3.58M	140K	20K	500K	251K	1.18M
June	Tweets	43.1K	51.1K	45.2K	129K	78.3K	65.4K	18.5K	57.9K	73.3K	80.8K
	Following	177	170	162	14	29	17	10	9	10	1,056
	Followed	740K	2.2M	859K	4.04M	3.71M	149K	19.2K	523K	260K	1.23M
July	Tweets	44.3K	52.6K	47.5K	132.2K	80.1K	66.5K	23.1K	60.9K	74.4K	82.9K
	Following	177	172	162	14	29	19	11	9	10	1,057
	Followed	813.4K	2.2M	906.7K	4.0M	3.8M	161.7K	22.0K	556.1K	266K	1.2M
August	Tweets	45.6K	54.2K	71.1K	134K	81.2K	67.4K	25.1K	64.4K	80.2K	84.9K
	Following	176	171	179	14	29	20	11	9	10	1,054
	Followed	886K	2.41M	920K	4.14M	4M	176K	23.1K	597K	285K	1.36K

harnesses a wide network of tweeters to keep abreast of developments through social media.

The rise of followers for all pan-Arab media channels during the five-month period suggests a clear enhancement of their engagement with audiences. Twitter has proved to be an effective communication tool for media organizations seeking to reach out to audiences in a timely and convenient way. It is also noteworthy that most pan-Arab media channels do not follow too many tweeters online, with most of them limiting their following volume to less than one hundred. France 24 is the only exception, with over 1,000 tweeters being followed by the channel. This is probably related to conceptions of Twitter as a good source of news to be reckoned with, especially in times of crisis, when average citizens play the role of journalists in reporting news from areas inaccessible to media staff.

Another set of data generated from social media analytics for the ten pan-Arab media channels shows interesting findings relating to audience engagement. It is clear from table 6.3 that all pan-Arab media organizations seem to enjoy good status in terms of their Klout rankings, which far exceeded the global threshold average of 40 for being an influencer. Sky News Arabia received 83.6 for its Klout score, followed by Al-Arabiya (72.8), Al-Jazeera (71.6), CNN Arabic (70.4), and BBC Arabic (69). Data generated for August 17, 2014, show that BBC Arabic followers had average followers of 158, while Al-Jazeera's have 335, Al-Mayadeen's 369, Alhurra's 1,224, and *Al-Hayat*'s 736. Since the higher Klout averages audience followers have, the more powerful those audiences are, the data suggest that followers of Alhurra, *Al-Hayat*, Al-Mayadeen, Al-Arabiya, and Al-Jazeera are influencers in their own social media communities. Average tweets for followers ranged from 191 for Al-Arabiya channel to 865 for *Al-Hayat* newspaper. Pan-Arab media outlets like Alhurra, *Asharq*

Table 6.3. Simply Measured Social Media Engagement (August 17, 2014)

Organization	*Followers*	*Average Audience Followers*	*Tweets*	*Average Audience Tweets*	*Klout Score*	*Average Audience Klout Score*
BBC Arabic	867,378	158	45,288	266	69.0	16.1
CNN Arabic	2,383,659	128	53,870	236	70.4	16.5
Sky News Arabia	902,406	154	71,090	319	83.6	16.0
Al-Jazeera	4,126,204	335	133,966	271	71.6	16.5
Al-Arabiya	3,960,517	260	81,001	191	72.8	16.7
Al-Mayadeen	171,975	369	67,120	418	64.1	16.9
Alhurra	22,994	1,224	2,458	824	53.0	16.7
Asharq Al-Awsat	590,306	265	63,720	504	66.8	17.1
Al-Hayat	199,580	736	55,822	865	67.0	19.6
France 24	1,348,550	198	84,507	212	67.4	16.3

Al-Awsat, and Al-Mayadeen had audiences with good average tweets, ranging from 418 for Al-Mayadeen to 824 for Alhurra. On the other hand, Klout averages for audiences suggest that *Al-Hayat Political* had the highest Klout audiences (19.6), while Sky News Arabia had the lowest (16). All Klout score averages for pan-Arab media followers are under the global benchmark of 40, which suggests that followers of pan-Arab media have more to do to get closer to the 40 score for influencers.

ARAB JOURNALISTS' AUDIENCE ENGAGEMENT ON TWITTER

Data obtained from Simply Measured social media analytics shows that the highest audience engagement was generated by Faisal Al-Kasim of Al-Jazeera channel, with 1,689,795 followers and an audience followers' average of 208 (see table 6.4). Al-Kasim had 42,876 tweets while his followers had an average of 279. With his highest Klout score of 71.6, Al-Kasim's audiences had a minimal 17 Klout score, which was not the highest for followers of other journalists covered by the study. Ali Al-Dfiri of Al-Jazeera had the next-highest number of followers (479,957), who had average followers of 537. Rima Maktabi and Taleb Kanaan of Al-Arabiya channel had 393,970 and 141,348 followers, respectively, with average audience followers of 529 and 296, respectively. Maktabi had a Klout score of 61, while Kanaan had 48. It is noted that some journalists had average

Table 6.4. Pan-Arab Media Journalists' Twitter Engagement

Journalist	*Followers*	*Average Audience Followers*	*Tweets*	*Average Audience Tweets*	*Klout Score*	*Average Audience Klout Score*
Ali Al-Dfiri	479,957	537	23,127	762	67.6	18.9
Faisal Al-Kasim	1,689,795	208	42,876	279	71.6	17.0
Hamad Al-Mahmud	1,135	4,949	3,386	3,845	49.1	24.1
Mohammed Al-Harthi	13,166	2,926	683	1,967	54.4	21.2
Jehad Al-Khazen	7,020	1,833	571	2,643	41.1	20.1
Khaled Al-Dakheel	97,469	2,256	7,082	1,822	61.8	22.6
Khadija Ben Ghana	48,940	736	5,502	1,946	62.8	21.3
Nour Eddine Zorgui	6,471	3,912	8,549	2,323	51.3	19.5
Rima Maktabi	393,970	529	5,864	215	61.0	16.6
Salman Al-Dossary	74,831	1,523	29,819	8,478	69.9	23.4
Samir Farah	5,209	2,044	856	3,208	46.1	19.4
Taleb Kanaan	141,348	296	6,327	651	48.0	14.5
Zeina Yazji	40,486	1,063	17,211	2,012	52.8	19.7
Faisal Ben Huraiz	3,086	1,691	754	2,197	43.0	18.1
Caroline Faraj	313	8,633	805	3,321	35.6	28.6

audience followers greater than or close to theirs. For example, Hamad Al-Mahmud of Sky News Arabia had 1,135 followers, while his audience had a follower average of 4,949, which made his audiences acquire the highest average Klout score in the group. Journalists with impressive average audience followers also include Mohammed Al-Harthi, who had 13,166 followers while his audience follower average was 2,926; Khaled Al-Dakheel of *Asharq Al-Awsat*, who had 97,469 followers while his audience follower average was 2,256; Nour Eddine Zorgui of BBC Arabic, who had 6,471 followers whose follower average was 3,912; and Salman Al-Dossary of *Asharq Al-Awsat*, who had 74,831 followers and an audience follower average of 1,523. Except for Caroline Faraj of CNN Arabic, all pan-Arab journalists had Klout scores above 40, which suggest their potential role as social media influencers in their communities.

CONCLUSION

Audience engagement in social space has stood out as the most outstanding feature of pan-Arab media use of social platforms in their communications. The study has shown that all ten pan-Arab media organizations employ both Facebook and Twitter to create conversations on issues of interest to the region and to the world. It was observed that Faisal Al-Kasim of Al-Jazeera channel was at the forefront of social media engagement among pan-Arab journalists, with over five million Facebook fans and around two million Twitter followers. All pan-Arab media engaged with their audiences on issues relevant to their news agendas; however, audiences were demonstrating reactions to the issues in the conversations based on their diverse social, political, and cultural backgrounds. It was not always clear how the narratives of Facebook conversations were playing out in the broader political public sphere of the region. But it was obvious that the thousands of media posts and tweets and those of journalists were creating considerable buzz in social space. Some media channels seemed to have tolerated all types of conversations, while others seemed to do some filtering of "unfavorable" comments. It is not clear how pan-Arab media handle the conversations they initiate through posts and tweets. All pan-Arab media have some forms of social media units that coordinate their social media traffic within their broad news management systems. However, it is not clear whether those media do follow-ups and further analyses of social media traffic to generate newsworthy news content or to improve their editorial policies and interactions with the audience. There has been no substantive signs of Arab media contributing to the conversations they had initiated. This could be an interesting topic to pursue in another research work.

Pan-Arab journalists covered by this study have generally generated good social media engagements, though Faisal Al-Kasim remains the most eminent Arab journalist in social space, at least within the parameters of this research project. With over five million Facebook fans and around two million Twitter followers, Al-Kasim has proved that pan-Arab journalists have the potential to gain a global influencer status. But if we considered the fact that Al-Kasim's social media traffic is dominated by his views about the conflict in Syria and in the region at large, we would realize that his social contributions were more reflective of his political/ideological views than of professional standards. To a lesser extent, political/ideological inclinations were driving social engagements by Al-Mayadeen journalists, who seem to advocate a pan-Arabist, secular, and pro-Syrian-Iranian line than other journalists in the group. Journalists working for non-Arab pan-Arab media such as BBC Arabic, CNN Arabic, Alhurra, Sky News Arabia, and France 24 seemed keen on following professional standards that are informed by their media organizations' practices in the media industry. In Saudi-owned media like Al-Arabiya, *Asharq Al-Awsat*, and *Al-Hayat*, journalists did their engagements by sharing their own stories or addressing issues with low political or ideological connotations.

NOTE

1. Simply Measured. http://simplymeasured.com/free-social-media-tools/#.

7

Social Media in Newsrooms

Chapters 5 and 6 analyzed pan-Arab media usage of social space in terms of generated traffic, but this chapter draws on interviews and secondhand observations to discuss the ways in which social media are used. One main function of social media usage is branding and visibility purposes measured mainly by the number of visits, "likes," and "shares." A few of these outlets also dedicate considerable resources to engaging with their audiences; despite the vast opportunities for two-way communication and interaction online, many news organizations around the world still maintain a one-way communication model, utilizing applications that post headlines automatically on Twitter and Facebook instead of engaging in two-way conversation with their users (Canter 2013, 491–92). The extent of engaging online (discussed in chapter 6) still depends on the individual journalists or the organizational routines, and, as such, the integration between journalists and audience is still rather limited (Singer et al. 2011). The main argument of this chapter is that social media have some impact on Arab journalistic practices: with the speed of disseminating information via social media sites, it has become imperative for those media to be present on social sites to provide not only news updates but also views and opinions. There are still ways to improve this service, which has an acute need to provide more in-depth analysis and background and to develop long-term strategies for audience engagement.

NEWS GATHERING GOES MOBILE

In this section, we discuss how social media platforms are harnessed by numerous pan-Arab media organizations as part of their newsroom operations. The discussion draws on qualitative interviews with media professionals and social media service operators in those organizations in order to provide an account of how they are integrated into news work.

The recent Arab uprisings are widely believed to have shaped the digital journalistic practices inside pan-Arab newsrooms such as Al-Jazeera. The channel noticed users' need for continuous updates, and social media provided a platform for this service, with the assignment of at least one staff member on each shift to handle social media updating and following users' tweets: "When you go to 24/7 rolling news, the way people expect their content to be delivered is different. We used to be hesitant to send out too many updates [on Twitter]. But when it's 24/7, they want to be flooded; they want to know everything [even if it's not big news]," said Mohamed Nanabhay, Al-Jazeera Online's chief (Ostrow 2011). Al-Jazeera also launched live blogs, which attracted a larger number of users following the blog than those following the lead story online; social media therefore have served as a means to engage users and turn them into loyal audiences: "What's behind [our social media success] is excellence in world-class journalism. The social media campaigns have been methods to get people to watch that content and make up their minds. Once you see it, you'll be hooked and come back" (Ostrow 2011).

Al-Jazeera has invested in multimedia platforms using Live Blog, Tumblr, Twitter, Flickr, Facebook, and YouTube as well as Audioboo to share audio content. The web team uses Scribble Live to edit and post user-generated content (UGC). The traffic on the Al-Jazeera website during the Egyptian revolution grew by 2,500 percent, thanks to the online live stream launched by the channel; during that time, protesters could dial a number and record a report, which would later be posted online, reposted on Audioboo, and then embedded on the Al-Jazeera website or shared on TV, said Riyaad Minty, head of social media at Al-Jazeera Network; even during the shutdown in January 2011 in Egypt, the channel had to readjust its strategy: "If there is a communication blackout, you need to know how you can connect a satellite to a mobile phone, because these are often the only things you may have with you. . . . That's the basis I've been working under—what is the minimum amount of equipment here, and what can we do?" said Safdar Mustafa, head of the mobile media unit at Al-Jazeera Network (cited in Ulbricht 2011, 30). Al-Jazeera's planning department investigates potential innovative projects, including the use of social media, but the continuous political conflicts in the region can also kick-start a project, even though it may still be at the preparation stage:

"When a war breaks out or there is mass protest, people really want a way to get information to us. Then, suddenly, the project takes off. There are a lot of half-baked projects in which you think, let's see if this flies. Some of them don't, and some of them really take off," declared Safdar Mustafa (Ulbricht 2011, 30). The channel's correspondents are equipped with the right mobile tools and prepared for communication blackouts. The mobile unit creates new applications to receive mobile content from citizens via Android or Blackberry phones.

Al-Jazeera used social media to push its media content toward the public by posting images and audiovisual material, which it redistributed online. Another way to engage with its users was through a dedicated user platform. Al-Jazeera English's platform for citizen journalism is called "Your Media," and in the sister Arabic channel it is called "Sharek" (or "Participate"). Such platforms expect users who have witnessed an event to contribute to the stories around it by e-mailing or completing a form on the site with pictures and videos if available (Ulbricht 2011, 31).

Al-Arabiya Network has a similar social media unit responsible for around forty-two accounts on social media sites such as Facebook, Twitter, Instagram, Google+, Vine, and LinkedIn, of which thirty-one are on Twitter alone. The unit has staff members representing different age groups, from twenty-two to sixty years old, which is "a good mix," according to the head of the unit, Sultan Batawi (interview, June 2014). Batawi said that the unit used software that automatically posts headlines on social media sites as well as on the channel's website: "We have more than four million subscribers on our 'breaking news.' Our unit is a linking point and a hub among all other departments. Our staff members roam between other departments. We recorded around twenty-five million visits to our website, of which 25 percent are recorded on our social media sites. This [social media unit] is the backbone of our newsroom." The unit contributes to the website if need be and also to television: "We [were] the first outlet to join the social media in 2010, but we intensified our operations after the Egyptian revolution in 2011. At that time, we had only two Facebook and Twitter accounts. In January 2011, there were hundreds of tweets on the account for just one day, which was why we launched different accounts like Al-Arabiya Misr, Arabiya Saudi, Arabiya Siyasa [politics], Arabiya Iqtisad [economics], Arabiya Thaqafa [culture], and Arabiya Sports, in addition to other accounts for Al-Arabiya television programs," Batawi said (interview, June 2014). The social media unit is responsible for analyzing social media data, using Socialbakers, including the number and country of visitors. It is estimated that the average age of Twitter users on Al-Arabiya is twenty-five and older, and around 40 percent of the Facebook users on the Al-Arabiya site are between twenty-four and thirty-five. The network has more than 4.7 million users, of which the majority come from Egypt, Saudi Arabia, Kuwait, and Lebanon (interview, June 2014).

The social media agenda on the Al-Arabiya Network closely follows the television news agenda after the content is adapted to suit the "audience's mood and age," according to Batawi, head of the social media unit:

> Social media can be used for interaction with our audience, for news gathering and for promotion. When we have new content, we seek interaction with our audience about it. One example is the Egyptian elections [May 2014]. We counted the tweets of each candidate [Hamdeen Sabahi and Abdel Fattah El-Sisi] and the words used by each candidate. When we have exclusive interviews, we depend on our users to post questions for the guest. We used hashtag #misralhadath [#egyptevent] which was very popular in Egypt even without advertising for [*sic*] it. We arrived at this hashtag after using #jom horiyajadeeda, which was not very common and did not get many visitors, so we used #misralhadath. Traffic on our Al-Hadath website [sister channel of Al-Arabiya] increased by 200 percent during the elections, thanks to the success of this Twitter campaign. Therefore, we use our social media sites to increase visibility and traffic either on our website or to our TV channels and we direct our audiences to either the website or the TV. We can, for instance, interact with our audience and tell them that their "tweets" will be picked up by an Al-Hadath TV presenter, in order to increase the number of viewers of the channels. When we compare ourselves with competitors, we see that the extent of engagement and interaction on our website is second only to CNN (interview, June 2014).

Al-Hayat newspaper, in a similar vein, had more than one account on social media sites, including *Al-Hayat* Misr [Egypt], *Al-Hayat* Syria, *Al-Hayat Siyasa* [Politics], and *Al-Hayat Iqtisad* [Economy], and these accounts were available on both Facebook and Twitter at the time of this research. The newspaper had a digital media unit which integrated social media into the main newsroom. The unit had a handful of journalists in addition to assistants, an editor, and a deputy editor, who together managed online news and social media sites and informed headquarters in Beirut and Jeddah: "We used to have one social media editor but this structure did not work and did not last long. We found out that each of us in the newsroom has to multitask and we always have ten windows open on our computer screen, so each of us can now write for the website and for social media sites simultaneously," says Fatima Rida, web content manager at *Al-Hayat* (interview, May 2014). It was particularly since the recent Arab uprisings that the unit gained a greater role inside the newsroom in order to reach out to its core audiences as well as new ones: "Social media is a good source of news. Now if [David] Cameron or [Saad Al-] Hariri tweeted something newsworthy, we cannot ignore it," Rida said. It is noted that Saad Al-Hariri, the former prime minister of Lebanon, left

Lebanon several years ago because he feared he would be assassinated like his father, Rafik Al-Hariri, who was murdered in 2005. Saad Al-Hariri said in an interview with British newspaper the *Guardian* that he would love to return to Lebanon but "there [were] huge challenges that face[d] Lebanon and one of the challenges [was] staying alive" (Chulov 2014). Rida asserted: "Although Saad Al-Hariri has not been in Beirut for five years, his tweets can still make headlines."

Rida cited another example: the tweet posted by the British ambassador to Lebanon, Tom Fletcher, commenting on his giving of blood following the suicide bombing in Beirut in November 2013: "His tweet about his donation and the picture he posted on Twitter made headlines here [in Beirut]. If he [had] not tweeted about it, we would never [have] know[n]," according to Rida. Mr. Fletcher's tweet and photograph were posted to show people the disaster near the Iranian embassy in Beirut in November 2013 caused by the two suicide bombers, who killed at least 22 people and injured more than 140. The tweet was also picked up by other outlets, such as the Lebanese online news site *Al-Nashra*, which published a brief article based on Mr. Fletcher's tweet (https://twitter.com/ukinlebanon/status/402847055321628672).

Fatima Rida also recalled an innovative example of using social media in news gathering for an article she published in *Al-Hayat* on May 21, 2014, about a Facebook group: "The group is about female Syrian refugees available for marriage and it has more than fifteen thousand 'likes.' I wrote about the group, interviewed relevant agencies, and I found that within one and a half hours only, the group grew to 18,000 members. It was shut down after the article was published, only to be relaunched again, shortly after, under a different name. My article about the group was shared by hundreds of readers. Without social media, I could not have found this news, and it would not have reached all those readers," Rida explains. The article triggered reaction from human rights organizations regarding marrying off Syrian minors. The Facebook group triggered a wave of insults against the creators of the page, casting doubt on the group's real intentions and accusing it of being involved in the trafficking of women and girls. Rida interviewed an activist for women's rights in Lebanon who called on everyone to report such defamations on social media in order to raise awareness about violence against women and girls. The group posted photographs of some Syrian girls and claimed that there were thousands of others who were interested in marrying any men from the Arab world. The article titled "Syrian Refugee Women for Marriage on Facebook" was published in the *Al-Hayat* newspaper on May 21, 2014.

The development of the situation in Egypt has also been one central theme in *Al-Hayat*'s social media site: "If you want to talk about Egypt, you cannot ignore social media and hashtags like 'intikhbou Al-Aars' [vote for the pimp]. The Lebanese Broadcasting Corporation (LBC) made a report about it, and the Egyptians on social media criticized it," says Rida. The hashtag went viral on social media in Egypt and the Arab region, and graffiti of the "pimp" hashtag appeared in the streets of Cairo, below Abdel Fattah El-Sisi's face. The word "pimp" is considered an extremely vulgar word in Egypt; consequently, several Egyptian television presenters, such as Khairy Ramadan of CBC Television, called for the government to block Twitter. He urged the presidential contenders, El-Sisi and Hamdeen Sabahi, to rebut this campaign, which he attributed to the Muslim Brotherhood: "The easiest thing the government could do here is to block Twitter or close YouTube. Of course the youth will ignite fire and say that we are back to dictatorship if this happens. But no one will pay attention to the fact that Erdoğan [Turkey's prime minister] has done so, and that after Erdoğan closed Twitter due to his leaks, he also closed YouTube" (quoted in Ajbaili 2014); on the other hand, the former publisher of *Al-Masry Al-Youm* newspaper, Hisham Qassim, said that such social media insults against El-Sisi could not be controlled: "The smear campaigns and insults, I believe, will win him popularity. . . . We . . . tried this [repressive action against such sites] previously. We shut down the whole Internet during Mubarak's era and the result was Mubarak's ouster. . . . If Mubarak had not shut down the Internet, many of those people who took to the streets against him would have stayed at home" (cited in Ajbaili 2014). What is posted on social media sites can indeed make headlines across pan-Arab and local newsrooms: "If Hamdeen [Sabahi] writes on Twitter about his losing or winning the [presidential] election, this would be news for us. I cannot follow everyone [on social media] but I tend to target influential people in topical places," says Fatima Rida of *Al-Hayat* newspaper (interview, May 2014). During the Egyptian presidential elections in May 2014, several Egyptian newspapers followed social media sites, hunting for reactions from voters. The Egyptian *Al-Youm Al-Sabei* (*Youm7* 2014) published an article on May 27, 2014, about the Egyptian actor Samir Ghanim, who appeared on several activists' Facebook accounts after posing for pictures with some Egyptian citizens in front of a voting post.

Other Arab outlets use social media to generate user reaction on topical news; for instance, the Saudi electronic news site *Al-Mowaten* published an article regarding the Saudi government's decision to allow restaurants to operate twenty-four hours a day. Posts collected from leading members' Twitter accounts were examined in order to see how many were in favor of the new law and how many were against (Al-Said 2013).

The Lebanese *Al-Mogez* newspaper (Salah 2014) published an article based on a tweet by the Lebanese-Palestinian former singer Fadel Shaker, wanted by the authorities for allegedly killing Lebanese soldiers. Shaker denied press reports about his arrest, accusing the media of lying: he tweeted that the media had used a "photoshopped" image of him behind bars. Shaker was a prominent singer before declaring his allegiance to a Salafist sheikh in 2011 and retiring from his music career on religious grounds; in 2013, however, he had admitted to killing two soldiers before he went into hiding, encouraging "Twitterers" to speculate on his whereabouts and led to his arrest. News sites also use social media to measure the general feelings regarding celebrities. A recent article in the Egyptian newspaper *Al-Youm Al-Sabei* (Gamal and Said 2014) attracted posts from the Twitter accounts of several fellow celebrities commenting on the news of the death of Egyptian actor and musician Hussein Al-Imam in May 2014. The Saudi award-winning journalist Badria Al-Bishr (over 250,000 Twitter followers) illustrated the use of social media for debating controversial issues such as women's rights in Saudi Arabia. One of her articles published in *Al-Hayat* newspaper on May 17, 2014, addressed the recording of an obscene conversation between a Saudi preacher and a young Saudi woman, which she posted on several social media sites. The woman lured the preacher to a meeting only to later disseminate the conversation on social media in order to reveal the hypocrisy of clergymen who lead fervent campaigns against assigning women to the Shura Council and allowing men and women to mingle in public spaces. The use of social media in this case was an attempt not only to circulate this particular incident but to hopefully continue an important debate concerning the general status of women in Saudi Arabia.

The opportunities associated with news and social media were the main reason for Abdel Bari Atwan, former editor in chief of the London-based *Al-Quds Al-Arabi* newspaper, to launch his own web-based newspaper *Rai Al-Youm* [*Today's Opinion*]: "I started thinking about this project three years ago," he said. "This is because the print press is facing harsh competition [from] the electronic press, the expenses of running a print copy are rather high, and the majority of our readers at *Al-Quds Al-Arabi* come from online [sites] anyway . . . readers do not wait until the newspaper is shipped to them a day after the events have already happened" (interview, April 2014). Atwan uses social media sites such as Facebook and Twitter to reach out to his audience on *Rai Al-Youm*. His personal Twitter account has more than four hundred thousand followers, and, he points out, his reputation (and name) also attracts new readers. The outlet is concerned with *Rai* [opinion] and not *Khabar* [news]. He explained: "It is called *Rai Al-Youm*, not *Khabar Al-Youm*, so it is based solely on opinion. News is available everywhere on the Internet and readers now want opinion and analysis. Journalism used to be about breaking news, but now it is about opinion and analysis or what is behind the news" (Atwan interview, April 2014). Readers interact with the news, he continued, by posting around one hundred comments for each editorial on *Rai Al-Youm*, but the outlet does not specifically request readers to send UGC because of the limited resources available to examine the material and verify the information it contains.

Roujina Yousef, online editor at the London-based pan-Arab newspaper *Asharq Al-Awsat*, says that "social media provide new media technology, and some may think that journalism has been negatively influenced by this fast-paced technology, especially with the vast number of users around the world. Social media provide platforms to disseminate short news items so we can communicate important information quickly" (interview, April 2014). The newspaper hired a professional company to produce statistics and reports about their social media sites, such as the number of visitors, "shares," and "links": "Our audience comes primarily from Saudi Arabia and Egypt. We use social media to know more about our audience. We use Facebook to publish more soft news with visuals while Twitter is for more hard political news." Yousef adds: "We have now moved to [the] beta platform in order to produce ticking news instantly." The newspaper used Twitter to post headlines for busy readers who wanted to access news and information quickly and who did not have much time to search for it on selected websites; therefore, they could access it directly on social media: "In the old days, readers used to subscribe to their favorite newspaper only to read about yesterday's news; now, they can access online news and read about the news as it unfolds," Yousef explained. "We do not yet know the full and long-term impact of social media on newspapers and whether online news would replace print media. The good thing is that traditional newspapers still appeal to the older [generation of] newspaper [readers] who prefer the hard copy of the paper with their morning coffee or prefer to read it on their way to work, while the new generation prefers online news," she added. The Internet consequently provides an infinite source of information that Arab users favor over buying a particular newspaper, a way to read analyses from a certain viewpoint, as all ideological trends are present, online. *Asharq Al-Awsat*'s integration of online and print departments allowed selected topics to be chosen for their daily news agenda, "but in the social media unit, we focus on breaking and brief news, and we leave analyses and details with background to be published on our website or in the printed paper," Yousef explained (interview, April 2014). The typical social media *Asharq Al-Awsat* site users are between twelve and twenty-eight years old, "and they use social media as their first preferred medium to communicate with others" (interview, April 2014).

REPACKAGING GLOBAL BRANDS

Arabic services on international outlets such as BBC Arabic, CNN Arabic, Deutsche Welle Arabic, or France 24 Arabic also utilize social media tools as part of their overall organizational strategy. Mohamed Abdel Qader, head of the social media unit at BBC Arabic, says that his unit uses social media tools such as Facebook, Twitter, YouTube, and Google+ for news gathering, especially if they do not have a correspondent in a certain area or have limited access to a news event. The unit is part of the Digital Media Department, which encompasses online news and online video and social media units. "We use social media to listen to our audience and follow online trends. Some of our television programs have their own Facebook and Twitter pages. We have more than two and a half million followers on Facebook, with Egypt and Saudi Arabia as the biggest markets for us" (Abdel Qader, interview, April 2014). The television has also sought to integrate interactive web features in its programming, and one illustration of this is the BBC Arabic flagship program *Talking Point*, which provides tri-media content. The fifty-minute program is aired five times per week on TV, followed by thirty minutes on radio. The program is hosted by a veteran radio presenter, assisted by members of the online team working with a TV director. It begins on the online discussion forum, where audiences contribute their views about topical issues. Some of those contributors are contacted by the online team and asked whether they would like to participate in the live discussion on TV, either by phoning in or via webcam. The show was launched in 2003 during the Iraq War, and it was molded after an English-speaking program. The English forum, *Have Your Say*, was launched shortly after the concept, which the Arabic service wanted to replicate as a supplement to, but not a replacement of, *Talking Point*. The result was a multimedia program that offered online postings and phone-in features on TV and radio with audience participation via video cameras. The program is now claimed to provide an exemplar for other foreign services, such as Persian TV, which has also launched its own *Talking Point*. *Talking Point*, or *Nuqtat Hiwar*, has been praised by a number of Arab commentaries for being a forum for diverse voices. One commentator, Fatima Kheir, argues that *Nuqtat Hiwar* enforces the culture of dialogue and debate by comparing it to other debate programs on rival channels such as Al-Jazeera. She claims that the British management sets the rules for a sober rational debate, unlike other programs on Arab satellite channels such as Al-Jazeera's flagship program, *The Opposite Direction,* which is characterized by its "shrieking and screaming" rather than genuine dialogue that accommodates diverse views (Hroub 2006, 104). She commends *Talking Point* for its use of SMS, video messages, e-mails, and webcams for transmitting viewers' comments and for its host's quiet and tranquil tone as debate moderator. This style, she argues, may be a direct impact from the British debate style (Kheir 2008). Another Arab commentator agrees that the program is molded according to the British moderation rules, and he compared it to Al-Jazeera's hosts whose loud voices had become characteristic of their programs (Khalifa 2008). The social media coordinator at BBC Arabic also monitored the tweets of influential Arab activists and politicians and selected some of their posts to present during the program. The debates held on BBC Arabic platforms were generally dominated by males between twenty-five to thirty-five years old. Facebook debates often included polarized views and comments made in colloquial Arabic, which sometimes contained indecent language. The traffic peaked during the Arab Spring, such as during the Egyptian revolution in 2011, and later declined to an average number of visitors once the crisis had died down. The traffic also peaked during crisis periods that were not adequately covered by other outlets such as Al-Jazeera and Al-Arabiya, for example, the conflicts in Saudi Arabia and Bahrain (Abdel-Sattar et al. 2012, 12–14).

The social media unit at BBC Arabic started a blog called *BBC Trends* that "reviewed the most popular topics. It is like a press review, but dedicated to social media trends. The trend report feeds into mainstream television and radio departments. The report is useful [for] a group of audience [*sic*] who do not have time to review all social media sites. We use dedicated links to analyze these trends divided by country and topic. Sometimes we choose a topic from these trends and expand on it in an online feature or an article. We also give television the material to use for their packages" (Mohamed Abdel Qader, interview, April 2014). Presenters also had their official accounts on social media sites where they posted news and comments about their programs, as part of the branding of the network provision, and as long as they did not express their personal views or show support for certain political or religious ideologies (as shall be discussed in chapter 8). One of the main anchors at BBC Arabic was Rasha Qandeel, who saw Twitter as one of the greatest inventions: "Twitter is a quick source of information but we have to verify its news. For presenters, it is a great invention to promote BBC and to interact with audiences, live. Following interviews, I can take a few quotes, in consultation with the editor, and post these quotes on my Twitter account to promote the program or selected news items. Twitter is not a luxury, it is important as a fast way to exchange information and to interact with [the] audience."[1]

Deutsche Welle Arabic also utilized social media as part of the network's branding strategy as well as for engagement with the audience. Samar Karam, social media editor at Deutsche Welle Arabic, said: "We started social media activities in 2010. Before that time, the TV team used to upload some of their programs on YouTube but there was no dedicated unit for social media. Later, we realized that we need[ed] a team dedicated to social media in order to interact with our audience. It is not enough just to upload material. There is software that helps post headlines and information automatically on social media sites. On Twitter, when we add breaking news manually, we add a hashtag to the title in order to ensure more interactivity and lively debate. On Facebook, we pick up light stories which satisfy users' curiosity, and we also add lots of diverse visuals. Soft news tends to elicit comments" (interview, April 2014). Karam said that the most popular social media sites within the Deutsche Welle network were the Arabic and Farsi sites: "It seems that the majority of users come from authoritarian countries perhaps to vent their views," she added. Her colleague, Rainer Sollich, Deputy Head, Arabic Service, said that in the Arabic Service "there is a social media editor and a social media assistant on duty, five days a week. Their main task is to encourage the audience to comment and take part interactively, to monitor our social media offerings and to monitor what is going on in the field of social media in general. The editors also post articles on Facebook and Twitter. We have a unit for all Deutche Welle programs responsible for research and monitoring of social media posts" (interview, May 2014). The overall aim is to engage with the audience: "We want to encourage the dialogue with our audience, and social media are nowadays the best ways and tools for it. We want our audience to play as active a part as possible. But of course we should and would not forget those who don't take part and don't want to comment on social media platforms," said Sollich. The social media unit seeks comments on topical issues such as the conflict in Syria and Iraq or the status of the Muslim Brotherhood in Egypt, in addition to topics suggested by users: "Picking up suggestions from our social media users, we ran stories on the situation of the Arab minority in Iran and about Muslim women wearing headscarves or *niqab* in Germany and whether they experience tolerance or discrimination within German society. We also regularly publish comments from our social media users online and present them once a week in our TV news journal. In our talk show, *Shabab Talk,* we ask our audience to post questions and comments for the presenter to pose to the guests," added Sollich (interview, May 2014).

Deutsche Welle network has, moreover, sponsored the "Bobs" Awards (Best of Blogs and online activism) in fourteen languages, including Arabic. The annual awards were launched in 2004, when blogs were regarded as a new type of media outlet worthy of being taken seriously, to promote dialogue across language barriers. Zahi Alawi, editor of the Arabic Bobs, said:

> We started when blogs were particularly strong in the Middle East, like in Egypt, Saudi Arabia, Tunisia, and Bahrain. We added more categories to the award such as social media, photo-log, video-log, best Twitter personality, best Facebook account, and best innovation. We have media partners and jurors like Tarek Amr [Egyptian activist] and before that, Amira Husseini [from Bahrain]. Our website is open for all to register in the competition, and we receive 2,000 to 3,000 suggestions in all languages. We choose the best ones in terms of sustainability and continuity. So, if the blog only has twenty likes, it may not be as active as we wanted it to be. Most of the blogs are political but there are also blogs about social topics. (interview, April 2014)

Pan-Arab outlets acknowledge the inevitable role of social media to help them reach out to young audiences. There is still an overall tendency, however, to follow the social media accounts of influential figures such as politicians or media professionals or observers. Western-subsidized outlets in particular adopt a strategy of engaging with members of the audience as debaters, commentators, or content contributors, but this engagement is still moderated by the journalists, as discussed in the following section.

DEMOCRATIZED DEBATE UNDER CONTROL

The debate on the political role of social media was intensified in the wake of the Arab uprisings across the region. There are those who call the recent uprisings the protests of Facebook generations, while others argue that the role of social media has been overstated (Aouragh and Alexander 2011). One of the key reforms needed in the region is the ability to maintain a rational debate in which diverse views are tolerated. Local or pan-Arab media outlets have already incorporated online forums and debates within their websites and social media sites. Moderation constitutes an important task for online journalists, although the paradox lies in the perceived liberating effect that social and new media have; while the latter forms of media have enabled users to interact freely with the news producers as well as with each other, the news professionals still have the power to moderate users' comments, eliminating some of them if deemed inappropriate. The BBC online forum, for instance, is subject to editorial moderation where improper comments are filtered out. An example is the *Have Your Say* forum, which invites readers' written comments on topical issues as well as users' pictures and UGC, but BBC journalists still moderate this UGC in order to meet the organization's professional standards (Thurman 2008, 7). BBC Arabic has a strict policy of moderating users' comments on the website; however, it is more difficult to control all posts on Facebook or Twitter prior to posting. The comments on the websites are premoderated, while those on social media are postmoderated by filtering out comments containing predefined words such as insults, racism, or sectarianism (Mohamed Abdel Qader, interview, April 2014). The moderation team does not seek to divide the posts and comments made online equally between those who oppose and those who agree with a certain view, which may be implausible on online forums and rather problematic to implement in social media sites. The team can follow loyal participants who regularly contribute to online forums and social media sites. BBC Arabic received nearly two million posts from its audience in response to questions about the developments in Egypt during and following the January 25 revolution in 2011 (Abdel Qader, interview, April 2014).

Deutsche Welle Arabic's operations were similar. Social media such as Facebook were used to pose questions relating to a topic of a televised program, and users were asked to respond to these; some were selected to be read during the televised program. "We can also add a view by a German expert specializing in the Middle East and leave it to the users to comment on that view," the social media editor at Deutsche Welle Arabic, Samar Karam, said. She also said that the online content was abundant and users "[were] used to getting news on their phones or via social media, so they [did] not have to make an effort to search for news. In the beginning of the Syrian revolution in 2011, we had a wave of comments which seemed targeted and we had to remove them from Facebook. On Twitter, it is difficult to control such comments. In general, we do not tolerate insults on religion or individuals. We do not want anyone to use our sites to insult others so we spend a lot of time on moderation. We do not support provocative comments such as 'they deserve to die'" (interview, April, 2014).

The Al-Arabiya Network social media team also filters users' posts in order to eliminate insulting language. Presenters do not express their political opinion or use such words as "martyrs." As part of the network's policy, Sultan Batawi, social media head, confirmed that "because words permanently remain on [the] Facebook platform, we have to be careful with the wording on our sites. It is our job to communicate the news but it is not our job to sway public opinion." The network does not frequently experience "electronic campaigns" by movements such as Islamist ones:

"When we face a guerrilla campaign, we deal with it in different ways. If we suspect a series of comments, we can either change the content, or post a poll for users to vote for a view but without commenting, and later we filter the content for a limited time until the repetitive comments cease," says Batawi (interview, May 2014). The Facebook page of Al-Arabiya may include forty news stories every day, of which some may elicit thousands of comments, and the social media team work on filtering these posts: "But if some users call us 'Hebrew channel' [to cast doubt on the credibility of the news] or insult us in some way, we tend to leave their comments unmoderated. They have the right to express their view about us," Batawi said. The state-controlled Electronic Committee, or the so-called Lagna Electroniyya, joined protest groups on Facebook during the 2011 Egyptian revolution, for instance, in order to post a flood of comments in an attempt to suppress the debates, either by casting doubt on the credibility of news or by posting the same message several times (Elsayed 2013).

Deutsche Welle Arabic's policy was also to encourage "free and open debates without tolerating hate speeches and discrimination," Rainer Sollich, deputy head of the Arabic Service confirmed: "Interaction with audience is much faster and very direct now. In former times the feedback came by mail; sometimes it took weeks to receive any feedback. Now we receive the feedback directly and can see the reactions of our audience, although one has to be careful in analyzing the feedback. Sometimes comments on Facebook are part of political campaigns. This happened to us at the beginning of the Syrian crisis, when we were bombarded with pro-Assad comments on Facebook. If there is an obvious campaign, then we need to moderate those comments, but not all of them" (interview, May 2014). His colleague Samar Karam sees that writing in colloquial "makes it easier to express insults and negative comments [than if the user attempts to use the written variety of Arabic]. But social media are not there to teach people better Arabic skills; it is there to help them express their views," says Karam (interview, April 2014).

Al-Hayat newspaper's new and social media team provided two venues for users' comments: the website and social media sites; the former is usually moderated while the second is much less so, according to the web content manager, Fatima Rida. The rival *Asharq Al-Awsat,* on the other hand, allowed users to comment only on the website (on any published item), and the social media sites were usually under staff scrutiny: "Our typical readers are educated, middle-class, and their comments are therefore well-informed and less insulting," according to Roujina Yousef, online editor at the newspaper. Words such as "spy," "agent," "traitor," "Shi'a," and "Sunni" were normally filtered out of social media content. There is also a moderation policy at *Rai Al-Youm* that eliminated insults and words like "traitor": "There are many people who do not add their real names and use names like Abu Mohamed, or Abu Arabi, and we monitor their comments, which can be indecent," Abdel Bari Atwan, editor of *Rai Al-Youm* said (interview, April 2014).

Moderation is consequently a controversial issue in modern newsrooms. Their aim is to engage audiences, yet journalists still act as gatekeepers with the power to filter comments, or, as a social media expert said: "The main reason for the media [using] comment fields is to make readers stay for a longer period on their websites, so that they can sell more advertising space. Also, traditional journalists are nervous. They feel threatened that readers are intruding upon the area that traditionally belongs to them" (cited in Trygg 2012, 21). Moderation is often seen as a means to ensure the quality of comments online (or on social media), as one British online editor said: "I am not concerned about free speech overall; there are enough places online where people can go to be heard. The paper is a brand like any other brand" (cited in Trygg 2012, 22). Unmoderated environments are regarded as less attractive forums for serious audiences. Meg Pickard, head of digital engagement at the *Guardian* (Trygg 2012, 21) said: "Commenting online is not a right, it is a privilege, albeit one which people have come to expect on publisher sites. We have a responsibility to care for the overall community. If people want to express perspectives that are inappropriate to appear on the *Guardian* site, according to our community standards, they are free to use other platforms such as private blogs, but on publisher sites, there need to be structure and rules. While moderation can sometimes be controversial, nonmoderated environments aren't places where people want to spend a lot of time."

CONCLUSION

Many pan-Arab newsrooms have embraced social media in their daily practices for different purposes, and chief among these is the use of social media for news gathering and for interacting with audiences. The newsrooms also actively use social media as part of their public relations strategy, which is more evident in global outlets such as the BBC Arabic, Al-Jazeera, and Deutsche Welle Arabic; social media, in this case, can be used as channels for branding and promoting programs and blogging posts by staff and presenters. Social media are also used as platforms to monitor trends and emergent stories, especially those that are building momentum and opening dialogue with active users. Other pan-Arab outlets such as pan-Arab newspapers have fewer resources and expertise to enable them to develop a flexible social media strategy that responds to emerging trends online. The degree of user engagement therefore varies across outlets, with some of them being more concerned with the number of "views" and "likes" on social media sites than with user interaction.

It is evident from talking to social media editors from selected pan-Arab outlets that social media sites have helped change the rigid news values, which have traditionally favored hard political news; light news is now favored, particularly on Facebook, although, as indicated in the interviews, political news is still on the top of the news agenda, partly because of the rising conflicts in the region and partly due to the openness and the new methods available to the younger Arab generation. They are not only able to obtain information and updates on the situation in their own and neighboring countries but also able to share links on social media sites. Social media, particularly Facebook, are used to interact with the audience, albeit by varying degrees in newsrooms, depending on the resources available and the number of staff responsible for social media coordination. Previous research (particularly Abdel-Sattar 2013) shows that innovation within Arab newsrooms can often come through experimentation by individuals within the newsrooms, including IT staff, while members of the senior management team are the decision makers and have the final say in approving or rejecting new technological projects. The business model in each newsroom can shape its multimedia strategy, whether it depends on handheld cameras or cutting-edge tools; above all, the political context and conflicts in the region impact on newsrooms' innovation and multimedia strategies (Abdel-Sattar 2013, 294–300).

Social media provide innovative platforms for news gathering and news dissemination, and these two functions are still largely underdeveloped in pan-Arab newsrooms. Future studies will show developments in those uses, especially with the challenge of verifying online content. There is still hunger for news and information in the Arab region, and consequently, news media have been expanding over the past decade. Another challenge (reviewed in the following chapter) is the possibility of supporting a rational online debate, which is largely attributed to contributors' tendency to use inappropriate language in their comments. This tendency justifies the development of the role of journalists as moderators in addition to being traditional gatekeepers and scrutinizers: "Technology now enables anyone to publish and disseminate news, but I think the journalist's role is not only confined to writing and spreading the news, but it is also to provide analysis and investigation. This unique role distinguishes online journalism, because scoop is no longer in communicating the news quickly, but in adding background information and analysis which helps users to understand events" (Roujina Yousef, interview, April 2014). The new role of journalists is implicit as the "relationship between producer and consumer of journalistic content and the borders between them . . . vanishes. This is a new challenge and it changes the traditional way of doing journalism," according to Rainer Sollich, deputy head of Deutsche Welle Arabic (interview, May 2014). The next chapter elaborates on this new role.

NOTE

1. See more at http://www.bbc.co.uk/academy/arabic/standards/socialmedia/article/art20140224133318974.

8

Citizen Journalists versus Traditional Gatekeepers

Internet users in the Middle East have reached over 113 million, according to Internet World Stats (2014). It is estimated that the Internet, and particularly social networking tools such as blogs, could play a critical role in promoting the civic engagement of Arabs all over the world. Al-Saggaf and Begg (2004), for instance, analyzed the Saudi political online community and found that the Internet prompted a vibrant discussion about local politics and internal public affairs. The increasing use of new and social media has paved the way for citizen journalism to be grounded in Arab media practices; bloggers communicate information to their followers through links to mainstream news sites, and Twitter has been used to retweet coverage from mainstream media, while mainstream journalists have used social media to supplement their investigations, and some have broken stories communicated to them directly by activists (Bossio and Bebawi 2012).

Nip (2006, 216–18) identified five models of journalism according to the role of journalists, from gatekeeping to participatory journalism. The first model is traditional journalism, in which journalists still act as gatekeepers who filter the news while the audience's participation is rather limited (sending op-eds or letters to the editors) and often moderated and edited to suit the journalistic norms and culture within the respective media outlet. The second model is public journalism, in which journalists are more concerned with finding out the public's views and they can, for instance, commission and publish polls; here, again, journalists act as gatekeepers in moderating public discussions. The third model is interactive journalism, in which journalists reach out to their audiences, requesting their comments on the news. The fourth model is participatory journalism, in which audiences can actively engage in the news process by sending images and content for publication, and finally, the fifth model is citizen journalism, in which citizens generate their content via social media, such as blogs, to be disseminated and published by professional journalists.

Participatory journalism, according to Singer and colleagues (2011), includes five stages: the first stage is observation, in which the story is generated and information as well as images are collected; this is followed by the filtering stage, in which data is sifted according to the journalists' needs; then comes the editing stage, in which the story is written and posted; and then, at the distribution stage, the story is disseminated; and finally comes the interpretation stage, in which the story is open to audiences' comments and discussion. Social media can be used for participatory journalism in order to link professional and citizen journalists as well as open up new communication channels between producers and consumers of news stories. Journalists may use social media for different purposes such as finding news sources, gathering news, maintaining a network of sources, following influential people such as political activists, following discussions on forums, unraveling current trends in society, disseminating stories, branding, or interacting with the audience. Journalists, moreover, often adopt user-generated content (UGC) to complement the information that they have gathered. They may also solicit this content; one example is Yahoo!'s initiative "You Witness News," launched in 2007 as a joint venture with MSNBC and Reuters, aimed at encouraging users to share stories, images, and videos (Potter 2007). This content could then be used on television or the web, although contributors do not receive financial remuneration for generating this content. Some American outlets such as the *New York Times* advise their staff to be cautious when handling social media material. NPR has issued a policy to help its staff use social media tools as an extension to traditional reporting (Cozma and Chen 2013).

Scholars have noted the emergence of networked journalism in addition to citizen journalism, or the result of collaborative journalistic work between professionals and amateurs on breaking news stories, linking to each other and sharing ideas such as reporting about bloggers' arrests, brutal police attacks, or sexual harassment (Duffy 2012, 8). The Al-Jazeera site, for example, launched the Ushahidi map, recording episodes of violence in Gaza during the Israeli strikes in 2009 (Duffy 2012, 11). One recent study (Duffy 2012) analyzed ten Arab media sites from UAE, Bahrain, Qatar, Egypt, Saudi Arabia, Oman, Jordan, Lebanon, and Iraq as well as the London-based *Asharq Al-Awsat*, showing their engagement in networked journalism with no embedded links to their news stories. The lack of such links indicates these outlets are "still stuck in print mind-set"

(Duffy 2012, 12). Some sites did not allow audiences to comment on all the stories, while others did not have this facility at all, despite the fact that they encouraged their readers to share articles via social media. Politically sensitive articles did not request audiences' comments, and site administrators moderated all comments on all other stories (Duffy 2012, 11).

Newsroom convergence has influenced the relationship between journalists, their sources, and audiences (Bruna 2013). Journalism convergence is a multidimensional process with technological, managerial, professional, and content-related features (Bruna 2013, 13). The technological aspect affects digitization and content sharing online and facilitates the exchange of images and sounds between users and producers. The managerial aspect refers to the organizational changes within the newsroom, with new units and departments set up to manage new and social media interaction with the audience. The professional aspect refers to the requirements on journalists to continually update their skills in order to enable them to handle multimedia platforms. Many outlets, such as the BBC, encourage television presenters and journalists to have professional social media accounts, which allows them to establish direct contact with their audiences regarding the content of their shows, thereby raising the profile of the presenter, the media content, and the media institution at large. The content-related aspect also refers to the amalgamation of users' and journalists' input via various features of interactivity.

This chapter provides an overview of the rising phenomenon of citizen journalism in the Arab region, with examples from pan-Arab newsrooms such as the BBC, Deutsche Welle, and Al-Jazeera.

ARAB CITIZEN JOURNALISM

One important outcome of the integration of social media in the news process in the MENA region is the rise of citizen journalism. An example of a specialized news service based on citizen journalism is the Egyptian news agency Rassd, launched on January 25, 2011, the same date that the revolution to topple Mubarak's rule began. Its aim was to cover the revolution using citizen journalists' material via a Facebook group; in a matter of three days, the Facebook group secured four hundred thousand users, turning the page into one important source for audio and visual material by documenting the protests. The cofounder of Rassd, Anas Hassan, told media that the service had been preceded by a range of citizen journalism initiatives during 2010 such as "Raqib" (monitor), "Sawwir" (take pictures), and "Dawwin" (blog), and Rassd was an acronym for the three initiatives (Elsayed 2013, 7). The group is open to user-generated content (UGC) created by members of the public and a large group of volunteers.

Rassd claimed to have received 6,500 reports a day during the 18 days of the January 2011 revolution, of which 4,000 were published (Elsayed 2013). The group utilized the limited resources needed on Facebook to launch their site instead of using a dedicated website, which might have required hosting and maintenance; on the other hand, Rassd was taken to task for publishing inaccurate information and siding with certain political movements, particularly the Muslim Brotherhood, of which many of Rassd's founders were members (Elsayed 2013).

At BBC Arabic, the quality and volume of UGC may have depended on the nature of current events. Saddam Hussein's execution, for instance, elicited overwhelming responses from audiences; in fact, the execution on December 30, 2006, following a fourteen-month trial on charges of killing 148 Iraqi Shi'as, not only attracted global media interest but also captured the attention of online communities. A mobile video version of the execution was circulated online, offering a censor-free look at the execution of a once-powerful Iraqi dictator (Salama 2007). Another example of UGC was the written and visual content posted online during the floods in Jeddah, Saudi Arabia, in 2011 and 2012: "We depended on social media to follow the search for people affected by the flooding. Social media are the best place to get information, images and comments when there is instability or unexpected weather conditions," said Sultan Batawi, head of social media at Al-Arabiya Network (interview, May 2014). Deutsche Welle Arabic encouraged users to send photographs and content, but the real challenge for social media teams was to authenticate the content: "We do not often do that [ask for UGC] because we do not have enough people to verify the images. There are professional companies that verify the images and content on social media and we might collaborate with them for news gathering in the future. But the instant feedback is good for our brand and content development," according to Samar Karam, social media editor at Deutsche Welle Arabic (interview, May 2014). The Libyan uprising was another challenge for citizen journalism, argued Alex Murray of the BBC: "You get hoax [material] on all stories such as [that in] Zawiya, where clashes erupted during [the] Libya[n] uprising, report footage showing a man stripped with a walking stick in his hand. Other broadcasters ran the footage but the BBC was suspicious because the footage was run a week before."[1] Al-Jazeera Network wrestled with the challenge of verifying materials sent by users: "There is a lot of noise that happens out there. . . . In a lot of countries, we try to identify people beforehand. We get phone numbers and location verification of people we could trust. . . . We started building a database of people we could follow," said Riyaad Minty, head of social media at Al-Jazeera Network (Ulbricht 2011, 31). The channel also aimed to search for citizen journalists who were already active online and regularly contributed with online content: "We try to get a phone number, an email address, to get direct contact with them to have a discussion to see where the information came from and when it was recorded," Minty said (Ulbricht 2011, 31). Even when the channel received citizen journalistic content that was three or four days old, it could still use it as background material after stamping the time and date of receiving it.

Ushahidi was used to create a platform in 2009 in order to collect data through different means, including SMS, e-mail, and the web to create a visualized output in response to crises manifested in its use during the Gaza War (2009). The Al-Jazeera site used that platform and integrated it with Twitter to receive updates on the war (Ekine 2009). Al-Jazeera English, for instance, depends on citizen journalism to gain access to places where its professional journalists may not be able to reach and also to engage users not only in the production but in the distribution of media content. Journalists at Al-Jazeera English are highly visible on Twitter, clearly indicating their affiliation with the channel's communicating journalistic messages related to their respective shows (Bruna 2013).

The recent uprisings in the region have triggered an increasing use of social media in journalism and activism. The Syrian conflict, for instance, was described as one of the most socially mediated events in contemporary history—social media content about the conflict was very high, and the activity reflected the convoluted situation in that country: Syrian citizens turned into storytellers and journalists in the wake of the uprisings, especially with the censoring of state media and the acute need to communicate to the world what was happening on the ground. Satellite television also turned to citizen journalism to obtain a wide range of views and information (Ismail 2012, 106). One editor said that the advance of technology made it possible to stream live videos from inside Syria and that there were a hundred thousand videos, despite the regime's prohibition of unauthorized filming; without this technology, the editor added, "the regime could have repeated what it did to its people in 1982 in Hama" (Ismail 2012, 109). It is known that the Syrian city of Hama witnessed a massacre in 1982 when the late president, Hafez Al-Assad, father of the current president, Bashar Al-Assad, crushed the Sunni rebellion in the city with heavy artillery fire for several days. The troops were accompanied by bulldozers that flattened neighborhoods after killing an estimated twenty thousand Syrians. The challenge currently facing citizen journalism in Syria is the credibility of materials posted on social media and the Internet; thus, it is not unusual for one group to upload a video on social media about the development in one particular town in Syria only to find another group posting another video showing a completely different picture of the situation in the same town (Ismail 2012, 115). Wall and el Zahed (2014) argued that citizen journalism in Syria provides a new information ecosystem challenging the state-censored media, with every city and every street having its own reporter (2). One of the first citizen journalism initiatives in Syria was the Local Coordinating Committees (LCCs), which claimed to run seventy reporting committees throughout Syria, and almost all citizen journalists made use of social media as their key platform (Wall and el Zahed 2014, 5).

Social media had consequently transformed the Syrian media scene, and new local news agencies were set up, including the Sham News Network (SNN) in February 2011, which depended on citizen journalism footage and images for its output (Ismail 2012, 115). Many newsrooms in at least seventeen countries used SNN content, including the *New York Times*, *USA Today*, *L'Express*, and the *Washington Post* (Wall and el Zahed 2014, 8). Similar agencies followed suit in catering for local audiences, such as Deer Al-Zour Agency, Baba Amro Network, and Homs Agency. One recent study showed that nearly 60 percent of those following the situation in Syria did not trust news and footage broadcast by state television, while they totally endorsed the need for citizen journalism to tell the world what was really happening there (Ismail 2012, 176). Syrian diaspora communities also helped to disseminate material collected by citizen journalists. Examples include Activists News Association (ANA), set up by Syrian Rami Jarrah (who fled the country for his own safety), which maintained a network of 350 Syrian grassroots reporters (Wall and el Zahed 2014, 11).

The coverage of the 2010 Iraqi election was another example of convergent journalism. Al-Jazeera English, for instance, distributed some flip cameras to opinion leaders in Iraq in order to collect material about the voting process: "Each of these videos features the perspective of a regular Iraqi, whose viewpoints and experiences are rarely shared in the news reports coming out of the country. Through video, we can listen to their voices, see their faces and gain a better understanding of what it was like inside Iraq on this important day" (quoted in Powers 2012, 9). The challenge for such departments is the verification of UGC. Al-Jazeera English, for one, received more than four hundred videos a day, which made it vital for the channel to work with communities of bloggers in an attempt to identify the most reliable sources within those communities (Bruna 2013). The Al-Jazeera Transparency Unit (AJTU) was launched in January 2011 as the Arab world's version of "WikiLeaks" and "a platform [for] send[ing] documents, multimedia content or plain clues and pieces of evidence, for the newsroom to consider using them in the editorial output" (Bruna 2013, 15). There are also dedicated interactive shows on Al-Jazeera English, such as *Listening Post* and *The Stream*. *Listening Post* is a twenty-five-minute weekly program recorded in Al-Jazeera's London studios. The program reviews the media coverage of selected international events in each episode, utilizing viewers' videos as well as interviews with professional journalists and experts. *The Stream* also comments on international news coverage with journalists as well as audiences from the region affected by the news. It presents itself as "a social media community with its own daily TV show on Al-Jazeera . . . in search of unheard voices, new perspectives of citizens on the ground and unreported angles on the most interesting stories of the day" (cited in Bruna 2013, 12). Bruna (2013) analyzed the Twitter activity of some of Al-Jazeera English journalists and also the interactivity features in their flagship programs, *The Stream* and *Listening Post*, in order to assess the means by which the audience participated in interactive broadcasts. The analysis of *Listening Post* showed that the most popular recording technology was the webcam, followed by cell phones, and most participants were journalists and media professionals from the United Kingdom and the United States as well as other countries such as Iran, Nigeria, and Libya. The high share of audiences from the United Kingdom is perhaps explained in terms of the popularity of the channel, which is available free on the air in the United Kingdom. Al-Jazeera's wide coverage during the start of the Arab uprisings prompted the launch of #DemandAlJazeera to encourage viewers in the United States to ask for the inclusion of Al-Jazeera English within the channels supplied by their cable providers (Bruna 2013).

User-generated content, including polls, "Have Your Say," Q & A, blogs, and comments on stories or message boards is the most favored source for media outlets, especially in places where there is limited access, although users may try to leverage UGC and social media forums in order to direct journalists to a specific viewpoint.

THE CHALLENGE OF VERIFICATION

Citizen journalism found new and strong grounds among Arab audiences, although it was not always regarded as a credible source of information. A recent study by El Semary and Al Khaja (2013) concerning social media users in the Emirates showed that in spite of citizen journalists being regarded as a credible news source, traditional media were still regarded as more trustworthy and professional due to their highly skilled correspondents and the depth of their coverage and analyses. Traditional media continued to function as gatekeepers, and when they picked up stories by citizen journalists, they were able to select the stories that suited their news agenda. During the recent uprisings in the MENA region, Arab mainstream media depended, to some extent, on information from social media sites such as Facebook and YouTube in order to avoid the dangers and considerable expenses of covering events in the affected countries (Ali and Fahmy 2013). Governments, however, continued to maintain a strong grip over traditional media through infiltration and blocking of social media sites. Social media have created a platform for citizen journalists to have their voices heard, on the other hand; however, traditional media have continued to practice their role as gatekeepers by selecting the information they require in order to communicate to a wider audience (Ali and Fahmy 2013). Citizen journalists are regarded as more honest than mainstream television reporters, perhaps due to the belief of minimal censorship of citizen journalism, while traditional television reporters are regarded as subject to harsher censorship practices; nevertheless, traditional television content is still valued as more professionally packaged and edited, compared with citizen journalism-generated content, and hence more credible and suitable for public interest. Seventy percent of the sample of young people believed in the credibility of traditional media, but they still saw both traditional media and new media as having a complementary rather than competitive relationship. Arab media, moreover, did not seem keen on engaging their audience, and not many newspapers quoted ordinary citizens, which reflects a lack of public political engagement in many Arab states (Duffy 2013). One recent study argued that some UAE-based newspapers prioritized state press releases over the attestations of Emirati citizens in the wake of the recent Arab uprisings (Duffy 2013).

Panelists at the plenary session of the Twelfth Arab Media Forum 2013 discussed the challenges of the new open digital spaces, which offered new sources that would reveal new consumption patterns. These platforms have been embraced by citizen journalists, but they can also be misused by both the state and opposition as propaganda tools, particularly with regard to the turbulent situation across the region: journalists' professional standards concerning objectivity and neutrality can be subjected to severe testing (Arab Media Forum 2013). Dhaen Shaheen, Executive Director and Chief Editor, *Al-Bayan* (newspaper), said:

> There is a major difference between the newsroom of today and that of yesterday. Today we have to prepare two sets of news: one for the online platform while the other for the next day's newspaper when most people have already heard about the news—to give them something new. However, with the influx of the social media, the print media has also fallen in the trap of sometimes publishing fabricated news, without verifying the facts. This is dangerous and we need to constantly guard ourselves against such practices. (cited in Arab Media Forum 2013)

Moreover, Thair Soukar, head of Digital Strategy, Sky News Arabia, said: "We are all under pressure to release news. But one must ensure accuracy and authenticity of the information. I do think that there is no conventional media anymore. There are conventional practices however—which is to ensure the right processes in verification, ensuring authentication and accuracy" (cited in Arab Media Forum 2013). On the other hand, Khaled Al-Farm, professor of political communication at Al-Imam University in Saudi Arabia, commented that the Arab Spring had led to the disintegration of state media across the region and the rise of what he termed "media chaos," with numerous privately owned broadcasting, print and online ventures. The situation now, he concluded, is that state media are no longer agenda setters while the new media can work without clear professional guidelines (cited in Abu Ne'ama 2013).

Social media have therefore created more opportunities for journalists to engage with their audiences in their capacity as users, eyewitness commentators, and contributors to the news content. The degree of engagement with the audience varies across the Arab region. It is safe to argue that the expectations of both journalists and news audiences have changed, as each side expects a more interactive tool and two-way communication platform for the provision of news and access to it. Social media still provide an untapped communication potential from users, not only inside the region but also among Arab diaspora communities across the world. Opportunities include utilizing social media in reporting crises, providing avenues for the marginalized voices in the region, and exploring new sources. Pan-Arab and local media outlets are expected to (re)design their new media strategies in this regard, to fully explore these potentials in the near future.

THE NEW ROLE OF JOURNALISTS

Some scholars (Lasorsa, Lewis, and Holton 2011; Hermida 2009) hail the role of Twitter for changing journalistic norms, particularly in sharing the gatekeeper's role with the audience and offering a more transparent news process. This new journalism, or "ambient journalism" (Hermida 2010a, 301), provides an array of tools to gather, share, and disseminate news and information, which can have a strong impact not only on the journalistic field but on the realms of citizenship; instead of talking about the function of the journalist being a gatekeeper, it has become more important to evaluate the new role of gate watching, defined as "the observation of the output gates of news publications and other sources, in order to identify important material as soon as it becomes available" (Bruns 2005, 2). Gate watching, then, "is an egalitarian, open-access medium which is particularly well suited to liberating the exchange of alternative, non-mainstream content and ideas" (Bruns 2005, 2). This model allows the user not only to consume but also to produce media content. Mainstream journalism for Bruns (2005) may be outmoded and in desperate need of reinventing itself, with users moving from being passive audiences to being producers and distributors of news content; if journalism's main aim is considered "to help enable, extend, and enhance public discovery, discussion and deliberation of the news," then citizen journalism such as blogging may be considered an authentic form of journalism (Bruns 2005, 317). The journalist's task, therefore, is not only to filter media content but to promote and evaluate newsworthy information on the web as a gate watcher.

Finding information has undoubtedly been one of the main challenges to the journalism profession in the Arab region, with states controlling the flow and dissemination of information, even with the proliferation of privately owned media. Social media have been regarded as an effective tool to counteract this deficiency, with Twitter, for instance, allowing immediate dissemination and sharing of information by citizens, activists, politicians, and celebrities as well as diaspora communities. Journalists now have tools to effectively gather, categorize, and share information, which is a paradigm shift in modern journalism (Pavlik 2001, 184). Social media have also been hailed as a tool for collective actions beyond state control, allowing the "explor[ation] of new ways to gather together and get . . . things done" (Shirky 2008, 22). Twitter can be an easy and fast source of news, but tweets can also be a platform for hoaxes and misinformation; sharing news stories via social media such as Facebook is expected to exceed referrals from search engines, making Facebook "one of the most influential players in driving news audiences" (*Economist* 2011).

Abdul Razzaq, a new media journalist at Al-Jazeera, saw dealing with social media inevitable and a "necessary evil" that has played a pivotal role in the dissemination of news and information by surpassing state control (Fal 2013). His colleague, Mohamed Sidi, stressed that social media should not be disregarded as proper media platforms simply because it is difficult to verify information on the Internet (Fal 2013). Social media pose an ethical challenge, a journalist at Aljazeera.net suggested, but it plays an important role in spreading the news and avoiding censorship:

> Social media have the advantage of spreading news quickly, especially among those who have not got the time to read the papers or watch television. It encourages ordinary citizens to provide journalistic input from places difficult for mainstream journalists to reach. But the drawback is the absence of code of ethics online, and lack of credibility such as rumors on twitters as well as hacking. (cited in Fal 2013)

Al-Jazeera has capitalized on the new and social media to reach out to a wider share of audiences. The managing director of the network explained that the web platform means more than just copying television broadcasts onto the website; with a large network of correspondents across eighty bureaus around the world, Al-Jazeera can accumulate a considerable amount of data in excess of what is required for television bulletins. The current tendency is to create a special package for television and post the full-length interviews, images, and audio files on the website (Bartlett 2014). The material which is not used in a two-minute television package can add value to digital users and a new opportunity for engaging with the content, or, as the managing director put it: "There is this massive information out there. We, as journalists, need to get the integrity of that information absolutely right, but we also need to make sure we're adding the value, we're adding the depth, we're giving the full picture, we're giving the background, and we're giving the content. If people want to know more, they can know more because of digital now" (quoted in Bartlett 2014).

Riyaad Minty, head of social media at Al-Jazeera Network, argued: "It's not about having a single dedicated social media team to handle everything. . . . We come up with the strategy and experiment with the tools to see how they can be handed over to the newsroom to own the project and try it themselves. . . . Everyone is open to bounce ideas and identify ways to move forward" (cited in Ulbricht 2011, 31).

JOURNALIST OR IDEOLOGUE?

Many journalists may see an opportunity in blog writing in order to comment on the news without the constraints of news corporations (Hermida and Thurman 2008); however, not all outlets allow their journalists to freely express their views. BBC Arabic, for instance, follows the overall BBC social media policy, which prohibits editorial staff from indicating their political allegiance and warns against posting offensive comments about BBC colleagues,[2] according to Liliane Landor, Controller of Languages, BBC Global News:

> The BBC journalist is not allowed to express their personal views online or support a certain party whether in homeland or in the UK or any other country. You must be objective and neutral at all times. Journalists can join cooking forums but not political forums. You are not allowed to criticize the BBC on Facebook or twitter. If one of your parents, relatives or friends is jailed in the homeland, you should not express your opinion on Facebook or twitter. I have been in the BBC for more than 20 years and I still do not know the political opinion of many colleagues here. . . . A BBC journalist can absolutely not be a fan, a friend or a follower of a politician or an activist from whatever country be it in your country, in Britain or someone else's country. They can follow as many people as they want on twitter because they need sources,

> but not to post opinion. You are not allowed to put your personal opinion in a blog even though you may have an avatar or a different name. At the end of the day, you're a BBC journalist who has a duty not to put in any doubt the impartiality and objectivity of the organization we work for. We rely on social media a great deal in the BBC. . . . We do not publish everything we get via social media. We run it through a robust system of verification and checks.[3]

Deutsche Welle does not usually impose restrictions on its staff members' articulating their views if they wish, "although television presenters might find it awkward to openly express their political views on social media sites," Samar Karam from Deutsche Welle Arabic argued (interview, April 2014).

Other Arabic-speaking media outlets, in contrast, allow their journalists to use social media to express their views, even if they end up publicly venting their problems. The tweets of veteran host Ahmad Mansour of Al-Jazeera have been followed closely by a number of Egyptian media outlets who accused him of using social media to incite public opinion against the Egyptian army and against the newly elected president, Abdel Fattah El-Sisi. An example was a Facebook post published in February 2014, allegedly one of Mansour's, in which there was an explicit incitement to kill Egyptian security officers. Mansour immediately denied that he owned a Facebook account and claimed that the post was fabricated in order to tarnish his name. The post was circulated via Ikhwan Online, the Muslim Brotherhood Internet portal, but the site later announced that the Facebook post attributed to Mansour was not verified by official sources and condemned the attack on him. Several mainstream media outlets, such as the newspaper *Youm El-Sabei* (*Youm7*) launched an offensive on Mansour, casting doubts on his motives for writing such a post, and two television anchors on Tahrir TV, Rania Badawi and Jihan Mansour, demanded the revocation of Mansour's Egyptian citizenship as a penalty for his alleged Facebook comment. The post also prompted the Egyptian Journalists Syndicate to threaten Mansour with dismissal from the syndicate, but Mansour retaliated by warning that he would seek all legal measures against the syndicate if it went ahead with its threat (Al-Jazeera 2014). Mansour tweeted his denial of ever writing the post on Facebook and accused the Egyptian authorities of misleading the media, including Ikhwan Online, by publishing the post under his name. Mansour did not hesitate to express his personal view in his tweets, and he never concealed his rejection of El-Sisi's government and its overthrow of the Muslim Brotherhood. One of Mansour's tweets, for instance, dated August 8, 2014, declared that the current president, "Abdel Fattah Al-Sisi, who stole the nation, army and Egyptians' will and wealth and hope, has stolen the Suez Canal project from President Mohamed Morsi" (https://twitter.com/amansouraja).

Following the eruption of the Gaza-Israel attacks in July 2014, a number of Egyptian and Al-Jazeera journalists engaged in exchanges on social media. Al-Jazeera's main anchor, Jamal Rayyan, criticized the Egyptian journalist Moustafa Bakri for his statements about the Egyptian role in solving the conflict in Gaza. Rayyan tweeted: "In an attempt to mislead public opinion, Moustafa Bakri on Twitter called for Israel to lift the blockade on Gaza, but he did not ask Al-Sisi to lift this blockade [of Rafah Crossing], why? If the Palestinian issue, Mr. Bakri, is the central matter for Egypt and the Arab world, then why should the Palestinians die on behalf of all Arabs?" (Al-Ansari 2014). The Egyptian talk show host Mazhar Shaeen volunteered to respond to Rayyan's tweets by saying: "If you want to talk about a media scandal, let's talk about your own channel [Al-Jazeera], and what you broadcast on your [suspect] channel [about] treason and hired conspiracy" (Al-Ansari 2014).

Fatima Rida, New Media editor at *Al-Hayat*, cited the danger of expressing one's opinion as a journalist or a high-profile official on social media. She was particularly referring to the incident of the dismissal of Lebanese Octavia Nasr from CNN because of one of Nasr's tweets (interview, May 2014). Nasr was fired after twenty years as the CNN senior Middle East editor because of a tweet she sent in 2010, following the death of Grand Ayatollah Mohammad Hussein Fadlallah, who helped found Hezbollah in Lebanon. Nasr wrote: "Sad to hear of the passing of Sayyed Mohammad Hussein Fadlallah. One of Hezbollah's giants I respect a lot." The tweet was picked up by the Simon Wiesenthal Center in the United States, which demanded that Nasr apologize to all victims of Hezbollah. Nasr later wrote on the CNN website that her tweet was an error of judgment and justified her respect for Fadlallah specifically for his stance on women's rights. The reason for sacking Nasr, as explained by CNN, was due to her jeopardizing her credibility as senior editor for Middle Eastern affairs and that the tweet did not meet the company's editorial standards. Commenting on the aftermath of her tweet, Nasr wrote: "Reaction to my Tweet was immediate, overwhelming and provides a good lesson on why 140 characters should not be used to comment on controversial or sensitive issues, especially those dealing with the Middle East" (Walker 2010). The incident prompted a debate about the so-called Twittercide in which high-profile users could fall foul of what they wrote in 140 characters (Walker 2010). Fatima Rida (*Al-Hayat*) also recalled how then British ambassador to Lebanon Frances Guy also tweeted in 2010 about Fadlallah's death, paying tribute to him as a man who was willing to reach out across faiths. The tweet caused some controversy, which made Guy remove the tweet and apologize for it.

THE NEW MULTISKILLED JOURNALIST

Several Arab journalists call for reemphasis on the editorial skills necessary for journalists working with new and social media. One of them is Samar Karam at the Germany-based Deutsche Welle Arabic, who said that "anyone can be online journalists who could jeopardize the professional journalistic standards, as evident in some Arab online sites [which publish inaccurate news]." She mentioned an example of an Arab news site that published a brief article claiming that the German chancellor, Angela Merkel, had banned iPhone sales in Germany, which could not be verified in any German or European news source: "Arab journalists could get the news from social media [such as Twitter] and actually believe it, and they may print it as news without verifying it first. Online journalism is a tool but it still has to comply with traditional professional standards," she said (interview, April 2014). Her colleague, Rainer Sollich, deputy head of the Arabic service at Deutsche Welle (DW), agrees that the new role of a journalist is to verify stories circulating online: "I believe there will always be a role for DW (and other) journalists, mainly research and verification. Professional journalism also needs to deal as objectively and neutrally as possible with content published on the social media platform. Internet and social media platforms are full of interesting content and information but someone has to check and filter this information and to transfer it into qualified journalistic content" (interview, May 2014).

Sultan Batawi, head of social media at Al-Arabiya, saw the role of an Arab journalist evolving around multiskills and the ability to work on multimedia platforms:

> A journalist has to move across all platforms, so writing for the web is not like writing for TV or for social media. I think journalists who work with social media are the ones who can adapt easily to writing to all platforms, because we adapt to a dynamic platform, unlike print journalists who tend to follow one particular style for a long time. TV journalism is even better because it forces you to imagine your audience when you write a news item, and this ability to imagine helps you adapt your writing to other platforms. I also write for the technology section, and in the old days I used to post a report together with a photo. Now I am asked to post an image on Instagram, write a report for TV and another for online. So we have to multitask. Everyone will have to move across platforms; it is like when the typing machine was invented, those who used it extensively were the early adapters. The same happened when the computer was invented. But now it is usual for everyone to be able to use computers and social media. Even state leaders use social media. (interview, May 2014)

Zahi Alawi, editor of the "Bobs" (Best of Blogs) Awards, sponsored by Deutsche Welle, considered it imperative for journalists to be familiar with social media uses: "Any journalist who does not use social media lacks a good source of news" (interview, April 2014). Journalists, for him, whether working on TV, print, or online, must comply with the journalistic standards and ethics, a view shared by Abdel Bari Atwan (*Rai Al-Youm* online news site), who confirmed that "all journalists, whether they work online or offline, have to comply with the same standards. Journalism is not about posting something online and updating it: it is about much more than that" (interview, April 2014).

Several Arabic-speaking outlets have injected additional capital into new and social media facilities. One example is the BBC, which has invested heavily in social media in an attempt to encourage more audiences to contribute to its coverage of major events such as the Asian tsunami. Part of this investment was in a new hub to process and authenticate user-generated material. The hub processes over ten thousand e-mail comments on a weekly basis in addition to one thousand still images and more than one hundred video clips (Newman 2009). There are cases in which it is rather difficult, if not impossible, to verify material such as that submitted during the Iranian protests in 2009, and here an editorial judgment has to be made about the material's authenticity. Such user-generated material is deemed valuable for enhancing the quality of the BBC's output, as judged not only by the BBC editors but also by the audience. In a MORI survey released in 2007, the majority of the BBC's audience sampled in the survey agreed that UGC enhances the quality of content (Newman 2009).

The BBC's investment in third-party social media networks, however, faces a challenge in authenticating and verifying material on the Internet. One example was during the Mumbai attacks in 2008, when the BBC was criticized for circulating unsubstantiated information via Twitter (Newman 2009, 9). Mohamed Yehia, head of digital media at BBC Arabic, said that verifying material on the Internet is an important but elaborate process (*Economist* 2011). There is no shortage of visual material on the Internet, but it is a complex task to examine this material to determine its authenticity, such as looking for street signs indicating the exact place or comparing weather reports with the weather conditions in a video or photograph. Authenticating the images or video is not the only task for professional journalists: they also have to make sure that such images do not identify and jeopardize people's lives (*Economist* 2011). The BBC developed its own verification methods in a special UGC hub in London staffed by more than twenty journalists who search videos, pictures, and content online to be used to supplement the content generated by the BBC staff and correspondents, including the Arabic service. The verification process of users' videos includes checking the local accents, the location, and the weather forecasts for that location (Sasseen 2012, 26). Arab videographers also quickly learned to authenticate their footage, for instance, by including a shot of a daily newspaper confirming the date or including a street sign (Sasseen 2012, 26). The BBC also established a dedicated news desk for Syria, staffed by senior editors and journalists from across the BBC network. The desk contributed to verifying UGC from Syria, defined as the "content supplied to the BBC via mobile devices as well as content submitted online, through social media sites or through the post [for example] video cassettes" (Harkin et al. 2012, 23).

Other networks, such as Al-Jazeera, had dedicated staff to check the quality of images and verify the UGC, which increased with the escalation of conflicts across the region. Sharek received more than two hundred videos per day from Syrian audiences during the first three months of the Syrian uprising, which remarkably increased on Fridays (Harkin et al. 2012, 22). Deutsche Welle journalists realized that there was much information online and the challenge now was "to verify this information and guide the audience not to believe anything online," said Samar Karam from the social media unit (interview, April 2014). What may look like open and abundant information on the World Wide Web may be questionable: on the one hand, it can ensure the dissemination of news and information necessary for a well-informed public, while on the other, some of the information may contain elements of factional agitation or incitement.

CONCLUSION

Social media, according to online Arab media practitioners, can be used in three different commercially viable ways:

1. *Planning*: Journalists use social media for news-gathering purposes, such as gaining access to new sources, checking rumors, networking, and disseminating news.
2. *Branding*: Journalists use social media in order to promote their own outlets as well as a particular output.
3. *Increasing market share*: Journalists may also use social media to engage with current and new audiences via online debates. The more engaged audiences are, the more loyal users they become. As such, social media can be used to maintain the link to this cohort of loyal audiences as well as in tracking new trends among them.

Pan-Arab journalists use social media for the above three purposes, although not all outlets can afford a high degree of engagement with audiences because of the human and financial resources required to maintain them. Social media is shaping the media sector as a whole, shaking up old monopolies and providing new networks of interaction between audiences and journalists, politicians, and activists.

NOTES

1. See http://www.bbc.co.uk/academy/arabic/standards/social-media/article/art20130702112134053.
2. BBC Editorial Guidelines, http://www.bbc.co.uk/guidelines/editorialguidelines/page/guidance-blogs-personal-summary.
3. BBC Academy, http://www.bbc.co.uk/academy/arabic/standards/socialmedia/article/art20130702112134054.

Conclusions

On March 17–18, 2015, Dubai hosted the first Middle Eastern social media event of its kind: the Arab Social Media Influencers Summit, where leading social media influencers were celebrated. In a significant way, the launch of this social media event in the MENA region suggested the growing importance of social space in the region's social, cultural, and political life. Though the summit featured a wide range of personalities and institutions with extensive and substantive social space engagement, media personalities and institutions were capturing much of the spotlight at the event. A major implication of that event was that for traditional media organizations and practitioners in the MENA region, social media are no longer a luxury but a central driver of mass communications' survival. Media-relevant discussions at the summit's panels showed that cyberspace is a gold mine for communications organizations and professionals to tap as they work to enhance their profile and foster audience engagement. Media personalities like Ali Jaber and Mustafa Al-Agha of MBC and Sultan Sooud Al-Qassemi, a freelance writer, made it clear to a huge audience that social media in the MENA communications environment are here to stay not only as enablers of conventional media survivors but also as media outlets in their own right.

Among other things, the Arab Social Media Influencers Summit strongly suggests that Arab media work and journalism in particular have come a long a way in the past two decades in terms of relevance to both global professional standards and regional audience needs. Socioeconomic, political, and technological transitions in the context of globalization were bound to shape journalism in a region long known for its inhibitive communication systems and low audience engagement. The advent of satellite television and the web, among other things, has put both Arab professional journalists and mass audiences face to face with new journalistic norms and practices that thrive on greater critical inquiries, pluralistic representations, and audience engagements. Historically, Arabs' firsthand encounter with Western journalism had taken place through overseas training programs, academic studies, and visits. But in the age of satellite television and the Internet, interactions with Western-style journalism have been brought to Arab homes through pan-Arab media outlets operating in a highly competitive environment. It is true that all Arabic-speaking media are turning more regional and global by virtue of their online presence or satellite reach; but media outlets with extensive operations, staff and professional standards, and substantive content diversity are rather limited in number. While those media diverge in their emerging journalism models drawing on independence, government control, and self-censorship, they share one common feature: their growing use of social media as an integral part of the journalism practice.

This book represents an analytical inquiry into how social media are harnessed by a range of pan-Arab communications outlets and journalists to enhance audience engagement. The basic assumption underlying this work is that since social space represents a source of empowerment for both pan-Arab media professionals and audiences, new media would most likely have a credible impact on how journalism is practiced. Given the participatory nature of social media platforms, journalism would be expected to be more interactive and symmetrical with audiences who are gaining more power in defining content and communication parameters. It is a central theme of this book that social media will be transforming the traditional model of journalism as practiced not only in North America and Europe but in the Middle East and North Africa as well. We have noted profound interest on the part of pan-Arab media institutions and journalists in being part of the social media space, though significant variations in usage patterns have been noted. The fact that pan-Arab media are investing in social media structures, technologies, and, more important, human resources suggests that Web 2.0 technologies are here to stay as key drivers of the pan-Arab journalism landscape.

But as we note in this book, while the use of social media in the pan-Arab communications landscape could enhance media organizations' power of reach as well as audiences' access to social conversations, they may not hold bright promises for journalists' aspirations to be independent communicators. As elsewhere, pan-Arab journalists are expected to handle social space within both in-house social media policies set by their employers and national regulations governing cyberspace. In the MENA region, the traditional role of the journalist is more that of an advocate who is expected to echo political, social, and cultural standards, in most cases in the spirit of patriotism and "development journalism." Arab journalism in the twenty-first century, as noted in chapter 1, continues to embrace many of the traditional values of nationalism and mobilization despite Arab Spring upheavals and neoliberal market reforms. Tensions between technologies as both socially emancipating and socially constraining will continue to define the emerging cyber Arab journalism landscape for years to come. Media regulations across the region, especially those applying to online communications, have only reinforced long-standing control traditions in the media sector. The opening up of media markets, especially satellite television and the audiovisual industry in general, to private entrepreneurs seems to have created a sense of optimism about a new journalism in the making. But in the past two decades, rising frustrations with heavy-handed state media regulations have given rise to disenchantment with the vision of the private sector as a savior.

But could new media make the difference? Conceptually, online journalism, as McQuail (2013) noted, is characterized by diversity of forms, freedom from mainstream media regulations, and relative delocalization. If new and social media are seen in the West as a novel challenge to the traditional role of the journalist as gatekeeper, here in the Arab region they seem to be perceived by Arab journalists as enhancing their role as culture custodians who are entrusted with safeguarding their societies against alien onslaughts. This sense of "advocacy journalism" has been most conspicuous in pan-Arab media channels whose mission is to reflect and sustain existing social and political traditions perceived to be central to the region's survival in the midst of global turbulence. In pan-Arab media outlets affiliated with foreign countries outside the MENA region, this sense of cultural custodianship seems to be almost virtually nonexistent. In significant ways, the emancipatory potential embedded in social media platforms seems to be profoundly diluted by the region's "physical world" realities. It is an important theme of this book that social media do have the potential to induce significant transitions in pan-Arab journalism; however, culture and politics would most likely continue to militate against the realization of that prospect.

If political and cultural traditions in the MENA region remain antithetical to the region's new communications development as a feature of emerging social empowerment, the momentum for investment in this sector would most likely continue to grow. As noted earlier in this book, oil-rich countries of the Gulf have been at the forefront of communications development, with billions of dollars invested in the information and telecommunications sector. The role of media convergence in economic development has never been appropriately recognized in most of those countries, where notions of knowledge society and knowledge economy seem to define national development strategies. On the other hand, the ICT picture does not seem to be shiny in other countries with more limited resources. Available data show countries experiencing political upheavals and instabilities are also characterized by poor information and telecommunications infrastructures. The main implication of this feature is that Arab or pan-Arab media in cyberspace are less accessible to audiences in communications-poor countries compared with those in Gulf Cooperation Council (GCC) nations. As the successive Arab social media reports in the past few years suggest, traditional media channels would most likely continue to shape public opinion in those countries while new media took lower profiles in national communications. For pan-Arab media organizations keen on communicating with audiences through social media, however, limited or no access to the web on the part of millions of potential followers would seem highly detrimental to their future development.

But despite the euphoria associated with the institutional and corporate diffusion of social media technologies in the region, the emerging cyberspace has created growing concerns on the part of governments over potential threats associated with agitation, slander, and incitement. Across the region, rising access to the Internet at large and the spread of social media in particular have triggered contradictory reactions by Arab governments. Many of the current Arab states have expressed their commitments to political as well as economic reforms while keeping a firm grip on the cultural industries. Cultural traditions are increasingly viewed as central to social and political survival and should be safeguarded against encroachments through satellite television and online media. The potential negative effects of those media have given rise to numerous regulations across the region, suggesting media as a double-edged weapon that can be used not only to mobilize public opinion but also to undermine the ideological foundations of Arab societies and states. The war-on-terror narrative has provided Arab states with more compelling rationale to exercise stricter control over media industries in the name of protecting their nations against terrorism. In many ways, those concerns have been quite inhibitive for pan-Arab media seeking to communicate with audiences in the region in a more free style. Channels like BBC Arabic, CNN Arabic, Sky News Arabia, and Al-Arabiya have demonstrated full use of social media in their traditional media settings; however, cyberspace regulatory regimes deployed in different countries seem to have diminished their engagement with audiences.

It is in this divergent technological and social communication environment that pan-Arab media channels have come to harness social platforms in the region to engage audiences. We have found that all pan-Arab media organizations covered by the study have been active users of the two leading social media platforms: Facebook and Twitter. If the ultimate goal of pan-Arab mass communications since the 1990s and before had been framed around building specific public opinions among the region's populations relevant to diverse political and ideological orientations, social media would have made that task the most achievable. Traditional regional media like BBC Arabic radio, the Voice of America, Radio Cairo (Voice of the Arabs), and Radio Monte Carlo had little success in engaging Arab populations partly because of lacking reliable audience data and of state censorship practices. In the age of social media, pan-Arab communications have made audience engagement most possible and measurable. The proliferation of new information and communications technologies among the region's populations has substantially enabled pan-Arab media organizations to reach out to audiences and engage them in global conversations on issues of high relevance to the Middle East. The steady flow of social media traffic from pan-Arab media organizations testified to the determination of pan-Arab media to make social platforms an integral centerpiece of their operations. The establishment of social media units and recruitment of social media specialists by all pan-Arab media outlets covered by the study suggest that those operations seem serious in going social not only for the sake of development but for survival as well. As elsewhere, social media have become the new frontier in the marketing not only of goods and services but of ideas and values as well.

Since our knowledge about social media's role in marketing communications and journalism continues to be severely constrained by underdeveloped methodologies and tools, more research is needed to understand how social platforms are harnessed in this pan-Arab communication sector. A more longitudinal investigation of pan-Arab media usage of a wider range of social tools could lead to more insightful ideas on where this emerging sector is heading. But as this study suggests, social media are here to stay as part of pan-Arab media operations. We are more likely to see greater expansions in social media integration into overall pan-Arab media operations affiliated with a range of ideologically and politically divergent organizations seeking to win hearts and minds in a constantly destabilized yet strategically important region. The region's experience with the so-called Arab Spring uprisings shows that people's voices do matter in shaping the Middle East future. Hence, engaging Arab populations with new ideas for constructive transitions is of paramount importance to ensure sound social, economic, and political transitions. We argue in this book that social media could be the most effective in achieving that goal!

The study reveals that a good number of pan-Arab newsrooms have embraced social media in their daily practices for different purposes;

chief among them is news gathering and audience engagement. Newsrooms actively use social media as part of their public relations strategies, most conspicuously in global outlets such as BBC Arabic, Al-Jazeera, and Deutsche Welle Arabic. Here, social media can be used for branding and promoting programs and blogging posts by staff and presenters. Social media are also used as platforms to monitor trends and emerging stories, especially those that are building momentum and opening a dialogue with active users. Other pan-Arab outlets, such as pan-Arab newspapers, have too limited resources and expertise to develop flexible social media strategies that properly respond to emerging trends online. Thus, the degree of user engagement varies across outlets, with some of them being more concerned with the number of views and likes on social media sites than with engaging with audience comments. It is evident from talking to social media editors in selected pan-Arab outlets that social media sites have helped change the rigid news values, which traditionally favor hard political news toward human interest features. Light-hearted news is favored particularly on Facebook, though political news is still on the top of the news agenda, partially because of the rising conflicts in the region and partially because of the new ways available to the younger Arab generations to keep abreast of developments in their own and other neighboring countries. Social media, particularly Facebook, are used to interact with the audience, albeit at varying degrees across pan-Arab newsrooms, depending on the quality of resources, especially manpower and telecommunications infrastructures. Business models in pan-Arab newsrooms can shape their multimedia strategies, while the political context and conflicts inside the region have an impact on newsrooms' innovation and multimedia strategies.

At the pan-Arab media practitioners' level, it is clear that the twenty-six journalists covered by the study have some form of engagement with social media at personal and professional levels. The volume of outbound traffic originating from those pan-Arab journalists suggests how increasingly integrated social media have turned in their journalistic practices. On the other hand, while all twenty-six journalists may be described as active social media users, the patterns of usage seem to vary according to social media guidelines defining work at their media organizations. Pan-Arab journalists' handling of social media assignments is governed by internal social media policies that define all types of engagement to be initiated by those journalists as both professionals and private persons. The study has identified two categories of social media users in the pan-Arab media sector: the users of advocacy journalism and the professional journalism users. The first category is inclusive of journalists working for Al-Jazeera and Al-Mayadeen channels, where clear political and ideological inclinations are being promoted in a rather conspicuous fashion. The second category includes journalists working for media channels with social media policies that discourage expression of personal opinions and emphasize professional standards in dealing with social space. This does not suggest that media in the first category have no guidelines for social media work. They actually do; but at the same time, their engagement with audiences as voices of their media organization's ideological line does not seem to be discouraged.

The study has found that pan-Arab media journalists use social media in distinctive ways: crowdsourcing ideas from audiences to enrich their programs; driving traffic to their own or their organizations' central websites/portals; sharing links with audiences on issues not directly addressed by employer organizations; and commenting on developments in the region and around the world. It was also found that journalists use social media for news-gathering purposes, such as gaining access to new sources, checking rumors, networking, and dissemination. Social media are also used in branding to promote their own outlets as well as particular contents and formats to increasing market share: journalists may also use social media to engage with current and new audiences via online debates. It has been clear from interviews that pan-Arab journalists seem to believe that the more engaged audiences are, the more loyal they would prove to be. As such, social media can be used to maintain the link to this cohort of loyal audiences as well as to track new trends among them. It was found that journalists working for the two ideologically oriented channels, Al-Jazeera and Al-Mayadeen, were active in using social media in the four patterns with a noticeable emphasis on advocacy facets of their social media traffic. It was also found that journalists had varying levels of engagement with audiences as based on their Facebook posts. Al-Jazeera's journalists were at the forefront in terms of engagement mainly because the topics they post carry huge potential controversies and were bound to generate highly sensational feedback. On the other hand, journalists in other media were receiving lower engagement, most likely due to the less dramatic nature of their posted topics.

A central component of this study relates to audience engagement in cyberspace. The study has shown that the ten pan-Arab media organizations employ both Facebook and Twitter to generate conversations on issues of interest to the region and the world. It was noticed that Faisal Al-Kasim of Al-Jazeera channel was at the forefront of social media engagement with over five million Facebook fans and around two million Twitter followers. All pan-Arab media engaged with their audiences on issues relevant to their news agendas; however, audience inputs into the conversations were mostly defined by the quality of their social, political, and cultural backgrounds. It was not always clear how the narratives of Facebook conversations were playing out in the broader political public sphere of the region. But it was obvious that the outbound Facebook and Twitter traffic was creating considerable buzz in the cybersphere. Some media channels seemed to have accommodated all types of contributions to the conversations, while others apparently did some filtering of "unfavorable comments." It is not clear how pan-Arab media handle the conversations they initiate through posts and tweets. All pan-Arab media have some forms of social media units that coordinate their inbound and outbound social media traffic within their existing news management systems. However, it is not clear whether those media do follow-ups and further analyses of social media traffic to generate insights and improve their editorial policies and interactions with the audience. There has been no sign of Arab media substantially contributing to the conversations they had initiated.

All pan-Arab journalists covered by this study generated good social media engagements, though Faisal Al-Kasim remains one of the most eminent Arab journalists in social space. With over five million Facebook fans and around two million Twitter followers, Al-Kasim has proved that pan-Arab journalists have the potential to gain a "global influencer" status. But when we consider the fact that Al-Kasim's social media traffic is dominated by his views about the conflict in Syria and in the region at large, we realize that his social contributions are more reflective of his political and ideological activism than of professional standards. To a lesser extent, political or ideological inclinations were driving social engagements by Al-Mayadeen journalists, who seem to advocate a pan-Arabist, secular, and pro-Syrian-Iranian line than other journalists in the group. Journalists working for non-Arab pan-Arab media, like BBC Arabic, CNN Arabic, Alhurra, Sky News Arabia, and France 24, seemed keen on following professional standards that are informed by their media organizations' guidelines and norms. In Saudi-owned media like Al-Arabiya, *Asharq Al-Awsat*, and *Al-Hayat*, journalists did their engagements by sharing their own stories or addressing issues with low political or ideological connotations.

The future of social media holds good promise for pan-Arab media. The development of new social measurements and analytics would hugely help those media to engage with their audiences across the region. The introduction of new applications and technologies coupled with the rise of a new generation of social media–savvy generations and the continued enhancement of information infrastructures would bode well for greater engagement. The book sees this as an opportunity that both media outlets as institutions and audiences as stakeholders in the cyber content generation could tap into with huge dividends. There are limitless opportunities for engagement and content dissemination through social media networks that pan-Arab journalists could consider. The communication model that defines the emerging social media landscape is that of user empowerment and value-added content. Pan-Arab media institutions with diverse agendas are now able to expand their reach and attract audiences throughout the region. Global conversations have been triggered through social media networks on issues long considered taboo from political and religious points of view. For pan-Arab media, the social media buzz is a good indicator of changing public opinions in the region and could be harnessed in effective ways to generate good content on traditional media platforms. As noted in the 2015 Arab Social Media Influencers Summit, the social media world is loaded with an abundance of opportunities the MENA region could not afford to miss out on.

But social media networks also come with big challenges that pan-Arab media have to address. The first challenge relates to their ability to provide the relevant content to their audiences through diverse social media networks. The study found varying levels of social media integration in the ten media organizations covered by the analysis. Organizations that have started with solid new media foundations or those that have invested much in upgrading those foundations have been found to lead in this area. On the other hand, organizations that place social media as secondary tools in their news operations have been found to lag behind in terms of traffic volume and engagement. Quality content requires the allocation of resources—human, technical, and financial—to keep social media operations up and running. The degree of integration with existing newsroom structures seems to define the quality of social media outputs and how engaging they are in cyberspace. Pan-Arab media with fully integrated social media systems are more likely to generate the fastest traffic and to attract the largest number of followers.

The challenges facing pan-Arab media are not only technological but social, cultural, and political. All ten pan-Arab media outlets are perceived by audiences as affiliated with some political or ideological points of view as defined by their sponsors or countries of origin. Traditionally, this feature has created big headaches for transnational media that came under fire for promoting certain political orientations that diminished their ability to be objective and independent. In the past, low audience perceptions of transnational media were reflected in low exposure to their contents as well as in critical academic and media discussions. But in the age of social media, audiences are getting more vocal in cyberspace in criticizing those media and the countries or groups they are affiliated with. In many cases, we noticed that some media outlets were triggering extremely negative remarks that could reflect badly on the organization. Pan-Arab media are becoming less able to control the conversations they initiate as part of their outbound traffic. In technological terms, limited audience access opportunities to cyberspace in a region that continues to rank low on international

Internet penetration indices is a big problem to be addressed. Low social media engagement from some parts of the MENA region would cause conversations to look more biased and imbalanced. The situation seems to be aggravated by the institution of more inhibitive cybermedia regulations that preclude an independent and free use of social space on the part of both media organizations and individuals.

While this book was meant to be an exploratory analysis of the emerging social space in the pan-Arab media sector, it can serve as a launching point for further future investigations of how Arab media at large engage with social platforms. We see promising prospects for significant scholarly investigations of this new frontier in media work to establish solid knowledge about how media professionals perceive social media at personal and institutional levels. This study drew on selective interviews with some pan-Arab journalists to described personal perceptions of social media tools and integration. But much more is needed to generate more systematic knowledge about those perceptions and how they vary across national or organizational media settings. By the same token, this study also briefly touched on selected social media integration cases in the MENA region, but the broader picture remains rather foggy. More research into newsroom practices and structures could provide insightful findings about convergence and integration as the central features of social media engagement. Finally, while this study addressed audience perceptions of pan-Arab media's outbound content based on the analysis of Facebook contestations, more could be done to address audience views of social media as an emerging component of the new communications landscape.

References

Abbassi, A. 2013. "Free-to-Air Satellite TV Channels in the Arab World: The Growth in Supply Continues." *Satellite Today*, November 18, 2013. http://www.satellitetoday.com/publications/2013/11/18/free-to-air-satellite-tv-channels-in-the-arab-world-the-growth-in-supply-continues.

Abdel Latif, Omayma. 2001. "The Medium Is the Message." *Al Ahram Weekly*, no. 526, March 22–28.

Abdel Nabi, Abdel Fattah. 1989. *Sociology of News* (in Arabic). Cairo: Al Arabi Books.

Abdel-Sattar, Nesrine. 2013. "Innovation in Arabic Online Newsrooms: A Comparative Study of the Social Shaping of Multimedia Adoption in Aljazeera Net, Almassae and Almasry Alyoum in the Context of the Arab Spring." PhD diss., Oxford Internet Institute, University of Oxford.

Abdel-Sattar, Nesrine, Mina Al-Lami, Marie Gillespie, Nermeen Sayed, and Marayam Wissam. 2012. "Media And BBC Arabic: A Case Study of *Nuqtat Hewar*." Research report, June, Open University, Milton Keynes. http://www.open.ac.uk/researchprojects/diasporas/publications/report/bbc-arabic-and-social-media-a-case-study-of-nuqtat-hewar.

Abderrahmane, Azzi. 1998. "Mass Media in the Grand Maghrib: Morocco—Algeria—Tunisia." Department of Communication, International Islamic University Malaysia. Accessed October 18, 2003. www.geocities.com/Athens/Ithaca/8257/maghrib.htm.

Abdulla, Rasha. 2013. *Mapping Digital Media: Egypt*. London: Open Society Media Program.

Abu Ne'ama, Hanadi. 2013. "Social Media Do Not Replace Traditional Media." *Al Emarat al Youm*, May 15. http://www.emaratalyoum.com/local-section/other/2013-05-15-1.575020.

Abu Zeid, Farouk. 1993. *Arab* Émigré Press (in Arabic). Cairo: Alam Al Kotub.

Ajbaili, Mustapha. 2014. "Egypt TV Presenters Tout Twitter Ban over Anti-Sisi Hashtag." *Al-Arabiya News*, March 31. http://english.alarabiya.net/en/media/television-and-radio/2014/03/31/Egypt-TV-presenters-tout-twitter-ban-over-anti-Sisi-hashtag.html.

Al-Ahram Al-Arabi. 2013. "Chaos of Syndicates Threaten the Future of Unions." October 10. http://arabi.ahram.org.eg/NewsQ/34618.aspx.

Al-Ansari, Jihad. 2014. "War of Tweets between Al Jazeera Anchor and Egyptian Journalists." Masr Al-Arabiya, July 31. http://www.masralarabia.com.

Al-Arabi, Othman. 2006. "Credibility of Arab Electronic Press in Saudi Arabia." In *Proceedings of the Conference Online Journalism in the Arab World—Realities and Challenges*, edited by Ali Abdulrahman Awad. Sharjah, UAE: University of Sharjah.

Al-Basami, Zakia. 2013. "Al Jazeera News Channel and Loss of Its Credibility after Arab Spring." November 10, 2013. *Zakia al Basami* (blog). http://ashjan101.wordpress.com/2013/11/10/al-jazeera-news-channel-and-loss-of-its-credibility-after-arab-spring.

Al-Faysal, Abd al-Ameer. 2006. *Electronic Press in the Arab World*. Amman: Dar el Shorouk.

Ali, Aggo. 2006. "Arab Electronic Press: Realities and Opportunities." In *Proceedings of the Conference Online Journalism in the Arab World: Realities and Challenges*, edited by Ali Abdulrahman Awad, 22–23. University of Sharjah, UAE.

Ali, Sadaf, and Shahira Fahmy. 2013. "Gatekeeping and Citizen Journalism: The Use of Social Media during the Recent Uprisings in Iran, Egypt, and Libya. *Media, War & Conflict* 6 (1): 55–69.

Al-Jaber, Khalid, and Barrie Gunter. 2013. "Evolving News Systems in the Gulf Countries." In *News Media in the Arab World: A Study of 10 Arab and Muslim Countries*, edited by Barrie Gunter and Roger Dickinson. London: Bloomsbury Academic.

Al-Jabri, Mohamed Abed. 1997. *Issues in Contemporary Thinking*. Beirut: Center for the Arab Unity Studies (in Arabic).

Al-Jazeera. 2014. "Ahmed Mansour Disowns an Article Inciting to Violence." Al Jazeera.net, February 25. http://www.aljazeera.net/news/arabic/2014/2/25/أحمد-منصور-يتبرأ-من-مقال-يحرض-على-القتل.

Alqudsi-Ghabra, Taghreed, Talal Al-Bannai, and Mohammad Al-Bahrani. 2011. "The Internet in the Arab Gulf Cooperation Council (AGCC): Vehicle of Change." *International Journal of Internet Science* 6 (1): 44–67.

Al-Rawi, Ahmed, and Barrie Gunter. 2012. "News in Iraq." In *News Media in the Arab World: A Study of 10 Arab & Muslim Countries*, edited by Barrie Gunter and Roger Dickinson, 58–90. London: Bloomsbury Academic.

Al-Saggaf, Yeslam. 2011. "Saudi Females on Facebook: An Ethnographic Study." *International Journal of Emerging Technologies and Society* 9 (1): 1–19.

Al-Saggaf, Yeslam, and Mohamed M. Begg. 2004. "Online Communities versus Offline Communities in the Arab/Muslim World." *Information, Communication & Ethics in Society* 2:41–54.

Al-Said, Saleh. 2013. "Twitter Discussion: Restaurants to Operate 24 Hours." *Al Mowaten*, April 22.

Al-Watan Voice. 2007. "Satellite Channels Lure Saudi Female Presenters." *Al-Watan Voice,* April 6. http://www.alwatanvoice.com/arabic/print.php?id=82590 (in Arabic).

Amin, Hussein. 2001. "Mass Media in the Arab States between Diversification and Stagnation: An Overview." In *Mass Media, Politics & Society in the Middle East,* edited by Kai Hafez. Cresskill, NJ: Hampton Press.

Anderson, Ashley A., Dominique Brossard, Dietram A. Scheufele, Michael A. Xenos, and Peter Ladwig. 2014. "The 'Nasty Effect': Online Incivility and Risk Perceptions of Emerging Technologies." *Journal of Computer-Mediated Communication* 19 (3): 373–87.

Aouragh, Miriyam, and Anne Alexander. 2011. "The Egyptian Experience: Sense and Nonsense of the Internet Revolution." *International Journal of Communication* 5:1344–58.

Arab League. 2008. "Satellite Television Charter." *Arab Media and Society* (March). http://www.arabmediasociety.com/?article=648.

Arab Media Forum. 2013. "Arab Spring Has Reshaped the Newsroom in the Arab World" (May 14). http://www.arabmediaforum.ae/en/media-center/press releases/arab-spring-has-reshaped-the-newsroom-in-the-arab-world.aspx.

Arab Media Outlook. 2007. *Forecasts and Analysis of News and Current Affairs Media in the Middle East.* Dubai: Price Waterhouse Coopers.

Arab Social Media Influencers Summit. 2015. *Arab Social Media Report.* Dubai.

"Arab Social Media Outlook." 2014. White paper, Mohammed Bin Rashied School of Government, Dubai (in Arabic).

Arab Thought Foundation. 2011. *Arab Knowledge Report 2010/2011.* Dubai: Arab Thought Forum.

"Arab World Online." 2014. White paper, Mohamed bin Rashid School of Government, Dubai (in Arabic).

ASBU (Arab States Broadcasting Union). 2010. *Arab Satellite Broadcasting: Annual Report 2010.* Tunis: ASBU.

———. 2011. *Arab Satellite Broadcasting: Annual Report 2011.* Tunis: ASBU. www.asbu.net.

———. 2012. *Arab Satellite Television: Annual Report 2012.* Tunis: ASBU.

———. 2013. *Arab Satellite Television: Annual Report 2013.* Tunis: ASBU.

Awad, Ali Abdulrahman, ed. 2006. *Proceedings of the Conference Online Journalism in the Arab World: Realities and Challenges, 22–23 November 2005.* Sharjah: University of Sharjah, UAE.

Ayalon, Ami. 1995. *The Press in the Middle East: A History.* New York and Oxford: Oxford University Press.

Ayish, Muhammad. 1991. "Foreign Voices as People's Choices; BBC Popularity in the Arab World. *Middle Eastern Studies* 27 (3): 374–88.

———. 1997. "Arab Television Goes Commercial: A Case Study of the Middle East Broadcasting Center (MBC)." *Gazette* 59 (6): 473–94.

———. 2001. "American-Style Journalism and Arab World Television: An Exploratory Study of News Selection at Six Arab World Satellite Television Channels." *Transnational Broadcasting Studies* 6 (Spring/Summer).

———. 2002. "Political Communication on Arab World Television: Evolving Patterns." *Political Communication* 19 (2): 137–54.

——. 2003. *Arab World Television in the Age of Globalization: An Analysis of Emerging Political, Economic, Cultural and Technological Patterns*. Hamburg: Center for Middle Eastern Studies.

——. 2013. "Broadcasting Transitions in the United Arab Emirates." In *National Broadcasting and State Policy in Arab Countries*, edited by Tourya Guaaybess, 13–27. Basingstoke: Palgrave Macmillan.

Bartlett, Rachel. 2014. "The Digital Strategy 'Journey' at Al Jazeera English." Journalism.co.uk, April 8. http://www.journalism.co.uk/news/the-digital-strategy-journey-at-al-jazeera-english/s2/a556335.

Bebawi, Saba. 2013. "Arab Spring: New Media, New Journalism, Same Old Tensions?" *The Conversation*, December 23. http://theconversation.com/arab-spring-new-media-new-journalism-same-old-tensions-19662.

Bora, Kukil. 2014. "Farah Baker, a Gaza Teenager, Becomes Social Media Phenomenon by Tweeting about War." *International Business Times*, August 11. http://www.ibtimes.com/farah-baker-gaza-teenager-becomes-social-media-phenomenon-tweeting-about-war-1654456.

Bossio, Diana, and Saba Bebawi. 2012. "Reaping and Sowing the News from an Arab Spring: The Politicised Interaction between Traditional and Alternative Journalistic Practitioners." *Global Media Journal: Australian Edition* 6 (2).

Boyd, D. 2001. "Saudi Arabia's International Media Strategy: Influence through Multinational Ownership." In *Mass Media, Politics & Society in the Middle East*, edited by K. Hafez. Crisskill, NJ: Hampton Press.

Brandwatch. 2013. "Sky News Arabia Transforms Social Analytics into Competitive Edge and Increased Engagement." Retrieved August 22 from http://www.brandwatch.com/sky-news-arabia.

Bruna, Samuel Negredo. 2013. "Participation in Al Jazeera English: Integrating Witnesses and Users to Broaden the Reach of the News." *Communication & Society* 26 (1): 1–21.

Bruns, Axel. 2005. *Gatewatching: Collaborative Online News Production*. New York: Peter Lang.

Bryant, J., and M. Beth, eds. 2009. *Media Effects: Advances in Theory and Research*. New York: Routledge.

Canter, Lily. 2012. "Web 2.0 and the Changing Relationship between British Local Newspaper Journalists and Their Audiences." Unpublished PhD thesis, University of Sheffield, UK.

——. 2013. "The Interactive Spectrum: The Use of Social Media in UK Regional Newspapers." *Convergence: The International Journal of Research into New Media Technologies* 19 (4): 472–95.

Chulov, Martin. 2014. "Saad Hariri: Culture of Impunity in Lebanon Must End before I Return." *Guardian*, January 17.

Cooper, Andrew F., and Bessma Momani. 2011. "Qatar and Expanded Contours of Small State Diplomacy." *International Spectator: Italian Journal of International Affairs* 46 (3): 113–28.

Cozma, Aluca, and Kuan-Ju Chen. 2013. "What's in a Tweet?" *Journalism Practice* 7 (1): 33–46.

Da Lage, O. 2005. "The Politics of Al Jazeera or the Diplomacy of Doha." In *The Al Jazeera Phenomenon: Critical Perspectives on New Arab Media*, edited by M. Zayani, 49–65. New York: Pluto Press.

Dingman, Alex. 2013. "Social Media as Confusing as Helpful in Crisis Situations." *Topeka Capital Journal*, April 22. http://cjonline.com/news/2013-04-22/social-media-confusing-helpful-crisis-situations.

Dubai Press Club. 2011. *Arab Media Outlook (2011–2015): Exposure and Transitions*. Dubai: Dubai Press Club.

Dubai School of Government. 2011. *Arab Social Media Report* 1 (2) (May).

———. 2012. *Arab Social Media Report: Social Media in the Arab World: Influencing Societal and Cultural Change*. Dubai: Dubai School of Government.

———. 2013. "The Arab World Online: Trends in Internet Usage in the Arab Region." Report, Dubai School of Government.

Duffy, Matt J. 2012. "Audience Engagement in the Middle East Press: An Exploration of 'Networked Journalism' amid the New Media Landscape." *Middle East Media Educator* 1 (2): 7–15. Available at http://ro.uow.edu.au/meme/vol1/iss2/2.

———. 2013. "'Cultures of Journalism' in Arabic- and English-Language Newspapers within the United Arab Emirates." *Journal of Middle East Media* 9 (1) (Fall). http://www2.gsu.edu/~wwwaus/JMEM_home.html.

Economist. 2011. "The People Formerly Known as the Audience." July 7. http://www.economist.com/node/18904124.

———. 2015. "Arab Media: A Guttering Flame." February 15. http://www.economist.com/news/middle-east-and-africa/21643192-after-brief-flickering-free-speech-being-snuffed-out-guttering-flame.

Ehab, Salma. 2013. "Experts: Online Journalism and Social Media Need Laws." *Al-Watan* (Bahrain), March 23, 4.

Eickelman, D., and J. Anderson. 1999. *New Media in the Muslim World: The Emerging Public Sphere*. Bloomington: Indiana University Press.

Ekine, Sokari. 2009. "Ushahidi Platform Used to Document Congo, Gaza Crises." PBS, January 9, 2009. http://www.pbs.org/mediashift/2009/01/ushahidi-platform-used-to-document-congo-gaza-crises009.

El Ahmad, Khaled. 2012. "Arabs' Most Influential on Twitter." Wamda, January 24. http://ar.wamda.com.

El-Nawawy, M., and A. Iskandar. 2003. *Al Jazeera: How the Free Arab News Network Scooped the World and Changed the Middle East*. Cambridge, MA: Westview.

Elsayed, Yomna. 2013. "Revolutionary Media on a Budget: Facebook-Only Social Journalism." *Arab Media and Society*, no. 17 (Winter). http://www.arabmediasociety.com/?article=814.

El Semary, Hebatalla, and May Al Khaja. 2013. "The Credibility of Citizen Journalism and Traditional TV Journalism among Emirati Youth: Comparative Study." *American International Journal of Contemporary Research* 3 (11): 53–62.

El-Sherif, Mahmoud. 1980. "The Arab Attitude to Mass Media." *Intermedia* 8 (2): 28–29.

Ennaji, M. 1995. "A Syntactico-Semantic Study of the Language of News in Morocco." *International Journal of the Sociology of Language* 112:97–111.

ESCWA (Economic and Social Commission for Western Asia). 2012. *Status of the Digital Arabic Content Industry in the Arab Region*. Beirut: ESCWA.

Fal, Ahmed. 2013. "Do Social Media Mean the End of the Professional Journalism?" Doha Centre for Media Freedom, February 24. http://www.dc4mf.org/ar/content/3339.

Falkow, Sally. 2014. "How Journalists Use Social Media to Report the News." *Proactive Report*, May 7.

Fox, Rebecca Suzanne. 2012. "Media Darlings: The Egyptian Revolution and American Media Coverage." Unpublished master's thesis, American University in Cairo.

France 24. 2011. "Who Are We?" France 24. http://www.france24.com/ar/company.

Freedom House. 2013. *Freedom of the Press 2013: A Global Survey of Media Independence*. Washington, DC: Freedom House.

Gamal, Islam, and Samar Said. 2014. "Twitter Users Pay Tribute to Hussein el-Imam." *Al-Youm Al-Sabei*, May 18.

Gelvanovska, Natalija, Michel Rogy, and Carlo Maria Rossotto. 2014. *Broadband Networks in the Middle East and North Africa: Accelerating High-Speed Internet Access*. Washington, DC: World Bank.

Gillespie, M. 2013. "BBC Arabic, Social Media and Citizen Production: An Experiment in Digital Democracy before the Arab Spring." *Theory, Culture & Society* 30 (4): 92–130.

Gomaa, Mahmoud. 2007. "Internet Language Threat to the Arabic Language." Al Jazeera.net, November 21.

Goode, L. 2009. "Social News, Citizen Journalism and Democracy." *New Media and Society* 11 (8): 1287–1305.

Grabowicz, P. 2014. "The Transition to Digital Journalism." Knight Digital Media Center, Berkeley. http://multimedia.journalism.berkeley.edu/tutorials/digital-transform/social-networks.

Guaaybess, Tourya. 2013. "Introduction: A Return to the National Perspective." In *National Broadcasting and State Policy in Arab Countries*, edited by Tourya Guaaybess, 1–12. Basingstoke: Palgrave Macmillan.

Hafez, Kai. 2002. "Journalism Ethics Revisited: A Comparison of Ethics Codes in Europe, North Africa, the Middle East, and Muslim Asia." *Political Communication* 19 (2): 242.

Hamid, T. 2014. "CNN Focuses on Social Media with Arabic Website Re-launch." *National*, January 20, 13.

Hanna, R., A. Rohm, and V. Crittenden. 2011. "We're All Connected: The Power of the Social Media Ecosystem." *Business Horizons* 54:265–73.

Harkin, Juliette, Kevin Anderson, Libby Morgan, and Briar Smith. 2012. "Deciphering User-Generated Content in Transitional Societies: A Syria Coverage Case Study." Report, Center for Global Communication Studies, Annenberg School for Communication, University of Pennsylvania.

Harrison, T., and B. Barthel. 2009. "Wielding New Media in Web 2.0: Exploring the History of Engagement with the Collaborative Construction of Media Products." *New Media & Society* 11 (1–2): 155–78.

Hashem, A. 2012. "The Arab Spring Has Shaken Arab TV's Credibility." *Guardian*, April 3. http://www.theguardian.com/commentisfree/2012/apr/03/arab spring-arab-tv-credibility.

———. 2014a. "The Islamic State's Media Warfare." *Al-Monitor*, October 22. http://www.al-monitor.com/pulse/originals/2014/10/islamic-state-media strategy-propaganda-iraq-syria.html#ixzz3Hvv5e0UX.

———. 2014b. "The Islamic State's Social Media Strategy." *Al-Monitor*, August 18. http://www.al-monitor.com/pulse/originals/2014/08/is-clinton-atrocities social-media-baghdadi-mccain.html.

Hawkes, Rebecca. 2012. "Mobile TV: One of Three Most Popular 3G Services in Arab World." *Rapid TV News*, January 23. http://www.rapidtvnews.com/index.php/2012012319017/mobile-tv-one-of-three-most-popular-3g-services-in-arab-world.html#ixzz2rPmAeGXa.

Hermida, Alfred. 2009. "The Blogging BBC: Journalism Blogs at 'the World's Most Trusted News Organisation.'" *Journalism Practice* 3:268–84.

———. 2010a. "Twittering the News: The Emergence of Ambient Journalism." *Journalism Practice* 4:297–308.

———. 2010b. "From TV to Twitter: How Ambient News Became Ambient Journalism." *M/C Journal* 13 (2). Retrieved February 18, 2011. http://journal.media culture.org.au/index.php/mcjournal/article/viewArticle/220.

Hermida, A., and N. Thurman. 2008. "A Clash of Culture." *Journalism Practice* 2 (3): 343–56.

Howard, Philip, and Muzammil Hussain. 2012. *Democracy's Fourth Wave? Digital Media and the Arab Spring*. New York: Oxford University Press.

Hroub, Khalid. 2006. "Satellite Media and Social Change in the Arab World." In *Arab Media in the Information Age*. Abu Dhabi: Center for Strategic Studies and Research.

Internet World Stats. 2014. http://www.internetworldstats.com/middle.htm.

IREX (International Research & Exchanges Board). 2006. *Media Sustainability Index: Middle East and North Africa*. Washington, DC: IREX.

Ismail, Hanan. 2012. "The Role of Citizen Journalism in the View of Media Leaders in Jordan, Kuwait and Egypt." Unpublished master's thesis, Middle East University, Jordan.

ITU (International Telecommunications Union). 2012. "Key ICT Indicators for Developed and Developing Countries and the World." Database, ITU, Geneva.

———. 2013. "Key ICT Indicators for Developed and Developing Countries and the World." Database, ITU, Geneva.

Janmohamed, Shelina Zahra. 2012. "Is Staying Faithful to Islam Compatible with Twitter?" *National*, February 18. http://www.thenational.ae/thenational conversation/lifestyle-comment/is-staying-faithful-to-islam-compatible-with-twitter#ixzz37OTnJZyV.

Jarvis, J. 2006. "Neworked Journalism." *Buzz Machine* (blog), July 5. Retrieved October 23, 2009. http://www.buzzmachine.com/2006/07/05/networked journalism.

Jenkins, Henry. 2006. *Convergence Culture: Where Old and New Media Collide*. New York: New York University Press.

Jones, Adam. 2002. From Vanguard to Vanquished: The Tabloid Press in Jordan. *Political Communication* 19 (2): 171–88.

Katz, E. 1987. "Communication Research since Lazersfeld." In "50th Anniversary Issue," supplement, *Public Opinion Quarterly* 51: S25–S45.

Kendall, Elisabeth. 1997. "The Marginal Voice: Journals and the Avant-Garde in Egypt." *Journal of Islamic Studies* 8 (2): 216–38.

Khalaf, Ramy. 2013. "Bridging the Arabic Language Gap on the Web." *Edge Magazine*, January 9. http://www.theedge.me/bridging-the-arabic-language-gap-on-the-web/#sthash.qR2GTIUm.dpuf.

Khalaileh, Yasser, and Nazzal Kisswani. 2013. "The 'Right to Privacy' v. Telecommunications Interception and Access: International Regulations and Implementation in the Arab Region." *International Review of Law* 2013 (2): 10. http://dx.doi.org/10.5339/irl.2013.10.

Khalifa, Waleed. 2008. "Nuqtat Hewar Which Annoyed Arab Satellite Stations." *Assiyasi*, July 30. http://www.alssiyasi.com/?browser=view&EgyxpID=4343.

Khalil, Joe F. 2013. "Towards a Supranational Analysis of Arab Media: The Role of Cities." In *National Broadcasting and State Policy in Arab Countries*, edited by Tourya Guaaybess, 188–208. Basingstoke: Palgrave Macmillan.

Khazen, Jihad. 1999. "Censorship and State Control of the Press in the Arab World." *Harvard International Journal of Press Politics* 4 (3): 87–92.

Kheir, Fatima. 2008. "Nuqtat Hewar from Abroad." *Al Youm Assabea*, October 30, 2008. http://www.youm7.com/News.asp?NewsID=47037.

Khodour, Adiib. 1997. *The Arab Media on the Verge of the Twenty-First Century: The Beginning, Development and Reality* (in Arabic). Damascus and Cairo: Arab Center for Strategic Studies.

Kraidy, Marwan. 2013. "Television Reform in Saudi Arabia: The Challenges of Transnationalization and Digitization." In *National Broadcasting and State Policy in Arab Countries*, edited by Tourya Guaaybess, 28–41. Basingstoke: Palgrave Macmillan.

Labor Watch. 2012. "An Independent Syndicate for Online Journalists," October 7. http://www.labor-watch.net/index.php?option=com_content&view=article&id=6582:2012-10-07-07-24-01&catid=1:latest-news&Itemid=142.

Lasorsa, Dominic, Seth Lewis, and Avery Holton. 2011. "Normalizing Twitter." *Journalism Studies* 13 (1): 19–36.

Lee, C. 2012. "News Sharing in Social Media: The Effect of Gratifications and Prior Experience." *Computers in Human Behavior* 28:331–39.

Livingstone, S. 1999. "New Media, New Audiences?" *New Media and Society* 1 (1): 59–66.

———. 2004. "The Challenge of Changing Audiences: Or, What Is the Researcher to Do in the Age of the Internet?" *European Journal of Communication* 19 (1): 75–86. Available at LSE Research Online. http://eprints.lse.ac.uk/archive/00000412.

Lotan, Gilad. 2014. Israel, Gaza, War & Data: Social Networks and the Art of Personalizing Propaganda. Huffington Post, July 8. http://www.huffingtonpost.com/gilad-lotan/israel-gaza-war-social-networks-data_b_5658557.html.

Lynch, M. 2004. "Shattering the Politics of Silence: Satellite Television Talk Shows and the Transformation of Arab Political Culture." *Arab Reform Bulletin* 2 (11): 3. http://www.carnegieendowment.org/publications/index.cfm?fa=view&id=16242.

McFadden, Tom J. 1953. *Daily Journalism in the Arab States*. Columbus: Ohio State University Press.

McQuail, Denis. 2013. *Journalism and Society*. London: Sage.

Mejdell, Gunvor. 2008. "What Is Happening to *Lughatunā L-Gamīla*? Recent Media Representations and Social Practice in Egypt." *Journal of Arabic and Islamic Studies* 8:108–24.

Melki, Jad, Yasmine Dabbous, Khaled Nasser, and Sarah Mallat. 2012. *Mapping Digital Media: Lebanon*. London: Open Society Media Program.

Mellor, Noha. 2005. *The Making of Arab News*. Lanham, MD: Rowman & Littlefield.

———. 2011. *Pan-Arab Journalists in Transnational Media*. New York: Hampton Press.

———. 2012. "The Culture of Witnessing: War Correspondents Rewriting the History of the Iraq War." *Journal of Language and Intercultural Communication* 12 (2): 103–17.

———. 2014. "Countering Cultural Hegemony: Audience Research in the Arab World." *Journal of Arab & Muslim Media Research* 6 (2–3): 201–16.

Middle East Publishers Association. 2013. *Newsletter* 55 (55) (September–October).

Mijatović, D. 2013. "Foreword." In *2013 Social Media Guidebook*, edited by C. Möller and M. Stone, 5–8. Vienna: OSCE Representative on Freedom of the Media.

Miles, H. 2003. *Al-Jazeera: The Inside Story of the Arab News Channel That Is Challenging the West*. London: Grove Press.

Mohammed, Hamza, and Barrie Gunter. 2012. "News Consummation and News Agenda in Egypt." In *News Media in the Arab World: A Study of 10 Arab & Muslim Countries*, edited by Barrie Gunter and Roger Dickinson, 116–51. London: Bloomsbury Academic.

Morozov, Evgeny. 2012. *The Net Delusion: The Dark Side of Internet Freedom*. New York: Public Affairs Books.

Murphy, Caryle. 2013. *A Kingdom's Future: Saudi Arabia through the Eyes of Its Twentysomethings*. Washington, DC: Wilson Center.

Negus, Keith. 2002. "The Work of Cultural Intermediaries and the Enduring Distance between Production and Consumption." *Cultural Studies* 16 (4): 501–16.

New World Encyclopedia. n.d. "Al Jazeera." Accessed July 15, 2014. http://www.newworldencyclopedia.org/entry/Al_Jazeera.

Newman, Nic. 2009. "The Rise of Social Media and Its Impact on Mainstream Journalism: A Study of How Newspapers and Broadcasters in the UK and US Are Responding to a Wave of Participatory Social Media, and a Historic Shift in Control towards Individual Consumers." Working paper, Reuters Institute for the Study of Journalism, University of Oxford.

Nip, J. 2006. "Exploring the Second Phase of Public Journalism." *Journalism Studies* 7 (2): 212–36.

Nussibeh, Zaki, and Roger Dickinson. 2012. "The Development of Palestinian News Media." In *News Media in the Arab World: A Study of 10 Arab & Muslim Countries*, edited by Barrie Gunter and Roger Dickinson, 91–115. London: Bloomsbury Academic.

Ostrow, Adam. 2011. "What the Egyptian Revolution Taught Al Jazeera about Digital." Mashable.com, March 5. http://mashable.com/2011/03/04/al-jazeera-digital.

Palumbo, D. 2014. "12 Social Media Tools for Journalists." Journalism.co.uk. http://www.journalism.co.uk/news/12-social-media-tools-for-journalists/s2/a557339.

Pavlik, John V. 1998. *New Media Technology: Cultural and Commercial Perspectives*. 2nd ed. Boston: Allyn and Bacon.

———. 2000. "The Impact of Technology on Journalism." *Journalism Studies* 1 (2): 229–37.

———. 2001. *Journalism and New Media*. New York: Columbia University Press.

———. 2003. "New Technology and News Flows: Journalism and Crisis Coverage." In *Digital Journalism: Emerging Media and the Changing Horizons of Journalism*, edited by Kevin Kawamoto, 75–89. Oxford: Rowman & Littlefield.

Pew Research Center. 2012. "News Attitudes and Habit." http://www.people-press.org/2012/09/27/section-3-news-attitudes-and-habits-2.

Picard, Robert G. 2009. "Why Journalists Deserve Low Pay." *Christian Science Monitor*, May 19. http://www.csmonitor.com/layout/set/print/Commentary/Opinion/2009/0519/p09s02-coop.html.

Pintak, Lawrence. 2011. "Arab Media Revolution Spreading Change." CNN, January 31. http://edition.cnn.com/2011/OPINION/01/29/pintak.arab.media.

Pintak, Lawrence, and Jeremy Ginges. 2008. "The Mission of Arab Journalism: Creating Change in a Time of Turmoil." *International Journal of Press/Politics* 13 (3): 193–227.

Potter, Deborah. 2007. "You Witness News." *American Journalism Review* (April/May). http://ajrarchive.org/article.asp?id=4316.

Powers, Shawn. 2012. "From Broadcast to Networked Journalism: The Case of Al-Jazeera English." In *Histories of Public Service Broadcasters on the Web*, edited by Maureen Burns and Niels Brügger, 207–21. New York: Peter Lang.

Ramarprasad, Jyotika, and Naila N. Hamdy. 2006. "Functions of Egyptian Journalists: Perceived Importance and Actual Performance. *International Communication Gazette* 68 (2): 167–85.

Ramsay, Gail. 2012. "What Kind of Arabic and Why? Language in Egyptian Blogs." In issue supplement, *Orientalia Suecana* 61:49–87.

Richter, Carola. 2013. "Libyan Broadcasting under al-Qadhafi: The Politics of Pseduo-Liberalization." In *National Broadcasting and State Policy in Arab Countries*, edited by Tuorya Guaaybess, 150–65. Basingstoke: Palgrave Macmillan.

Rinnawi, Khalil. 2006. *Instant Nationalism: McArabism and Al-Jazeera: Transnational Media in the Arab World*. Lanham, MD: University Press of America.

Saadi, Emile. 2013. "New Saudi Authority for the Regulation of Audio and Visual Media." Altimimi and Co. http://www.tamimi.com/en/magazine/law-update/section-5/march-4/new-saudi-authority-for-the-regulation-of-audio-and-visual-media.html#sthash.TCj4XPPx.dpuf.

Saghiya, Hazim. 2006. "The Arab Press and Various Sources of Repression." In *Arab Media in the Information Age*, edited by Emirates Center for Strategic Studies and Research, 543–66. Abu Dhabi: Emirates Center for Strategic Studies and Research.

Sakr, Naomi. 2006. "The Impact of Commercial Interests on Arab Media Content." In *Arab Media in the Information Age*, edited by Emirates Center for Strategic Studies and Research, 61–86. Abu Dhabi: Emirates Center for Strategic Studies and Research.

Salah, Mohamed. 2014. "Fadel Shaker Tweets That His Arrest Was a Rumour." *Al Mogez*, January 14.

Salama, Vivian. 2007. "Death by Video Phone: Coverage of Saddam Hussein's Execution." *Arab Media & Society* (March). http://www.arabmediasociety.com/articles/downloads/20070327122124_AMS2_Vivian_Salama.pdf.

Sasseen, Jane. 2012. *The Video Revolution*. Washington, DC: Center for International Media Assistance.

Schudder, Tom. 2007. "An Interview with Hala Sarhan." *MEB Journal* (January/February). Accessed July 11, 2007. http://www.mebjournal.com.

Schwartz, Sharona. 2014. "Twitterverse Declares: 'Hitler Was Right.'" *The Blaze*, July 13. http://www.theblaze.com/stories/2014/07/13/twitterverse-declares-hitler-was-right.

Seib, P. 2010. "Transnational Journalism, Public Diplomacy, and Virtual States." *Journalism Studies* 11 (5): 734–44.

Semiocast. 2011. "Arabic Highest Growth on Twitter." http://semiocast.com/en/publications/2011_11_24_Arabic_highest_growth_on_Twitter.

Shirky, Clay. 2008. *Here Comes Everybody: The Power of Organizing without Organizations*. New York: Penguin.

Singer, J. B., D. Domingo, A. Heinonen, A. Hermida, S. Paulussen, T. Quandt, Z. Reich, and M. Vujnovic. 2011. *Participatory Journalism: Guarding Open Gates at Online Newspapers*. Chichester, UK: Wiley-Blackwell.

Skoler, M. 2009. "Why the News Media Became Irrelevant—and How Social Media Can Help." *Nieman Reports* (Fall): 38–40.

Strauss, M. 1991. "Redefining the Captive Audience Doctrine." Hastings Constitutional Law Quarterly 19:85–122.

Sweis, Rana, and Dina Baslan. 2013. *Mapping Digital Media: Jordan*. London: Open Society Media Program.

Talahma, Thair Mohamed. 2012. "Gatekeeping and Interactive Media on the Palestinian News Sites on the Internet." Master's thesis, Middle East University.

Thurman, Neil. 2008. "Initiatives by Online News Media Forums for Citizen Journalists? Adoption of User Generated Content." *New Media Society* 10 (1): 139–57.

TRA (Telecommunications Regulatory Authority). 2013. "Instagram." White paper, TRA, Abu Dhabi, UAE.

Trygg, Sanna. 2012. "Is Comment Free? Ethical, Editorial and Political Problems of Moderating Online News." Report, *POLIS Journalism and Society*. http://blogs.lse.ac.uk/polis/files/2012/01/IsCommentFree_PolisLSETrygg.pdf.

Tunstall, Jeremy. 2007. "So How Did the US Media Lose Its Way?" *Independent*, March 19.

Ulbricht, Melissa. 2011. "Aljazeera's Curious Experimental Approach." *Rhodes Journalism Review* 31 (September): 30–31. http://www.rjr.ru.ac.za/rjrpdf/rjr_no31/Al_Jazeeras_curious_approach.pdf.

Walker, P. 2010. "Octavia Nasr Fired by CNN over Tweet Praising Late Ayatollah." *Guardian*, July 8. http://www.theguardian.com/media/2010/jul/08/octavia-nasr-cnn-tweet-fired.

Wall, Melissa, and Sahar el Zahed. 2014. "Syrian Citizen Journalism." *Digital Journalism* 3. doi:10.1080/21670811.2014.931722.

Week. 2014. "Gaza Conflict: The Social Media Front Line." *Week*, July 18. www.theweek.co.uk/middle-east/59554/gaza-conflict-the-social-media-front-line.

Winder, Bayly P. C. 2014. "The Hashtag Generation: The Twitter Phenomenon in Saudi Society." *Journal of Georgetown University-Qatar Middle Eastern Studies Student Association* 2014:6. doi:10.5339/messa.2014.6.

Youm7. 2014. "Social Media Users Circulate a Picture of Samir Ghanem after He Cast His Ballot," May 27.

Youssef, Ahmed Magdy. 2013. "On Al-Jazeera's Lopsided Coverage of Egypt." Open Democracy, August 2. http://www.opendemocracy.net/ahmed-magdy-youssef/on-al-jazeeras-lopsided-coverage-of-egypt.

Zaid, Bouziane, and Mohamed Ibahrine. 2011. *Mapping Digital Media: Morocco*. London: Open Society Media Program.

Zayani, M., ed. 2005. *Al Jazeera Phenomenon: Critical Perspectives on New Arab Media*. New York: Pluto Press.

Zayani, Mohamed, and Sofiane Sahraoui. 2007. *The Culture of Al-Jazeera: Inside an Arab Media Giant*. Jefferson, NC: McFarland.

ZenithOptimedia. 2013. "Executive Summary: Advertising Expenditure Forecasts September 2013." http://www.zenithoptimedia.com/wp-content/uploads/2013/09/Adspend-forecasts-September-2013-executive-summary.pdf.

Ziani, A., S. Fahmy, and M. Elareshi. 2014. "Arabic-Language Newscasts in Four Non-Arab TV Channels: Form and Content." *Global Media Journal* (Arabian edition) 3 (1): 38–55.

Index